Nineteenth-Century Settler Emigration in British Literature and Art

Edinburgh Critical Studies in Victorian Culture
Series Editor: Julian Wolfreys

Recent books in the series:

Rudyard Kipling's Fiction: Mapping Psychic Spaces
Lizzy Welby

The Decadent Image: The Poetry of Wilde, Symons and Dowson
Kostas Boyiopoulos

British India and Victorian Literary Culture
Máire ní Fhlathúin

Anthony Trollope's Late Style: Victorian Liberalism and Literary Form
Frederik Van Dam

Dark Paradise: Pacific Islands in the Nineteenth-Century British Imagination
Jenn Fuller

Twentieth-Century Victorian: Arthur Conan Doyle and the Strand Magazine, *1891–1930*
Jonathan Cranfield

The Lyric Poem and Aestheticism: Forms of Modernity
Marion Thain

Gender, Technology and the New Woman
Lena Wånggren

Self-Harm in New Woman Writing
Alexandra Gray

Suffragist Artists in Partnership: Gender, Word and Image
Lucy Ella Rose

Victorian Liberalism and Material Culture: Synergies of Thought and Place
Kevin A. Morrison

The Victorian Male Body
Joanne-Ella Parsons and Ruth Heholt

Nineteenth-Century Settler Emigration in British Literature and Art
Fariha Shaikh

The Pre-Raphaelites and Orientalism
Eleonora Sasso

The Late-Victorian Little Magazine
Koenraad Claes

Coastal Cultures of the Long Nineteenth Century
Matthew Ingleby and Matt P. M. Kerr

Dickens and Demolition: Literary Allusion and Urban Change in the Mid-Nineteenth Century
Joanna Robinson

Artful Experiments: Ways of Knowing in Victorian Literature and Science
Philipp Erchinger

Victorian Poetry and the Poetics of the Literary Periodical
Caley Ehnes

The Victorian Actress in the Novel and on the Stage
Renata Kobetts Miller

Forthcoming volumes:

Her Father's Name: Gender, Theatricality and Spiritualism in Florence Marryat's Fiction
Tatiana Kontou

The Sculptural Body in Victorian Literature: Encrypted Sexualities
Patricia Pulham

Olive Schreiner and the Politics of Print Culture, 1883–1920
Clare Gill

Dickens's Clowns: Charles Dickens, Joseph Grimaldi and the Pantomime of Life
Johnathan Buckmaster

Victorian Auto/Biography: Problems in Genre and Subject
Amber Regis

Culture and Identity in Fin-de-Siècle Scotland: Romance, Decadence and the Celtic Revival
Michael Shaw

Gissing, Shakespeare and the Life of Writing
Thomas Ue

The Arabian Nights and Nineteenth Century British Culture
Melissa Dickson

The Aesthetics of Space in Nineteenth Century British Literature, 1851–1908
Giles Whiteley

For a complete list of titles published visit the Edinburgh Critical Studies in Victorian Culture web page at www.edinburghuniversitypress.com/series/ECVC

Also Available:

Victoriographies – A Journal of Nineteenth-Century Writing, 1790–1914, edited by Diane Piccitto and Patricia Pulham
ISSN: 2044-2416

www.eupjournals.com/vic

Nineteenth-Century Settler Emigration in British Literature and Art

Fariha Shaikh

EDINBURGH
University Press

Edinburgh University Press is one of the leading university presses in the UK. We publish academic books and journals in our selected subject areas across the humanities and social sciences, combining cutting-edge scholarship with high editorial and production values to produce academic works of lasting importance. For more information visit our website: edinburghuniversitypress.com

© Fariha Shaikh, 2018, 2019

Edinburgh University Press Ltd
The Tun – Holyrood Road,
12(2f) Jackson's Entry,
Edinburgh EH8 8PJ

First published in hardback by Edinburgh University Press 2018

Typeset in 11/13 Adobe Sabon by
IDSUK (DataConnection) Ltd, and
printed and bound in Great Britain
by CPI Group (UK) Ltd, Croydon,
CR0 4YY.

A CIP record for this book is available from the British Library

ISBN 978 1 4744 3369 3 (hardback)
ISBN 978 1 4744 3370 9 (paperback)
ISBN 978 1 4744 3371 6 (webready PDF)
ISBN 978 1 4744 3372 3 (epub)

The right of Fariha Shaikh to be identified as the author of this work has been asserted in accordance with the Copyright, Designs and Patents Act 1988, and the Copyright and Related Rights Regulations 2003 (SI No. 2498).

Contents

List of Illustrations vi
Acknowledgements vii
Series Editor's Preface ix

Introduction 1

1. Printed Emigrants' Letters: Networks of Affect and Authenticity 31

2. Emigrant Shipboard Newspapers: Provisional Settlement at Sea 63

3. Fragmentary Aesthetics: Susanna Moodie and Catharine Parr Traill in the Canadian Bush 95

4. Emigration Paintings: Visual Texts and Mobility 130

5. Emigration Aesthetics: Elizabeth Gaskell, Charles Dickens and Catherine Helen Spence 161

Conclusion: Structures of Mobility 191

Bibliography 196
Index 235

List of Illustrations

Figure 1: Sockett's Introductory Lines for Mary Holden's Letter, King's College London, Foyle Special Collections Library — 53

Figure 2: Close-Up of Mast of the *Alfred*, State Library of New South Wales, Mitchell Library, A1680 — 66

Figure 3: Sample First Page of an Issue of the *Alfred*, State Library of New South Wales, Mitchell Library, A1680 — 67

Figure 4: Front Page of First Issue of the *Open Sea*, State Library of New South Wales, Mitchell Library, A1645 — 69

Figure 5: 'Engraving' of Jeremy Diddler in the *Open Sea*, State Library of New South Wales, Mitchell Library, A1645 — 84

Figure 6: *The Last of England*, 1855, Ford Madox Brown, oil on panel, 82.5 x 75 cm © Birmingham Museums Trust — 134

Figure 7: *The Emigrant's Last Sight of Home*, 1858, Richard Redgrave. Purchased with assistance from an anonymous donor 1977. Oil on canvas, 69.9 x 98.4 cm ©Tate, London 2017 — 135

Figure 8: *A Letter from the Colonies*, 1852, Thomas Webster. Presented by J. G. Milner 1986. Oil on wood, 41.3 x 52.1 cm, ©Tate, London 2017 — 141

Figure 9: *Answering the Emigrant's Letter*, 1850, James Collinson, oil on panel, 70.1 x 91.2 cm, Manchester Art Gallery, UK / Bridgeman Images — 145

Figure 10: *Second Class – The Parting*, 1854, Abraham Solomon, oil on canvas, 76.3 x 54.5 cm, Southampton City Art Gallery, Hampshire, UK / Bridgeman Images — 152

Acknowledgements

This book began as a doctoral project under the supervision of Professor Josephine McDonagh at King's College London. Without Jo's wisdom, encouragement and acute judgement, this project would not have been possible, and I am profoundly grateful for her support of, and belief in, me. Like many of the texts studied here, this book is a mobile artefact: in moving from a doctoral project to monograph, it has also moved between different countries and institutions. Professor Nicholas Daly at University College Dublin was a wonderful mentor, taking me out for tea and lunch whenever I needed it as I navigated my own period of being an emigrant and coming to terms with my new environment. The final changes to this manuscript were made as I joined the University of Birmingham and I am grateful to my new colleagues for their warm welcome.

I am grateful to the Arts and Humanities Research Council for funding the initial research for this book, and to the Irish Research Council for providing me with the time and resources I needed to bring this project to fruition. An Australian Bicentennial Scholarship from the Menzies Centre, King's College London funded a research trip to the Mitchell Library, Sydney, for the research which appears in the second chapter of this book.

Grateful acknowledgement is made to the following sources for their permission to reproduce images from their collections. Every effort has been made to trace copyright holders, but if any has been inadvertently overlooked the publisher will be pleased to make the necessary arrangement at the first opportunity: Sockett's Introductory Lines for Mary Holden's Letter, King's College London, Foyle Special Collections Library; Sockett's Introductory Lines for Mary Holden's Letter, King's College London, Foyle Special Collections Library; Sample First Page of an Issue of the *Alfred*, State Library of New South Wales, Mitchell Library, A1680; Front Page of First

Issue of the *Open Sea*, State Library of New South Wales, Mitchell Library, A1645; 'Engraving' of Jeremy Diddler in the *Open Sea*, State Library of New South Wales, Mitchell Library, A1645; *The Emigrant's Last Sight of Home*, 1858, Richard Redgrave (b. 1804, d. 1888). Purchased with assistance from an anonymous donor 1977. Oil on canvas, 69.9 x 98.4 cm ©Tate, London 2017; *A Letter from the Colonies*, 1852, Thomas Webster (b. 1800, d. 1886). Presented by J. G. Milner 1986. Oil on wood, 41.3 x 52.1 cm, ©Tate, London 2017; *Answering the Emigrant's Letter*, 1850, James Collinson, oil on panel, 70.1 x 91.2 cm, Manchester Art Gallery, UK / Bridgeman Images; *Second Class – The Parting*, 1854, Abraham Solomon, oil on canvas, 76.3 x 54.5 cm, Southampton City Art Gallery, Hampshire, UK / Bridgeman Images.

I owe enormous thanks to the people whose lives have crossed with mine in the process of writing and researching this book. Dublin was made a much happier time through the friendships of Lara Atkin, Sarah Comyn, Treasa De Loughry, Alison Garden and Grainne McEvoy. They give me reason again and again to go back to Ireland. The guidance and support of Sharae Deckard and Fionnuala Dillane throughout my time at UCD was invaluable. Valerie Norton at UCD Humanities Institute was a warm and kind source of support throughout. Back home, James Grande, Ruth Livesey, Rebecca Mitchell, Brian Murray, Matthew Rubery, Mark Turner and Cathy Waters have always been on hand to answer any questions I have had. Philip Aherne, Ellie Bass and Hannah Crummé keep me grounded and my head above water when I need it the most.

To my siblings, who have made my life richer and fuller in myriad ways, I'd be lost without you all. And, finally, to my parents whose own multiple migrations I can only admire as they move from country to country, I have no words to express my thanks. For all of globalisation's advanced telecommunications and the collapsed sense of time and distance, nothing can make up for the solid presence of your touch. I dedicate this book to you both.

Series Editor's Preface

'Victorian' is a term, at once indicative of a strongly determined concept and an often notoriously vague notion, emptied of all meaningful content by the many journalistic misconceptions that persist about the inhabitants and cultures of the British Isles and Victoria's Empire in the nineteenth century. As such, it has become a by-word for the assumption of various, often contradictory habits of thought, belief, behaviour and perceptions. Victorian studies and studies in nineteenth-century literature and culture have, from their institutional inception, questioned narrowness of presumption, pushed at the limits of the nominal definition, and have sought to question the very grounds on which the unreflective perception of the so-called Victorian has been built; and so they continue to do. Victorian and nineteenth-century studies of literature and culture maintain a breadth and diversity of interest, of focus and inquiry, in an interrogative and intellectually open-minded and challenging manner, which are equal to the exploration and inquisitiveness of its subjects. Many of the questions asked by scholars and researchers of the innumerable productions of nineteenth-century society actively put into suspension the clichés and stereotypes of 'Victorianism', whether the approach has been sustained by historical, scientific, philosophical, empirical, ideological or theoretical concerns; indeed, it would be incorrect to assume that each of these approaches to the idea of the Victorian has been, or has remained, in the main exclusive, sealed off from the interests and engagements of other approaches. A vital interdisciplinarity has been pursued and embraced, for the most part, even as there has been contest and debate amongst Victorianists, pursued with as much fervour as the affirmative exploration between different disciplines and differing epistemologies put to work in the service of reading the nineteenth century.

Edinburgh Critical Studies in Victorian Culture aims to take up both the debates and the inventive approaches and departures from convention that studies in the nineteenth century have witnessed for the last half century at least. Aiming to maintain a 'Victorian' (in the most positive sense of that motif) spirit of inquiry, the series' purpose is to continue and augment the cross-fertilisation of interdisciplinary approaches, and to offer, in addition, a number of timely and untimely revisions of Victorian literature, culture, history and identity. At the same time, the series will ask questions concerning what has been missed or improperly received, misread, or not read at all, in order to present a multi-faceted and heterogeneous kaleidoscope of representations. Drawing on the most provocative, thoughtful and original research, the series will seek to prod at the notion of the 'Victorian', and in so doing, principally through theoretically and epistemologically sophisticated close readings of the historicity of literature and culture in the nineteenth century, to offer the reader provocative insights into a world that is at once overly familiar, and irreducibly different, other and strange. Working from original sources, primary documents and recent interdisciplinary theoretical models, Edinburgh Critical Studies in Victorian Culture seeks not simply to push at the boundaries of research in the nineteenth century, but also to inaugurate the persistent erasure and provisional, strategic redrawing of those borders.

Julian Wolfreys

*To Abba and Amma,
for everything,
and more*

Introduction

On 10 August 1852, a twenty-three-year-old man, Charles Henry Lines, finally set sail for Melbourne in the *Ballarat*. Thinking that the *Ballarat* would sail on Friday 6 August, Lines had travelled down from his home in London, to Gravesend, only to find that the ship would in fact arrive the following morning, on Saturday 7 August. To pass the time, Lines met with friends at Gravesend and, as the ship had not arrived yet, spent the night on shore. The atmosphere was one of feverish buoyancy: Lines described the night as 'spreeish and expensive, as might be expected of young fellows bidding adieu to the pleasures of City life'. The next day, the *Ballarat* arrived, and Lines took a boat out with his friends to her, 'where a new World, complete in itself, met our view and claimed us as its citizens'. Waking up on Sunday morning, he breakfasted on board the ship, received some friends in his cabin and then went ashore to take tea with them. A fire had been lit in the neighbourhood; a chill that he had caught the previous night on board the ship tempted him to spend the night on shore. The following morning, on Monday 9 August, he woke up, had breakfast and went on board the *Ballarat*, where to his utmost surprise, he found his mother waiting for him. 'I received a most unexpected visit from my poor dear Mother,' he wrote, 'who, as unexpectedly, gave me a Sov[ereign].'[1] Lines's mother's surprise visit and her equally surprise gift of a sovereign are marked by a quiet poignancy. Both she and her son knew that they would never see each other again in their lives. Against this sense of loss, the sovereign can be read as a symbolic gesture of hope that Lines realises his search for gold.

Lines's ship is a 'world' before the 'new' world, and by acquiescing to be a citizen of it, Lines renegotiates his own relationship to Britain. Yet, although he is ready to embrace this 'new' world, he cannot leave the 'old' one behind. Only ten days after sailing, he writes:

> We have lost the last traces of Old England some days, and the same trackless view of land and water, meets the view at every moment, the Sun invitingly shining, has involuntarily caused me several times to look over the ship's side as if expecting to see the green peacefully picturesque scenery of our Boyhoods [sic] home.[2]

The image of his childhood landscape superimposed onto the seascape around him is more than a trick of the light and imagination. Far from constituting a clean break from his previous life, the voyage out is a jumble of places and times, a place where Lines's youth and present, his childhood and future homes are all imbricated in each other. Crossing the ocean is a confused and confusing experience: loss is twinned with hope; home is simultaneously left far behind and yet to be made. The story of Lines's departure encapsulates the spatial and temporal reconfigurations necessitated by nineteenth-century settler emigration. The late ship and initial missed meeting with his mother are indications of the delayed terms through which he would correspond for the rest of his life with his family back in England. In the mid-century, letters between England and Australia took an average of sixty days to reach their destination: news from both parties was received with a fresh urgency even though it arrived belatedly. Lines's experience of the voyage out can be found in a diary he kept on the *Ballarat*. The steady record day by day – even when there is nothing much to record – strongly suggests an attempt to bring the spatial and temporal confusion of emigration, and the entangled thoughts, experiences and emotions, into an ordered chronology within the space of the diary.

In 1833, Alexander Stinson, Master of the Armoury at Tipperary and former captain of the Roscommon Militia, wrote to his eldest child, John, who had emigrated to Canada earlier in the year, telling him that he had purchased a copy of Martin Doyle's emigrant handbook, *Hints on Emigration to Upper Canada* (1831). At fifty-three years of age, Stinson was contemplating moving with the rest of his children to join John. Despite never having been to Canada himself, Doyle's book was considered an authoritative source of information for intending emigrants like Stinson: it was published and circulated in Dublin, Edinburgh and London. Addressed to the 'middle and lower classes of Greater Britain and Ireland', Doyle's book provided information on Canada's climate, the cost of land, what kinds of agricultural produce to grow, and the indigenous peoples. In Stinson's correspondence with his son, however, *Hints on Emigration* becomes more than a simple how-to-emigrate guidebook. John writes back, telling him that 'by reference to the map attached to that book, you may trace my route from Quebec to Easthope, by Montreal, Prescot, York, &c. also in the map of the Huron Tract [. . .] you can see how beautifully intersected that part of the block where I live is, with rivers and streams'. In asking his father to 'trace' his journey since arriving in Canada, John personalises the generic nature of the map. He adds a few more lines to his letter, writing, 'since I wrote the above [lines], I looked over Martin Doyle [. . .] in the 14th and following pages, and in the 28th page at the 12th line you will find an account of the road on which I live, it is a very public one, the stage coach will soon be running on from York to Goderich, every day'.[4] John's specific references instruct his father how to read Doyle's book so that he can familiarise himself with his new home before he emigrates out himself. Recontextualising Doyle's general advice to make it fit his own personal circumstances, both Alexander and John connect through their separate copies of Doyle's handbook: their intertwined reading experiences point to the way in they are embedded in a shared print network which extended from the shores of Britain to the settler world.

In 1851, a poor eighteen-year-old orphan, Isabella Wyly, arrived at Port Adelaide, Australia. She had no friends or family in the country. Within a short time of arriving, she found herself a job in a draper's shop and later on, she married her employer. Six years after she emigrated, she wrote to her sister-in-law, 'I hope I wont tire your Pations [patience] with this crible, but I seem Not *not* to be able to say envoy[?], when I think of it going 16 thousand miles.'[3] Enunciating the distance of '16 thousand miles' highlights both the geographical distance that separated Isabella from her family in Ireland and the ability of her letter to cross it and connect them. The length of the letter – at around 1,800 words – stands as testimony to the eagerness for that contact – and her apologetic tone seeks to conceal her fear of being forgotten by those who had known her all her life. The ease with which she imagines her letter reaching her family belies the complexity of the relationships between settler emigration, epistolary practices and textual mobility.

Lines's diary, Alexander and John's use of Doyle's manual and Wyly's letter point to the multifarious and competing ways in which nineteenth-century settler emigration intersected with nineteenth-century print culture and textuality. This book takes as its focus the confluence of space, time and text in the context of nineteenth-century settler emigration. It argues that rather than being peculiar to the experiences of one particular emigrant, the complex interrelationships between all three categories defined nineteenth-century settler emigration between the years 1830 and 1870. Over the course of the nineteenth century, hundreds of thousands of people left the shores of the British Isles in search of better lives in the colonies in Australia, Canada and New Zealand, and in North America. Emigration statistics are notoriously difficult to calculate due to the paucity of records: for much of the first half of the century, close tabs were not kept on the numbers of people leaving the country, and when they were, it is often difficult to distinguish between which were emigrants and which were visitors. Furthermore, there was no distinction between British and Irish born passengers.[5] Nonetheless, a rough estimate of the number of people leaving Britain from the beginning of the century to 1869 stands at slightly over six million: in the first part of the century, 3,466,110 passengers were recorded as leaving UK ports, and between 1853 and 1869, 2,682,001 migrants were recorded as leaving.[6] This number covered an astonishingly broad range of people in addition to gold-rush emigrants: parish-assisted poor emigrants, single women looking for work or escaping prostitution, middle-class families who had fallen on hard times, those fleeing the Great Hunger in Ireland, large numbers of children, both who were orphaned and whose parents could not afford to keep them, and single and married young men, all moved out in search of better lives in the colonies. *Nineteenth-Century Settler Emigration* argues that this demographic shift was textually constituted. Keen to support the outward flow of population, emigration societies published emigration manuals, guidebooks, pamphlets and newspaper articles. These provided practical knowledge of emigration, but at the same time, sold the general public a glowing report of the colonies: life outside of Britain, regardless of whether it was in Canada, Australia or New Zealand, was materially better than it was in Britain. Emigration was the topic of the day. Bills, Acts and reports all publicly debated the pros and cons of emigration. Emigrants produced their own texts: they recorded their experiences of the voyage out in diaries, sometimes sending them back to their families in Britain as evidence of their having arrived. On board the ship, and with little else to do, they made periodicals, put on plays, wrote letters to their families back in Britain. In the colonies, they continued to write to their families and produced accounts of their settlement to be published.

For those intending to emigrate, this body of literature would have been, in part, an invaluable resource. Emigrant guidebooks impressed upon their readers the necessity of perusing a wide variety of such material before they committed to moving abroad. Readers of one such guidebook, *Counsel for Emigrants*, were reminded in the epigraph that '[i]n the multitude of Councillors there is safety'.[7] This 'multitude' refers both to the miscellany of information in *Counsel*, which reproduced excerpts from newspaper accounts, other emigrant manuals and letters, but also to the vast amount of literature available on the market. The epigraph thus affirms the validity of the information that *Counsel* contains and prescribes a moral economy of reading: to read more is to know more, to safeguard oneself against the dangers and pitfalls of emigration. '[F]lights of imagination,' the editor informs the reader, 'are migratory excursions which we ought to indulge in as little as possible'; it is far better to 'sit down to the consultation', 'call witnesses', 'examine documents', and 'ask advice from every one whom we may think capable of giving it'.[8]

There was certainly no shortage of available information on emigration in the nineteenth-century print market. Regardless of whether the publishers were big, with strong colonial identifications, or whether they were small and hoping to make a quick profit, they were keen to produce texts on emigration. Accounts of emigration and settlement, emigrant manuals, emigrant letters, periodical articles, pamphlets, as well as official documentation on emigration flooded the market. As James Belich argues, 'the sheer scale' of publishing in literature aimed at 'boosting' the popularity of emigration was 'impressive': 'booster' literature was 'one of the largest genres in nineteenth-century English literature'.[9] John Barnes et al. echo this when they argue that, '[a]lthough many such publications were produced non-commercially by settlement agencies and religious organisations, the books that hundreds of thousands of emigrant readers took with them served to make this little-regarded genre one of the most remunerative areas of publishing in the nineteenth century'.[10] Nineteenth-century settler emigration, however, gave rise to an array of genres and texts which did not always act as propaganda. Instead, these texts can be placed under the broad and expansive category of 'emigration literature'. In this study, 'emigration literature' is used to denote texts that were produced directly out of the practices of emigration, and thus this term includes the manuscript shipboard periodicals discussed in the second chapter. As such, the term recuperates a broad number of different genres. In *Replenishing the Earth*, James Belich calls the literature which intended to 'boost' emigrant numbers 'booster literature'.[11]

Emigration literature, on the other hand, includes texts such as manuscript letters, periodicals, poetry, diaries and the more formal 'booster literature', such as bills, pamphlets, manuals and advertisements. Across these different genres, however, there are a number of key features which stand out and allow me to talk about emigration literature as a specific kind of writing. As I will show over the next few pages, this body of texts perform distinct cultural work from emigration novels or short stories. Emigration literature employs a rhetoric of nation-building, where emigrants are expected to be loyal to Britain, but also to the new country of settlement. The trajectories within emigrant narratives inevitably point to a future where success is inevitable: everyone can make it in the colonies, as long as they are prepared to work hard and undergo initial privation. Whether letter, periodical or autobiography, emigration literature is concerned with its own status as an authentic text: the first three chapters of the book examine how the texts of emigration literature muse on their own ability to cross physically the distance separating Britain from its colonies and yet still narrate authentically the realities of life in the colonies to a reading public in Britain. These key features across all the texts that I discuss in the first half of the book allow me to make the claim that the separate, distinct genre of emigration literature arises in the nineteenth century.

It is impossible to talk of the processes and experiences of settler emigration without taking into account the array of genres and media that were produced by, and responded to it. If emigration was the bodily experience of moving through space and time to settle in new and foreign places, then the texts of emigration literature were the objects that mediated this move and produced new ways of thinking about it. While it is imperative that we attend to the different agendas and audiences of the vast range of texts that fall under this label, nonetheless, we can make some broad claims for the cultural impact of emigration literature. Emigration literature redefined people's relationship to place. The complicated circuits of textual exchange between metropole and colony meant that emigration literature was physically on the move: emigrants' letters travelled between Britain and the colonies, manuscript shipboard newspapers were produced en route to Australia, and settler fiction was written in the colonies, but was often initially published in Britain and pirated in America. Thus, much like travel literature, emigration literature delocalised the places that emigrants wrote about: distinct locales were mediated through the circulating text. This mediation involved a fine balance: on the one hand, the colonies had to be rendered sufficiently similar to Britain so as to be comfortingly familiar, but they also had to maintain the sense of being different enough that it would allow people to lead a better life in the colonies.

Crucially, however, emigration literature is not travel literature: while there might be significant areas of overlap between the two genres, the important, fundamental difference lies in emigration literature's emphasis on the notion of home. As much as being a genre defined by the conditions of being mobile, the key preoccupation of emigration was the question of settlement and how to make a new home. This is both in the material sense, as the practicalities of settler life in the bush were a far cry from life in Britain, but also in the emotional sense. For all the emphasis in emigration literature on the similarities between Britain and the colonies, the lived experience of newly-arrived emigrants could be a startling exposure to a different way of life. For some emigrants, writing proved a way of integrating themselves into their new environments; in other cases, emigrant guidebooks and manuals advised emigrants on how to build that emotional attachment to their new homes – without completely breaking off relations with Britain.

Through exchanging texts and other gifts, emigrants and their families maintained and extended their kinship ties over time and space. It was one of the ways in which friends and family members separated by vast distances could imagine or feel that their loved ones were near. Distance became more than a geographical measurement in the context of emigration: as something to be felt or perceived, it gained a strong affective charge. In doing so, emigration literature produced its own very distinctive spatial imaginaries: through mediating this multi-layered sense of belonging to both colony and Britain, emigration literature collapsed and enlarged the sense of the distance between the two places. Thus at the same time as expanding people's notions of an inhabitable world, emigration literature simultaneously aimed to reduce the distance separating emigrants from their family back home. Far from being an objective fact, the distance between the colonies gained a representational force which could be aestheticised in multiple, competing ways.

Nineteenth-century settler emigration 'touched the lives of everyone, everywhere' in Britain.[12] Even those who spoke out against emigration were forced to acknowledge how deeply emigration and its literature pervaded everyday life. The author of 'The Emigration Cry', for example, noted that the mania for emigration pervaded every aspect of cultural life:

> What is the almost universal cry of the sons and daughters of England? Emigration. What is the advice that England gives to her distressed children? Emigrate. How does England apologise for her neglect of health, light, air, and wholesome food for body and soul? Let them emigrate, and they will fare better. What is England's recompense to the forlorn sister of her own shame, Ireland? Emigrate again. That one word rings on the platforms of public assemblies, echoes through the walls of literary institutions, stares one in the face in colossal placards, thrusts itself into one's hands in the form of tailors' outfitting advertisements.[13]

If emigration was an ever-constant theme in the everyday lives of people, then so were the cultural concerns of its literature. Emigration literature provided artists and novelists with a different way of imagining the relationships between Britain and the colonies. This distance gained an affective charge in emigration literature, and artists and novelists took on this aesthetic, exploring, extending and critiquing the cultural effects of emigration literature in their own work.

From Emigration to Colonisation

In 1798, Thomas Malthus wrote *An Essay on the Principle of Human Population*. The work was to prove hugely influential, going through six editions in twenty-eight years. Malthus's basic premise was that an unchecked human population 'increases in a geometrical ratio', while 'subsistence increases only in an arithmetical ratio'.[14] He predicted that, as human population grows at a faster rate than agricultural production can keep up with, there would come a time when the human population would outstrip food resources. By the 1830s, his words took on a frightening resonance and his prediction of a human population unable to feed itself seemed to be becoming true. The end of the Napoleonic Wars left hundreds of thousands out of employment. Industrialisation, as well as the Corn Laws, played their part in intensifying the difficulties of unemployment and social unrest. In 1815, 'the Corn Law pushed the price of a loaf of bread to one shilling, at a time when wages ranged from eight shillings per week for farm labourers, to thirty-six for the best skilled workers in London'. The agricultural depression of the 1830s, followed by the Hungry Forties, meant that for many, the future seemed very bleak. For Thomas Carlyle, all the unrest of the 1830s could be attributed to overpopulation, the 'grand anomaly', which was bringing 'all other anomalies to a crisis'.[15] He argued that the problem of unemployment extended to people of *all* classes: '[L]anguishing in all courthouses, hiding in obscure garrets, besieging all antechambers', are a surplus of 'trained men, educated to pen and practise, to administer and act', of 'briefless Barristers, chargeless Clergy, taskless Scholars', and of 'Half-pay Officers of both Services, wearing themselves down in wretched tedium', all of whom are 'in passionate want of simply one thing, Work'.[16]

But, if in England the '"tide of population" swells too high', the colonies in contrast were supposedly empty lands, waiting to receive the emigrants:

> in a world where Canadian Forests stand unfelled, boundless Plains and Prairies unbroken with the plough; on the west and on the east, green desert spaces never yet made white with corn; and to the overcrowded little western nook of Europe, our Terrestrial Planet, nine-tenths of it yet vacant or tenanted by nomads, is still crying, Come and till me, come and reap me![17]

In an attempt to correct the conceived population imbalance, when the government passed the Poor Law Amendment Act in 1834, they allowed parishes to use the money raised for the relief of the poor for the purposes of 'defraying the expenses of the emigration of poor persons having settlements in such parish, and willing to emigrate'.[18] In the early years of the decade, the government laid the foundations of the Colonial Land and Emigration Commission. Through the 1830s, Commissioners were appointed to explore the possibilities concerning emigration and on 14 January 1840, the Commission formally came into existence.[19]

At the same time as introducing emigration as a solution to social problems, the Poor Law Amendment Act consolidated public stigma associated with emigration. The history of North America as a former, and Australia as a current, penal colony set it firmly in people's minds that emigration was a means of siphoning off an unwanted section of society, and the Poor Law institutionalised the idea that emigration was for the labouring poor who did not have the means to feed themselves. As opponents of assisted schemes were quick to point out, emigration was not a solution in and of itself. The practice of giving away or selling at an extremely low price large tracts of land was often counter-productive as many of the newly-arrived emigrants did not have the requisite skills or knowledge to work the land to their advantage. Edward Gibbon Wakefield, the most prominent opponent of such assisted emigration schemes, campaigned strongly to change both the economic basis on which emigrants would move out, and concomitantly, to remove the stigma associated with emigration. In 1830, he published *A Letter from Sydney*, under the pseudonym of the radical Robert Gouger. Wakefield pointed out that the owners of big estates in the colonies did not have the means of getting the labour they needed in order to make their lands productive. He argued for a means of 'systematic colonisation', which would ensure that both labour and capital would be exported to the colonies: land would be sold at a high enough price for labour to be available to capital and yet low enough for labourers to be their own masters in four to five years of arriving. In impressing upon the government the 'need for money as well as migrants, instant townships, joint stock companies [and] genteel settlers',[20] Wakefield aimed to redefine how people thought about emigration.

Just over a decade later, Charles Buller was able to assert confidently in his 1843 speech to Parliament that, 'This change in the character of colonisation – this great change in the estimation in which it is held, is of greater moment than the mere provision of means for conducting emigration with no cost to the public.' He famously argued that a means of emigration which focused on relieving distress without looking at the larger picture 'aimed at little more than shovelling out [. . .] paupers to where they might die, without shocking their betters with the sight or sound of their last agony'.[21] Instead, what was needed, Buller argued, was Wakefield's notion of systematic colonisation, which would both go beyond the mere removal of unwanted people from Britain to build a more sustainable colony and would raise the estimation of emigration in the minds of the people.[22] If emigration was the disorganised helter-skelter of the rabble who had no choice about where to go, colonisation was the 'extension of civilised society'. Buller argues that 'within the last three or four years', the colonies have been filled with 'tradesmen and artizans [sic] of every kind [. . .] Clergymen and schoolmasters, and competent men of every liberal profession [. . .] artists and men of science'. The resulting settlement is one to which 'men of birth and refinement are tempted to emigrate; they do so in great numbers'.[23]

This was neither an exaggeration nor a cause for universal celebration. In 1852, an article in *Sharpe's London Magazine* argued that emigration was nothing but 'our inability to keep our people at home'. 'We are not an English people,' the author notes wryly, 'for we may all be gone tomorrow.' Fearing that the huge numbers of people emigrating from England were debilitating any nation-building agenda, the author argues that 'we are [...] daily robbing ourselves of thousands who might have worked for our own prosperity'.[24] Advocates of systematic colonisation, such as Buller and Wakefield, however, saw emigration as a means of 'augmenting the resources of the empire and the employment of the people'. Colonisation was not just a means of temporary relief to parishes at home. As Buller points out, 'his [the emigrant's] absence is only the first relief which he affords you'. Given a little time, the emigrant in Canada or Australia, will soon find that 'by applying his spare time and energies to raise additional food [...] he can obtain that which he can exchange for luxuries of which he never dreamed at home'. Given a little extra time, the emigrant then 'raises some article for export' – and crucially – '*appears in your market as a customer*'.[25] Theoretically, at least, systematic colonisation would create new markets with which Britain could trade and compete, and thereby economically strengthen itself and its colonies.

Wakefield's theory of systematic colonisation was part of a widespread shift towards positive public attitudes to emigration. As early as 1832, with no knowledge of the famine that was to hit Ireland, Martin Doyle, the author of the emigrant handbook, *Hints on Emigration to Upper Canada*, noted that whereas emigration was once 'a measure of relief [...] hitherto embarrassed with cost and difficulty', it is '*now* assuming a more attractive form, and recommending itself to all the honest and industrious classes'.[26] By mid-century, for the vast majority of people, emigration was a national colonial endeavour: it was a move that strengthened the nation, and realised Britain's global aspirations. As Angela Woollacott argues, settlers' 'world views' were marked by a sense of 'colonial connectedness': settlers 'understood that their own prosperity and security were linked to the fortunes of the British empire in other colonies'.[27] In addition to the emigration schemes of Caroline Chisholm and Charles Dickens, which I explore in greater depth in the first and last chapters of this book, there were a prolific number of philanthropic schemes in the middle of the century that encouraged people to emigrate. The existence of such schemes can be read as part of a more widespread move to systematise and organise the outward flow of people, but it also attests to a shift in public sentiment towards a more positive attitude to emigration. It is worth remembering, for example, that only a small minority of people emigrated out on assisted schemes: the vast majority of emigrants in the nineteenth century were free emigrants who had gone of their own choice and paid for their own passage.

The Expansion of Greater Britain

Looking back and reflecting on the events of the century in 1883, the Cambridge historian John Robert Seeley reflected that, 'Whether good or bad then, the growth of Greater Britain is an event of enormous magnitude' and 'evidently the great fact of modern English history'.[28] In numbers, certainly, the explosion of the settler colonies remains a staggering historical fact. As James Belich points out, 'Settler Australasia grew from 12,000 people in 1810 to 1.25 million in 1860, expanding over a hundredfold in fifty years [. . .] In Canada, Ontario grew twenty-threefold from about 60,000 people in 1811 to 1.4 million in 1861.'[29] But for Seeley, the 'magnitude' lay in the 'moral and intellectual consequences of this movement', just as much as in the statistical fact. Arguing that there is something distinctive about the staying power of British emigration, he points out that 'we see a constant stream of emigration from Germany to America, but no Greater Germany comes into existence'. He continues:

> It is not simply that a population of English blood is now found in Canada and in Australia, as in old time a Greek population was spread over Sicily, South Italy and the Western Coast of Asia Minor [. . .] Greater Britain is a real enlargement of the English State; it carries across the seas not merely the English race, but the authority of the English Government. We call it for want of a better word an Empire.[30]

Importantly, for Seeley, the white, Anglophone colonies constituted an empire quite different from that of India, for example:

> it strikes us at once that this enormous Indian population does not make part of Greater Britain in the same sense as those ten millions of Englishmen who live outside of the British Islands. The latter are of our own blood, and are therefore united with us by the strongest tie. The former are of alien race and religion, and are bound to us only by the tie of conquest.[31]

In Seeley's eyes, the settler colonies were triply bound to Britain through 'three ties': 'community of race, community of religion, community of interest'.[32] As Duncan Bell says, this 'vision of an integrated globe-spanning polity', which 'would incorporate the continental expanses of Canada, at its heart the British Isles, and stretch over the South Pacific to include the colonial territories of New Zealand and Australia' represented an 'unprecedented spatial stretching of the state to accommodate a [. . .] constellation of territories whilst simultaneously embodying a vision of moral order in which a superior Anglo-Saxon race [. . .] offered leadership and stability to a chaotic world'.[33] While 'the settler empire' was often imagined 'as a single transcontinental political unity',[34] the question of how to imagine the relationship between them was far more complex. 'Straddling oceans and spanning continents',[35] the 'fragmented form and vast extent' of the settler empire rendered unity and homogeneity 'an impossible dream'.[36] Seeley knew of this when he wrote:

> People cannot change their abodes, pass from an island to a continent, from the 50th degree of north latitude to the tropics or the Southern Hemisphere, from an ancient community to a new colony, from vast manufacturing cities to sugar plantations or lonely sheepwalks [sic] in countries where aboriginal savage tribes still wander, without changing their ideas and habits and ways of thinking, nay without somewhat modifying in the course of a few generations their physical type.[37]

In the cultural imagination, the unity between Britain and the colonies was a deep-seated bond. Metaphors of Britain as the benevolent mother country to which the colonies, as her children, owed their allegiance became the dominant mode of phrasing the relationship. Settler colonialism in particular relied heavily on the cultural capital of the family unit, because of the 'regenerative capacity' at the heart of settler societies. As Lorenzo Veracini astutely argues, 'settler migration operates within a register of sameness', where the future of new colonies depends on the success in which it can 'reproduce' older forms of communities.[38] The family literalises this notion of 'reproduction': it was no coincidence that a young healthy man, with a wife and children became the enduring image in the century of the 'ideal' coloniser.

Emphasising the familial nature of the bond between Britain and the colonies was one way of collapsing the sense of distance, but as the century wore on, this sense of distance was also overcome by technological advances. As Seeley put it so eloquently, Britain was: 'a nation so widely dispersed that before the age of steam and electricity its strongly natural bonds of race and religion seemed practically dissolved by distance'. But now, 'Science has given to the political organism a new circulation, which is steam, and a new nervous system, which is electricity'; 'political union over vast areas has begun to be possible, so soon Greater Britain starts up not only a reality but a robust reality'.[39] Technological developments of the telegraph, shorter sailing times, better postal services and the production of new routes to the colonies (such as the Suez Canal in 1869) meant that towards the end of the century, the sense of distance separating the colonies from Britain had been reduced. While this by no means contributed to a homogeneous experience of emigration, such changes reframed the contexts within which people were emigrating.

During the years 1830 to 1870, however, the distance between the colonies was and seemed immense. The colonies were at once metonymic projections of 'home' and frighteningly unfamiliar, distant places. The task of emigration literature was to assert that sense of similarity and overcome that sense of distance to produce a sense of familiarity. Concerns over how to negotiate the miles between Britain and her colonies shaped the aesthetics of emigration literature, but in turn, emigration literature set into play new ways of imagining the connections between homes, both near and afar. These seeped into established genres such as narrative paintings and novels. As we shall see, the texts of emigration, be they maps, letters, or periodicals, become a recurrent motif in novels and art as sites of enquiry into what it meant to be part of, and produce, a world that was simultaneously expanding and, at the same time, coming into closer contact with itself.

Mobility and Materiality

It was not only technological advances which produced new ways of experiencing and imagining the geographical distances between Britain and the colonies. Emigration literature also produced its own aesthetics of distance, at once shrinking the expanse to render the colonies ostensibly familiar locales and simultaneously maintaining the sense that they were different enough to allow for better and more successful lives to develop there. Texts of emigration literature, whether printed letters, diaries, periodicals or manuals, were inherently mobile as they travelled between Britain and the colonies, or as they were produced at sea, in the spaces that connected them. Their mobility opens up new ways in which we can understand the cultural work of literature in shaping how people understand their place in a changing world.

Various critics have made claims for the novel as *the* Victorian genre of mobility. In *Portable Property*, for example, John Plotz argues that the novel lies 'at the heart of Victorian reflections on portability', because it is a mobile artefact. '[N]ew forms of rapid transit' coupled with 'the triumphant explosion of book and periodical production and consumption' in the nineteenth century meant that novels circulated through local, regional, national and international networks.[40] The arrival of the railway, for example, meant the emergence of 'a profoundly mobile readership, for whom travel was an occasion for, rather than an impediment to, immersion in printed matter'.[41] The idea that novels moved between countries and continents, often for the purposes of colonial subjugation as well as for British settlers, is not new.[42] As Josephine McDonagh argues, novels were 'loved' by travellers and emigrants because they 'tell powerful and complex stories about people's relationships to places': they 'served to remind readers of their love of home, while simultaneously encouraging them to make emotional connections to new landscapes and environments'.[43] However, Plotz lets the mobility of the text fade into the background of the argument, and focuses instead on the mobile material world in the novel, arguing that the novel 'reflects'[44] on portability through its depictions of that world. In novels, even the most simple, ordinary, everyday objects become 'precious relics overseas' that 'connote family, England, and the prospect of ready cash all at once'.[45] Thus, although he recognises the mobility of the novel, he does not take into account the fact that novels – and a broad range of other textual material – often moved *with* people.

In *British Settler Emigration in Print*, Jude Piesse argues that the context of the novel's periodical publication needs to be taken into account if we are to understand fully the relationships between settler emigration and printed texts. She argues that the periodical's 'dependence upon new technologies of motion and transport, transnational range, and fluid formal dynamics' both contributes to the periodical's 'circulatory drives' and makes possible a 'new way of understanding it as an intrinsically migratory form'. The Victorian periodical was 'an inherently mobile form', with 'an unrivalled capacity to register emigration'.[46] Piesse thus convincingly argues that engaging with the mobility of periodicals is central to our understanding of the relationships between settler emigration and print.

Periodicals were a key feature of colonial settlement: in the vast majority of cases, periodicals, and not novels, were the first pieces of literature to be produced. British periodicals were shipped over to the colonies, where they were read, and excerpted by colonial periodicals. But periodicals and novels were not the only texts that moved between England and her colonies in the context of nineteenth-century emigrants. Mobility is a key aspect of emigration literature: letters, diaries, regulations for the voyage and journals were all embedded in a network of circulation of people, texts and goods. Extending our analysis from the particular genre of the novel or the periodical, and embracing a more expansive approach allows us to understand the literary contexts of nineteenth-century settler emigration more broadly. Positioning ephemeral texts, like shipboard manuscript newspapers, alongside mainstream settler accounts, canonical novels and art allows us to perceive just how deeply entwined the mobile world of the text is with the movement of people. The texts of emigration literature are not static entities with fixed spatio-temporal markers, but objects that are determined by the 'geographies' of their production and consumption.[47] Analysing in detail the contexts in which they are produced and consumed forces us to see texts of emigration literature as material objects, subject to the conditions of their formation and circulation. When *Cranford*'s narrator, Mary, posts her letter to Miss Matty's long-lost brother in India, she tries to imagine how the letter, which had 'but an hour ago [seemed] so familiar and common-place', would be changed by the journey: the letter 'would get tossed about on the sea, and stained with sea-waves perhaps; and be carried among palm-trees, and scented with all tropical fragrance'. Mary's letter is a tactile object; the shock of it leaving her hands leaves her standing looking at the 'gaping split' of the postbox hole which 'divided' her from that which was 'but a moment ago in my hand' and now 'gone from me like life – never to be recalled'.[48] Nineteenth-century emigrants too frequently wrote with fondness of the letters and books that people had sent them because they had been previously touched by loving hands. For example, Arthur Richardson, a young Irish emigrant to New York in the 1830s wrote home acknowledging receipt of a 'great many papers' from his mother, but more importantly, he notes from 'your handwriting on them that you are well'.[49] Catherine Langthorn, an Irish working-class woman in her late fifties, kept up correspondence, despite struggling with arthritis and failing eyesight, with her son who emigrated to Australia from Pinner in the 1880s. In one letter, she writes if you will let me know when your son and air is coming iwill try and send him his first shirt and boots if ican but iam afraid they will not be my own hand work for iam sorry to tell you that my other eye is nearly gone ifear you will not be able to read this for icanot see ionly rite it be guess but ithought you would be more likly to answer it if you saw it was my hand [*sic*].⁵⁰

Handwriting carried a deeply affective charge for those separated by emigration. For Langthorn, it does not matter whether her son is able to read the letter: the poor handwriting, the best form of her 'own hand work' that she can muster at this present time, is both an indication of her ill health, and also, as the reference to her grandson's boots and shirt indicate, a means of conveying her love for her son. More than what it linguistically conveys, the material qualities of handwriting itself – the materials with which it is written as well as its visual form – become signifiers of meaning in these letters.

From Plotz's 'portable property', to Elaine Freedgood's 'ideas in things' to Suzanne Daly's 'empire inside', critics have recently turned their attention with vigour to tracing the mobile world of objects in novels to track the cultural flows within empire.⁵¹ Emigration literature is unique in this respect because of its intertwined aesthetics of mobility and materiality, which require us not only to consider how these texts have moved and to where, but also presses upon us the need to consider how the very fact of their mobility has changed their material form. On the one hand, the mobility of the text of emigration literature – the manuscript or printed letter, the loose sheets of the shipboard periodical – generates a culture of suspicion.⁵² How were people to know the text had not been tampered with during its travels? How were they to know if accounts of distant places were not fabricated? In an attempt to make itself believable, emigration literature frequently used the material world to construct and refer to itself. To use the words of Elizabeth Ermarth, 'the language that appears referential, innocently pointing toward an objective world beyond it' is also 'self-reflexive, gesturing toward its own principles of operation'.⁵³ Emigration literature is filled with the stuff of everyday settler life – nails, seeds, foodstuff, tools, for example – but while the material world in the text ostensibly refers to the contexts of emigration, it simultaneously 'gestures' to the processes of its own production in an attempt to convey to the reader that its authenticity has not been compromised by its mobility. Accounts of the materiality of settler life are intended to show the reader that the author really had emigrated, and that the text authentically relates the facts of settler life.

These shared aesthetics of mobility and materiality in the context of emigration literature held greater sway over the nineteenth-century cultural imagination than has been previously granted.[54] When emigration makes it into the visual and novelistic folds, it does so in textual form: the texts of emigration culture, be they letters, or colonial magazines and periodicals, all become motifs in novels and paintings, and the site of a complex enquiry into what it means to move away and remake a home elsewhere. Emigration literature, so deeply concerned with its own materiality and mobility, itself becomes a textual object in novels and art and in so doing shapes the aesthetic representations of distance, mobility and home.

Interconnected Zones

Migration from Britain to her colonies shapes the modern world as we know it today. Studying the textual outputs of this demographic moment comes with its own challenges. A fuller story of white settlement in the colonies needs to acknowledge that nineteenth-century settler emigration was a messy entanglement of people, ideas and things in motion: it does not fit into the model of a metropole-colony binary where there is an outward surge of emigrants, who nostalgically look back to Britain for literary and artistic modes through which to articulate their experiences. While it interrogates how people conceived of the relationship between Britain and her colonies in the context of emigration, this book simultaneously recognises that this is one strand in a complex network of global connections. Colonial newspapers reprinted news from India, South East Asia, New Zealand and elsewhere. Emigrants to Australia would have stopped off at ports in Africa, the Indian Ocean, South East Asia and South America, while those across the Atlantic may well have disembarked in North America before travelling up to their final destinations. As Woollacott argues, settlers 'had personal connections to and knowledge of many places around a rapidly globalizing world'.[55] Furthermore, countries other than Britain in the nineteenth century were also experiencing multiple forms of emigration. In his travelogue *Greater Britain*, Charles Dilke writes of 'the introduction of a mixed multitude of Bengalees, Chinamen, South Sea Islanders, and Malays to cultivate the Queensland coast plantations'.[56] In 1858, an article in *Household Words* expressed anxiety over the large numbers of

'Chinamen' who, 'contrary to their long-established usages and habits [. . .] are swarming (no other word is so expressive of the manner of their emigration) into other climes'.[57] Taking the focus away from Britain and her colonies shows that other countries were also experiencing the widespread effects of emigration as people across Europe, Asia and Russia uprooted themselves to make new homes elsewhere.[58] Nineteenth-century British settler emigration was truly part of a much more global story of human migration. It is imperative that we recognise that the colonies were determined by multiple points of contact and were imbricated in complex circuits of exchange that involved many other countries. From the earliest days of its settlement, when the First Fleet was driven by starvation to trade with India, China and Jakarta, Australia established trading routes with India.[59] Furthermore, as recent important research has shown, the Indian Ocean was a rich network of trade relations.[60]

The networks of mobility which constitute nineteenth-century settler emigration is made more complicated by the fact that emigrants rarely settled down immediately once they had arrived in their new destinations. Some moved from settlement to settlement, in search of jobs or the best lands, or to be near their friends and family. Others returned to Britain. As little record of international movement was kept at the time, it is difficult to arrive at a statistic for back-migrants. Their motives for returning are multiple and varied. Wilbur Shepperson argues that it was because they were 'disenchanted' by what they had seen, or by the discrepancies between what they had read and what they had experienced (a phenomenon that is explored in the third chapter of this book).[61] As Dudley Baines argues, back-migration was a way in which '[p]otential emigrants received information about overseas countries'.[62] Emigrants returned with personal anecdotes about both the costs and benefits of emigration: 'if the bulk of the returned emigrants had been failures, they would have been less likely to induce the emigration of others'.[63]

Gary Magee and Andrew Thompson assert in *Empire and Globalisation* that attending to the '"networks" of contact and communication forged by migrants' is a means of 'analysing with greater precision [the] long-distance connections over extended periods of time'. This method of enquiry allows 'an interconnected zone constituted by multiple points of contact and complex circuits of exchange' to emerge. Magee and Thompson argue that this networked, interconnected zone is 'not just the preserve of an "official mind" in Whitehall', but 'a field of enterprise for the whole of British society',[64] an important point that underpins the scope of this book, which takes a more expansive approach and understands emigration and its textual culture as a general phenomenon that affected nineteenth-century Britain. Widening the field of analysis from the mid-century novel to include ephemeral material, such as printed emigrants' letters and manuscript shipboard newspapers, and narrative painting allows us to gauge the pervasive cultural effects of emigration literature that cut through different genres and classes of society. Telling the story of white settlement using source material from emigrants themselves has its challenges as it raises issues of which voice is privileged over others, but it is hard to ignore the fact that the shape and demography of the world as we know it today is a direct result of nineteenth-century migration.

The particular strand of British emigration to her colonies in this complex network of global migrations warrants our attention. Firstly, against current hysteria over various patterns of migration today, it reminds us that, for much of the nineteenth century, the predominant colour of voluntary migration was white. It is important, perhaps now more than ever, to be able to tell this story of nineteenth-century settler emigration without fearing that we lay ourselves open to the charge of 'Anglo-bias'. As Belich argues, the tacit reluctance to talk about an 'Anglo-world' is 'partly denial' and 'partly an inverse tendency to see the Anglo-world as normative' because we 'still live in or with the Anglo-world'.[65] Returning our attention to nineteenth-century settler emigration thus forces us both to correct this historical amnesia and at the same time to lay open the underlying conditions of this normative state. Secondly, as Alex Murdoch argues, '[i]n the nineteenth century emigration became part of the popular culture of Britain'.[66] 'Emigration history', he continues, 'has attracted the interest of economic and social historians and demographic specialists [. . .] but has been viewed more generally as peripheral to British history, almost as if British emigrants were no longer part of British history once they had left Britain.'[67] Eric Richards similarly argues that settler emigration is 'rarely given prominence' as a 'feature of modern British history', yet it is 'Britain's most fundamental and enduring legacy to the modern world'.[68]

Part of this 'enduring legacy' is a history of the erosion of peoples and cultures. The other side of emigration is the question of settlement: the emphasis on settlement and the creation of new homes abroad sets emigration literature apart from travel literature. This concern with a potential rootedness and belonging is all the more important because of the mobile conditions that emigration necessarily set into play. Settlement – the problems and politics of moving away and making a new home – is central to emigration literature and is thus an overarching concern in this book.[69] Belich argues that the term 'settler' became a more popular word than 'emigrant' over the course of the century. According to him, without the class implications of the term 'colonist' or the stigma of the term 'emigrant', and holding the promise of success, it is easy to see why 'settler' became such a popular term.[70] Given that the terms 'emigrant' and 'colonist' both have ideological implications, it is interesting that Belich picks up on the word 'settler' without pausing to comment on the central meaning of this word: to settle.

One of the problems of the term 'settle' is its stress on rootedness and belonging, without attending to the conflict embedded in the act of settling. Eric Richards is particularly blind to this when he writes, 'the people of the British Isles clearly set the pace, pioneering mass migration, sustaining the outward flows, and *helping to repopulate other continents*'.[71] As Sarah Nuttall argues, the term 'settler' is steeped in the 'politics of conquest and subjugation':

> The notion of the settler, which always also implies a native, carries with it in its originary sense a master-slave dialectic based on land: a relationship based on conquest and ownership on the one hand and on dispossession and subjugation on the other, in which one party acts and the other is acted upon; a relationship of response rather than co-intervention.[72]

At all times, this book is sensitive to these acts of wilful textual and physical repression. For the most part, as texts of colonisation, emigration literature holds out the promise that the new lands are not populated, and thus propagates the myth of empty spaces. This book recognises that encounters with indigenous peoples in the texts it studies are rare, but it pays close attention to these moments when they do occur. While the central concern of the book is with British emigration to the colonies, it asserts that it is not possible to tell this story of global modernity without taking into account the physical violence of settlement and the occasional moments of intimate contact that occur.[73]

David Harvey argues that globalisation, even in its early forms, can be described as a form of 'time-space compression', a phrase which refers to the 'speed-up in the pace of life, while so overcoming spatial barriers that the world sometimes seems to collapse inwards upon us'.[74] This is particularly true of the Victorian era: improvements in travel and communication technologies, postal services and global trade, for example, brought far-off and distant places into contact with each other. When critics have talked about the Victorian world 'shrinking', they have usually done so in terms that assert the progress and development of Britain.[75] Emigration was a key feature of these moments of Victorian modernity and globalisation, and there is no doubt that it was affected by these developments. However, this is only one side of the story of nineteenth-century modernity and emigration. Although the extension of kinship ties and feelings of national bonding were enabled by these technologies, at times the world could also seem enormous to emigrants and their families. Over and over again in their letters, emigrants stressed that they would most likely never see their families again, but hoped to meet them in the hereafter. And, while emigration extended the parameters of the knowable world for Britain and her inhabitants, a widening world for British settlers simultaneously meant a shrinking world for indigenous peoples.[76]

The first three chapters of this book respectively examine three genres arising directly out of the practices of nineteenth-century settler emigration: printed emigrants' letters, manuscript shipboard periodicals, and settler narratives. Collectively, these three chapters bring into focus some of the critical ideas of emigration literature and explore how emigration texts negotiate the temporal and spatial distance that separated Britain from her colonies. The chapters demonstrate that, across a variety of genres, writing is shown to produce a sense of settlement: it brings disparate ideas together and stabilises the confusing experiences of emigration into a textual form. At the same time, the authority of these texts was destabilised by the geographical distance between themselves and the places they described. In the printed texts of emigration literature – the letters and Moodie and Parr Traill's accounts of settlement – this destabilisation was seen as something to be overcome in order for the reader's trust to be gained. Manuscript shipboard periodicals, on the other hand, embraced this destabilisation, and between the gap of manuscript and print found a space in which to perform settlement.

Chapter 1 looks at printed emigrants' letters, a genre that has hitherto been neglected in both literary and historical studies of emigration, on account of their dubious authenticity. Publishers saw emigrants' letters written to friends, family, emigration societies and philanthropists as a valuable source of information on emigration. Letters were often printed and circulated in a wide array of places, from periodicals to emigration society reports, pamphlets to edited collections. This chapter explores the ways in which printed emigrants' letters manage the text's transition from manuscript to print. The letters provide first-hand accounts of emigration, of the colonies and of settling. They exude an intimate, personal tone and provide readers with a vicarious experience of emigration. At the same time, however, printed letters have been taken out of the context of small, personal networks of circulation and placed in the larger, and more public, circulation of print. Editors were keen to impress upon a suspicious reading public that the letter's mobility, as it travels from the colonies back to Britain and into print, had not compromised its authenticity. Producing the effect of being authentic was an integral part of these letters' commodity status: potential emigrants had to be convinced that the tales of the colonies in the letters really were true if they were going to buy them.

Chapter 2 takes up the concerns of the first chapter regarding the grey areas between public and private spheres and the binaries of manuscript and print, in the context of two manuscript shipboard periodicals, the *Alfred* (1839) and the *Open Sea* (1868). These were periodicals that emigrants themselves had made during the voyage to Australia. Whereas success is the inevitable narrative conclusion of printed emigrants' letters (and other propaganda), shipboard periodicals remain distinct from these genres because of their ostensible lack of participation in these narratives. Manuscript shipboard periodicals aim to invest themselves with the qualities of printed, land-based periodicals through their mimicry of them. Thus, rather than focusing on the *colony* as a place of settlement, these periodicals produce a culture of settlement *on board the ship*. In constructing the voyage out as a preparatory stage to the actual task of settlement in the colonies, the periodicals participate in the colonial push to turn emigrants into successful settlers.

Chapter 3 focuses on the semi-autobiographical accounts of settlement by Susanna Moodie and her sister, Catharine Parr Traill. It argues that the sketch form as practised by Moodie in *Roughing it in the Bush* (1852) and by Parr Traill in *The Backwoods of Canada* (1836), is an attempt to counter the tall tales of success circulating in booster literature. In this way, it takes on the concerns raised in the second chapter of what form is suitable for expressing the experiences of settlement. It argues that the sketch is intimately linked to the female experience of settlement: sketches could be written in the small hours of the night when the day-time chores were finished and children were in bed. Sketches thus capture a sense of these snatched fragments of time and simultaneously evoke the fragmented sensibility which comes when faced with such new surroundings.

The second part of this book examines the ways in which the tropes, concerns and rhetoric of emigration literature are absorbed into genres and media that are not directly related to settler emigration. The almost ubiquitous presence of emigration as a narrative resolution in novels, and the number of paintings that take emigration as a subject matter, frame the central assumption of the book that emigration was a pervasive cultural concern in the nineteenth century. The last two chapters of the book, which focus on narrative painting and novels respectively, interrogate the ways in which emigration literature shapes the aesthetic representations of emigration. While asserting that emigration is represented in these paintings and novels in particular ways, the second part of the book also seeks to establish the ways in which these genres produce alternative ways of thinking about and critiquing emigration.

Chapter 4 looks at representations of emigration in narrative paintings. The chapter explores how emigration is rendered into its textual components in narrative painting. It focuses in particular on five paintings of the mid-century: Ford Madox Brown's *The Last of England* (1855), Richard Redgrave's *The Emigrant's Last Sight of Home* (1858), Thomas Webster's *A Letter from the Colonies* (1852), James Collinson's *Answering the Emigrant's Letter* (1850) and Abraham Solomon's *Second Class – The Parting* (1854). The chapter argues that these emigration paintings eschewed the standard narrative of successful emigration that circulated in print. Instead, they construct a dynamic between image and text in order to emphasise the pain and uncertainty of emigration. In each of the paintings, emigration is depicted through a text, whether an emigrant's letter, a map, a shipping advertisement or the name of the ship. Thus, even when emigration is incorporated into visual culture, it still manifests itself through the texts of emigration literature.

Chapter 5 takes up this reading and interrogates the ways in which emigration literature becomes a trope in Charles Dickens's *Martin Chuzzlewit* (1844) and *David Copperfield* (1850), Elizabeth Gaskell's *Mary Barton* (1848) and Catherine Helen Spence's *Clara Morison* (1854). Part of the reason this book culminates in the mid-Victorian novel is because of emigration literature's own emphasis on 'narrative'. Emigration is a narrative, where the beginning is the point of departure, the middle is the difficulty of making a new settlement into a home, and the end is invariably a happy and industrious emigrant family. This chapter asserts that to ask how central or liminal emigration is to the plot of the novel is to miss the point. What is far more interesting is the ways in which the novels discussed here register the effects of emigration. They draw on the familiar tropes of emigration literature, but at the same time, they imagine a world in which emigration literature connects emigrants and their families and weaves them into the larger global network of the British Empire. Thus, collectively, the last two chapters of this book demonstrate the hold that emigration literature had over the nineteenth-century cultural imagination. Not only does it produce a stock of common tropes that other genres and media drew on, it also *becomes* a motif in them, a site of interrogation of the texts that produced a widening settler world.

Notes

1. Charles Henry Lines, *Papers, 1850–91, including Diary, 15 August–5 November 1852, Kept on a Voyage from Gravesend to Melbourne, on the Clipper* Ballarat, p. 1 [15 August 1852]. Sydney, Mitchell Library, MLMSS 3348: Microfilm CY 3943.
2. Ibid. p. 2 [20 August 1852].
3. David Fitzpatrick, *Oceans of Consolation: Personal Accounts of Irish Migration to Australia* (Cork: Cork University Press, 1994), p. 118, original emphasis.
4. *Copies and Extracts of Letters from Settlers in Upper Canada* (London: Marchant, 1833), p. 4.
5. Dudley Baines, *Migration in a Mature Economy: Emigration and Internal Migration in England and Wales, 1861–1900* (Cambridge: Cambridge University Press, 1985), p. 47.
6. Stephen Constantine and Marjory Harper, *Migration and Empire* (Oxford: Oxford University Press, 2010), p. 2.
7. *Counsel for Emigrants, and Interesting Information from Numerous Sources; With Original Letters from Canada and the United States* (Aberdeen: John Mathison, 1834), title page. Volume subsequently referred to as *Counsel*.
8. Ibid. p. ii.
9. James Belich, *Replenishing the Earth: The Settler Revolution and the Rise of the Anglo-World, 1783–1939* (Oxford: Oxford University Press, 2009), p. 153.
10. John Barnes et al., 'A Place in the World', in David McKitterick (ed.), *The Cambridge History of the Book in Britain, 1830–1914*, 6 vols (Cambridge: Cambridge University Press, 2009), vi, pp. 595–634 (p. 602).
11. Belich, *Replenishing the Earth*, p. 153.
12. Alexander Murdoch, *British Emigration 1603–1914* (Basingstoke: Palgrave Macmillan, 2004), p. 6.
13. 'The Emigration Cry', *Sharpe's London Magazine* (July 1852), pp. 352–61 (p. 352).

14. Thomas Malthus, *An Essay on the Principle of Population*, ed. Geoffrey Gilbert (Oxford: Oxford University Press, 2004 [1798]), p. 13.
15. Thomas Carlyle, *Chartism* (London: James Fraser, 1840), p. 108.
16. Ibid. p. 112.
17. Ibid. For more information on Carlyle's changing views on emigration, see Chris R. Vanden Bossche, *Carlyle and the Search for Authority* (Columbus: Ohio State University Press, 1991), p. 96 and pp. 114–15.
18. *The Act for the Amendment of the Poor Laws with a Practical Introduction, Notes and Forms by John Frederick Archibald* (London: Saunders and Benning, 1834), p. 101. The Poor Law did not specify to which colonies the poor were to be sent. The Act went on to stipulate that people who had agreed to emigrate out and then refused to, or if they returned home once having emigrated, were required to return the money paid to them for defraying the expenses of their emigration to the parish. Gary Howells argues that pauper emigrants were not always 'passive victims of the elite "shovelled out" and thoughtlessly dumped into a new world', but could actively negotiate the terms on which they emigrated out ('"For I was tired of England Sir": English Pauper Emigrant Strategies, 1834–60', *Social History* 23 [1998], pp. 181–94 [p. 181]).
19. Fred H. Hitchins, *The Colonial Land and Emigration Commission* (Philadelphia: University of Pennsylvania Press, 1931), pp. 9–11 (p. 44).
20. Belich, *Replenishing the Earth*, p. 147.
21. Charles Buller, *Systematic Colonization: Speech of Charles Buller* (London: John Murray, 1843), pp. 50–1. Buller's speech was reviewed favourably in the periodical press, including for example, 'Colonisation – The Only Cure for National Distress – Mr Charles Buller's Speech', *Fraser's Magazine* (July 1843), pp. 735–50.
22. Buller, *Systematic Colonization*, p. 28.
23. Ibid. p. 50.
24. 'The Emigration Cry', p. 354.
25. Buller, *Systematic Colonization*, p. 28. Emphasis added.
26. Martin Doyle, *Hints on Emigration to Upper Canada, Especially Addressed to the Middle and Lower Classes in Great Britain and Ireland*, 2nd edn (Dublin: William Curry, 1832), p. 3, original emphasis. Martin Doyle was the pseudonym of the Irish philanthropist and writer, William Hickey (1787–1875).
27. Angela Woollacott, *Settler Society in the Australian Colonies: Self-Government and Imperial Culture* (Oxford: Oxford University, 2015), p. 4.
28. J. R. Seeley, *The Expansion of England*, ed. John Gross (Chicago: University of Chicago Press, 1971 [1883]), p. 16 and p. 15.
29. Belich, *Replenishing the Earth*, p. 83.
30. Seeley, *The Expansion of England*, p. 38.

31. Ibid. p. 14.
32. Ibid. p. 15.
33. Duncan Bell, 'The Victorian Idea of a Global State', in Duncan Bell (ed.), *Victorian Visions of Global Order: Empire and International Relations in Nineteenth-Century Political Thought* (Cambridge: Cambridge University Press, 2007), pp. 159–85 (p. 160 and pp. 161–2).
34. Duncan Bell, *The Idea of Greater Britain: Empire and the Future of World Order, 1860–1900* (Princeton: Princeton University Press, 2007), p.1.
35. Ibid.
36. Ibid. p. 63.
37. Seeley, *The Expansion of England*, p. 16.
38. Lorenzo Veracini, *Settler Colonialism: A Theoretical Overview* (Basingstoke: Palgrave Macmillan, 2010), p. 3 and p. 4.
39. Ibid. p. 61 and p. 63.
40. John Plotz, *Portable Property: Victorian Culture on the Move* (Princeton: Princeton University Press, 2008), p. 5.
41. Ibid. p. 6 and p. 5.
42. See, for example, Priyamvada Gopal, *The Indian Novel in English: Nation, History, and Narration* (Oxford: Oxford University Press, 2009), pp. 15–17.
43. Josephine McDonagh, 'Place, Region and Migration', in John Kucich and Jenny Bourne Taylor (eds), *The Nineteenth-Century Novel, 1820–1880* (Oxford: Oxford University Press, 2012), pp. 361–76 (pp. 371–2).
44. Plotz, *Portable Property*, p. 6.
45. Ibid. p. xv.
46. Jude Piesse, *British Settler Emigration in Print, 1832–1877* (Oxford: Oxford University Press, 2016), p. 2.
47. See Miles Ogborn and Charles W. J. Withers, 'Introduction: Book Geography, Book History', in Miles Ogborn and Charles W. J Withers (eds), *Geographies of the Book* (Farnham: Ashgate, 2010), pp. 1–25.
48. Elizabeth Gaskell, *Cranford*, ed. Elizabeth Porges Watson, intro. Dinah Birch (Oxford: Oxford University Press, 2011 [1863]), p. 127.
49. Arthur Richardson, *Emigrant Letters from Arthur Richardson in America to his Family in Springfield, Lurgan, Ireland 1838-1843* (Dublin, National Library of Ireland, MS 46.759).
50. Jim Golland (ed.), *Pinner to Paradise: The Langthorn Letters* (Pinner: Pinner Local History Society, 1995), p. 109.
51. See Elaine Freedgood, *The Ideas in Things: Fugitive Meaning in the Victorian Novel* (Chicago: University of Chicago Press, 2006) and Suzanne Daly, *The Empire Inside: Indian Commodities in Victorian Domestic Novels* (Ann Arbor: University of Michigan Press, 2011).
52. For a more detailed account of suspicion and reading, see 'Interpretation as Exercise of Suspicion', in Paul Ricoeur, *Freud and Philosophy:*

An Essay on Interpretation, trans. Denis Savage (London: Yale University Press, 1970), pp. 32–6 and Alison Scott-Baumann, *Ricoeur and the Hermeneutics of Suspicion* (London: Continuum, 2009) pp. 93–5.
53. Elizabeth Deeds Ermarth, *Realism and Consensus in the English Novel: Time, Space and Narrative* (Edinburgh: Edinburgh University Press, 1998), p. xiii.
54. See Paul Basu and Simon Coleman, 'Introduction: Migrant Worlds, Material Cultures', *Mobilities* 3 (2008), pp. 313–30.
55. Woollacott, *Settler Society*, p. 13.
56. Charles Dilke, *Greater Britain: A Record of Travel in English-Speaking Countries during 1866 and 1867*, 4th edn (London: Macmillan, 1869), p. 299.
57. [Frank Vincent and Henry Morley], 'John Chinaman in Australia', *Household Words* 17 (April 1858), pp. 416–20 (p. 416).
58. See for example Jan Lucassen and Leo Lucassen, *Globalising Migration History: The Eurasian Experience: 16th– 21st Centuries* (Leiden: Brill, 2014).
59. Geoffrey Blainey, *The Tyranny of Distance: How Distance Shaped Australia's Memory* (London: Macmillan, 1966), p. 51.
60. See Devleena Ghosh and Stephen Muecke (eds), *Cultures of Trade: Indian Ocean Exchanges* (Newcastle-upon-Tyne: Cambridge Scholars, 2007) and H. V. Bowen, Elizabeth Mancke and John G. Reid (eds), *Britain's Oceanic Empire: Atlantic and Indian Ocean Worlds, c.1550–1850* (Cambridge: Cambridge University Press, 2012).
61. Wilbur Stanley Shepperson, *Emigration and Disenchantment: Portraits of Englishmen Repatriated from the United States* (Norman: University of Oklahoma Press, 1965). See also Marjory Harper, 'Introduction', in Marjory Harper (ed.), *Emigrant Homecomings: The Return Movement of Emigrants, 1600–2000* (Manchester: Manchester University Press, 2005), pp. 1–14 for a general introduction to back migration, and Eric Richards's essay in that volume, 'Running Home from Australia: Intercontinental Mobility and Migrant Expectations in the Nineteenth Century', pp. 77–104, for a focused discussion of back migration from Australia. Nineteenth-century shipboard periodicals produced on the voyage back provide a fascinating insight into the experiences of emigrants and their motivations for returning. See for example, P. M. Braidwood and A. J. Cape (eds), *The Parramatta Times* (Liverpool: D. Marples, 1886), produced on an 1886 voyage from Sydney to London.
62. Baines, *Migration in a Mature Economy*, p. 23.
63. Ibid. p. 29.
64. Gary B. Magee and Andrew S. Thompson, *Empire and Globalisation: Networks of People, Goods and Capital in the British World*,

c.1850–1914 (Cambridge: Cambridge University Press, 2010), pp. 16–17.
65. Belich, *Replenishing the Earth*, p. 5.
66. Murdoch, *British Emigration 1603–1914*, p. 6.
67. Ibid. pp. 6–7.
68. Eric Richards, *Britannia's Children: Emigration from England, Scotland, Wales and Ireland since 1600* (London: Hambledon and London, 2004), p. 3.
69. See also Tamara S. Wagner, 'Introduction: Narrating Domestic Portability: Emigration, Domesticity and Genre Formation', in *Victorian Settler Narratives: Emigrants, Cosmopolitans and Returnees in Nineteenth-Century Literature* (London: Pickering & Chatto, 2011), pp. 1–22.
70. Belich, *Replenishing the Earth*, pp. 149–50.
71. Richards, *Britannia's Children*, p. 3. Emphasis added.
72. Sarah Nuttall, 'Subjectivities of Whiteness', in *Rethinking Settler Colonialism: History and Memory in Australia, Canada, Aotearoa New Zealand and South Africa*, ed. Annie E. Coombes (Manchester: Manchester University Press, 2006), pp. 245–62 (p. 245).
73. See Mary Louise Pratt, *Imperial Eyes: Travel Writing and Transculturation*, 2nd edn (London: Routledge, 2006), especially 'Introduction: Criticism in the Contact Zone', pp. 1–12. For accounts of the violence and exploitation of colonial settlement in Australia, see Janine Roberts, *Massacres to Mining: The Colonisation of Aboriginal Australia* (Bristol: Investigative Media Productions, 2008) and Henry Reynolds, *The Other Side of the Frontier: Aboriginal Resistance to the European Invasion of Australia* (Sydney: University of New South Wales Press, 2006 [1982]). For accounts specific to Canada, see Celia Haig-Brown and David A. Nock (eds), *With Good Intentions: Euro-Canadian and Aboriginal Relations in Colonial Canada* (Vancouver: University of British Columbia Press, 2006).
74. David Harvey, *The Condition of Postmodernity: An Enquiry into the Origins of Cultural Change* (Oxford: Blackwell, 1989), p. 240. See also Anthony Giddens, *Modernity and Self-Identity: Self and Society in the Late Modern Age* (Cambridge: Polity Press, 1991), pp. 21–7 for an alternative account of the relationship between print culture and spatio-temporal relationships.
75. See, for example, Peter J. Hugill, 'The Shrinking Victorian World', in Martin Hewitt (ed.), *The Victorian World* (London: Routledge, 2012), pp. 73–89.
76. The 'shrinking world' of native people was troubling for some living in the nineteenth century as well. For a brief introduction, see David A. Nock, 'Horatio Hale: Forgotten Victorian Author of Positive Aboriginal Representation', in Celia Haig-Brown and David A. Nock (eds),

With Good Intentions: Euro-Canadian and Aboriginal Relations in Colonial Canada (Vancouver: University of British Columbia Press, 2006), pp. 32–50, and the Appendix in that volume, 'The Fair Play Papers – The Future of our Indians', pp. 321–30, which is a collection of Hale's writings in which he talks of 'the scattered remnants of a people, who against their will, had been forced to give up their old customs, laws and traditions' (p. 323). A more general and widespread sentiment, however, was that the rapidly decreasing numbers of indigenous peoples were a result of evolutionary 'progress'. See Patrick Brantlinger, *Dark Vanishings: Discourse on the Extinction of Primitive Races, 1800–1930* (London: Cornell University Press, 2003), especially Chap. 8, 'Darwin and After', pp. 164–88. For a more general introduction covering Canada and Australia, see Julie Evans et al., *Equal Subjects, Unequal Rights: Indigenous Peoples in British Settler Colonies, 1830–1910* (Manchester: Manchester University Press, 2003).

Chapter 1

Printed Emigrants' Letters: Networks of Affect and Authenticity

In 1833, a man by the name of Frederick Hasted left his Midhurst home in Sussex for Adelaide, Upper Canada. In his former life, Hasted was well-known as a hawker, travelling with his small carriage drawn by dogs through Sussex, Hampshire and their adjacent counties selling books, newspapers and other printed matter. Agricultural Sussex had been hard hit by the recession of the 1830s. With the end of the Napoleonic Wars, large numbers of military men were now without employment and the shift in supply and demand necessitated by a country now at peace, as well as technological advances, meant that agricultural labourers were being laid off. Frustrated with their situation, rural labourers rioted, 'burning ricks and barns, destroying the threshing machines that were taking their winter work, and joining forces to demand higher wages and more job security'.[1] Hasted had been indirectly affected by the Swing Riots and rural poverty. Tired of eking out a living and frustrated by the lack of economic opportunity, he took the passage out with his daughter to make a new life for himself as a labourer in Upper Canada. He initially settled in Adelaide, where there was a sizeable number of emigrants from Sussex. The presence of familiar faces provided him with a ready community in a foreign environment: he was well-known by the emigrants he travelled out with and he frequently bought land from and sold land to them and offered them work.[2] However, Hasted was unwilling to relinquish his previous relationships altogether. Despite the fact that the cost of sending letters to England came 'heavy' to him, he was an avid letter writer to his friends back home. In the first nine months after he arrived, he wrote at least four letters to friends, telling them of the colony and outlining his hopes for the future. '[A]s I had forgot something of material consequence to you,' he writes near the beginning of his fourth letter, to his friend 'John' in England, 'I thought I would spend 2s. 2d. more for your sake.' He writes to retract an offer of 'some land for house and garden'³ that he had made to John, but he envisages another important function for his letter. He ends with the following request:

> For the good of the poor, and the satisfaction of my friends, and all, whom it may concern, I shall be glad if Mr. Tripp, Mr. Sockett, or some one else, would have this letter printed, either in bills, books, or newspapers; bills I think would be best, as they could be sold at 1d. each, or given away.⁴

Hasted had strong connections with 'Mr Sockett', the man who designed and oversaw an assisted emigration scheme from Petworth, Sussex, that many of Hasted's neighbours in Adelaide had travelled out on. Although Hasted did not himself travel out on Thomas Sockett's emigration scheme, his connections with Sockett helped him find avenues which disseminated his letters as widely as possible. His letter was printed in 1834 in a pamphlet with another emigrant's letter, by William Marchant, a London publisher on Fenchurch Street who frequently published emigration literature, and it appeared in the *Brighton Herald* on 17 May in the same year.⁵ Hasted's desire to have his letters printed continues well after he has settled and Sockett took a strong interest in printing them. In 1839, six years after he arrived in Canada, Hasted ends another letter to his friend, writing, 'I also request you to send this by the Petworth postman, to Mr. Sockett, and I should feel obliged, if he would have the kindness to get it printed, and send a copy of it to each of the undermentioned persons [. . .].'⁶ In another letter dated 1841, Hasted mentions in passing that he has enclosed 'a copy of a letter I sent to a friend in England, which the Revd. T. Socket [sic] Rector of Petworth got printed, and sent me two copies back last spring'.⁷ Hasted was evidently keen for his letters to break out of personal, intimate circles and circulate in the more open world of print. Although he posits this as a benevolent gesture, a move that is for 'the good of the poor', for the 'satisfaction of [his] friends',⁸ and because he is a 'welwisher [sic] to the country',⁹ it is also rooted in a desire to be remembered by being kept in the public eye.

In reality, however, Hasted's letter joined hundreds of thousands of other emigrants' letters that were flooding the nineteenth-century print market. Emigration was an ever-constant topic in the nineteenth century: even if one did not emigrate oneself, it was more than likely that a family member or friend had done so. News and stories from the colonies and North America filled periodicals and newspapers;

roadside walls in villages and hoarding boards in towns were plastered with advertisements of emigration schemes and details of the next ship out; emigration manuals and guidebooks advised emigrants on where to go and what to take. It is no surprise that the rise in the number of emigrants in the nineteenth century is simultaneous with advances in print technology: the two were co-constituted. An example of a self-perpetuating market, the print market encouraged people to emigrate and in turn published the written works of these emigrants, thus ensuring a constant supply of material.

Yet this proliferation made it easier to circulate *mis*information: authors and editors took advantage of the chances of uncovering conflicting advice to assert that, unlike *other* texts in circulation, *theirs* contained the facts. '[F]inding that many contradictory reports and ideas have been circulated' on the subject of New Zealand's 'prosperity', Charles Heaphy, the artist and surveyor to the New Zealand Company from 1839 to 1841, writes that he has 'been induced, at the request of a considerable number of persons, both here in Britain and in the colony, to write a brief account of the present state of settlements in that country [New Zealand]'.[10] On the one hand, Heaphy was well-placed to offer his opinion: he had gained considerable first-hand experience when he sailed with the Company on their first expedition to New Zealand in 1839. During his three years' service with it, he joined the Company's expedition that founded Nelson in 1841 and travelled extensively around the country. On the other hand, he was well aware that his association with the Company made him open to the charge of being biased. He had been contracted by the Company to produce visual material for their publicity campaign and, in this capacity, he produced a wide range of landscape watercolours and of Maori and settler life, many of which were reproduced as lithographs.[11] '[I]t may be imagined,' he writes, 'that I am interested in upholding [the company's] principles, and am now writing by its dictation', but this, 'however, is not the case':[12] 'I must disclaim any participation or interference of it in my writings.'[13] Like much of booster literature, Heaphy's account walks a fine line between providing authentic facts and selling fantastical tales. Printed emigrants' letters were no exception to this. These were letters that ordinary, everyday emigrants had written home to their families and friends, which were then published. They were printed in an astonishing array of places: national and local newspapers, periodicals, pamphlets, leaflets, at the back of emigrant guidebooks, and in stand-alone edited collections. *Household Words* regularly published letters from emigrants, as did newspapers and society magazines which had their own emigration schemes, such as the *Ragged School Magazine*. Almost invariably, the letters contained positive stories of emigration. While they might begin with an acknowledgement of a difficult voyage and initial problems with settling, the conclusion of most, if not all, is a resounding story of success in the colonies.

The range of places in which printed emigrants' letters appeared, as well as the sheer volume of them that were in circulation, stand as testimony to the popularity of the genre. Despite this, printed emigrants' letters have been largely marginalised in studies of emigration literature. In *Invisible Immigrants*, leading historian of nineteenth-century settler emigration, Charlotte Erickson, argues that '[r]eliance on government documents, pamphlet literature, and the immigrant and trade union press' give us a 'distorted picture' of emigration.[14] William Jones reiterates this concern when he argues that all too often, writers of published emigrants' letters are not 'socially representative' and it is difficult to track down biographical information on them in order to 'offset the bias evident in their contents'.[15] David Gerber similarly argues that including printed letters in his edited collection of manuscript letters, *Authors of Their Lives*, would have introduced the 'imposing and time-consuming' 'problem of authentication':[16] one cannot test for 'mischievous editing' as source manuscripts have rarely survived.[17] Unlike Gerber, Wendy Cameron et al. include published letters in their collection of letters, but their decision seems to be forced by circumstance, rather than made out of choice. Recognising that their decision is unusual as most editors 'have excluded all but those in manuscript form' in their collections, Cameron et al. justify themselves by arguing that the 'small amount of extant correspondence from poor immigrants who went to early nineteenth-century Upper Canada does not offer that *luxury*' of working solely with manuscript letters.[18] They console themselves by 'tak[ing] comfort'[19] in Erickson's argument that '[p]rivate letters were no more unbiased than published ones':[20] Cameron et al.'s words border on lament here, an elegy for the aura of the manuscript that print cannot replace.

Yet despite these reservations, it is important to bring printed emigrants' letters to the debate. Doing so allows us to come to a fuller understanding of the connection to distant places that emigration literature created on personal and national levels. This chapter focuses on volumes of printed letters which were connected to a particular emigration scheme or company. As such, the volumes are consummate examples of booster literature: examining them in depth allows us to situate the critical concern over their authenticity in a wider context. Rather than seeing the 'very real problems and limitations'[21] of working with printed letters identified above as obstacles to interpretation, this chapter views them as opportunities to reinterpret print culture in new ways. Instead of centring on the revelatory function of printed emigrants' letters and asking what they can tell us about 'social change and economic conditions in the British Isles',[22] we need to ask instead what kinds of cultural work this body of texts performs within a contemporary context. Originally written for personal consumption, but circulating in the more open world of print, printed emigrants' letters negotiate the history of their manuscript origins by performing their own authenticity. Extending the field of analysis to printed emigrants' letters allows us to understand one of the ways in which the nineteenth century engaged with the problems of knowing distant places through text. Emigrants' letters bought news of the colonies to the reading public's field of reference at home. The connection across time and space between different peoples and places they created was ambiguous and troubled: there is no doubt that the origins of printed emigrants' letters are the result of *dis*connection and *dis*continuity. Their interest lies in their attempt to overcome this and present emigration as the unbroken extension of communal ties.

Narratives of Success

Printed emigrants' letters resound with stories of success. These narratives of success were mostly oriented around the availability of work, food and community in the colonies. Edward Boxall, for example, an ex-soldier who fought in the Napoleonic Wars in the 36th Regiment, wrote home, 'I was very fortunate, in bringing my discharge with me; for I found [. . .] that all who could shew their discharge, was entitled to a hundred acres of land, from the crown for their service, which I accordingly got.'[23] Boxall was travelling out with the first group of emigrants on the assisted emigration scheme from Petworth organised by Thomas Sockett, mentioned at the beginning of this chapter. Supported by the Earl of Egremont, Sockett sent out eighteen hundred men, women and children between the years 1832 and 1837 (when Egremont died) to Upper Canada through his Petworth Emigration Scheme. The scheme was one of the better-organised ones in the early nineteenth century: emigrants were provided with an outfit, transportation to Portsmouth, and money upon arrival in Toronto; some emigrants travelling further than this received extra help. Ships chartered in Egremont's name sailed with fully-assisted emigrants from Petworth, as well as emigrants who were sponsored through other emigration schemes, such as the Dorking Society for Emigration. These societies published their own collections of letters to promote themselves, but in his collections, Sockett drew on letters of *all* emigrants on Petworth ships, regardless of the sponsoring parish. Boxhall was a Petworth emigrant, and his acquisition of land was not unique: it was corroborated by the accounts of his accompanying emigrants who similarly wrote home with their good news. William Phillips, for example, boasts of his and his fellow emigrants' success at having 'each' received a hundred acres of the 'best land in Upper Canada': 'it is well watered and level, not a stone to be seen [. . .] for forty miles. I have plenty of timber on my land'.[24] The presence of family members in Canada created opportunities for work for Boxall and Phillips's relatives back at home: having acquired so much land, they needed hands to maintain it. Boxall writes, '[I]f either of my nephews, or both of them, should like to come over here, I will give them some land to work upon.'[25] Phillips urges his father that, 'I would not advise you to come here, if I did not know it would be to your advantage [. . .] bring uncle Carpenter with you [. . .] I can get you both a farm, if you want one'.[26] Letters such as Boxall and Phillips's, which project a vision of the colonies as places of bounty and plenitude, were important to Sockett for promoting his emigration scheme. After the first group of emigrants had arrived and started writing back home, he collected their letters to their friends and families and published them on single sheets and pamphlets, which he priced at either a penny or tuppence, or gave away free. Once he had amassed enough letters, he republished them along with some new ones in *Letters from Sussex Emigrants*, the edited collection in which Boxall and Phillip's letters appears. The volume was hugely popular: priced at two shillings, it went through two editions in one year. Sockett knew the importance of using printed matter to keep the success of his emigration scheme in the public eye. He campaigned heavily, placing 'broadsheet advertisements in public places in villages and along the main roads where toll gates offered a stopping point and a convenient wall'.[27] The following year, in 1834, he published an account of the second voyage of emigrants, written from the superintendent's perspective, *Narrative of a Voyage, with a Party of Emigrants, Sent out from Sussex* and *Canada: Letters from Persons who have Emigrated to Upper Canada*. In 1836, again, after another batch of emigrants had been sent out, he published *Continuation of Letters from Sussex Emigrants in Upper Canada*.[28]

In *Migration and a Mature Economy*, Dudley Baines argues that assisted emigration and colonisation schemes, whether government-funded or philanthropic, were 'most important' during the first half of the nineteenth century.[29] The economics varied from scheme to scheme. In 1849, Caroline Chisholm set up the Family Colonisation Loan Society. Whereas Egremont's assistance to Petworth emigrants was a 'gift',[30] Chisholm's society lent small, interest-free loans, which had to be paid back within two years, to emigrants who had saved most of the costs of emigration themselves. The aim was to keep the family unit intact, so entire families, or those intending to join their families in Australia, were given priority.[31] Chisholm drew on almost a decade of experience gained in Australia to set up her society. She had moved with her family from Madras, India, where her husband had been stationed, to Sydney in 1839. In 1841, she set up a 'Home' for young female emigrants who had arrived at Sydney but had been unable to find a job. She found jobs for these girls in the bush, often for sometimes double the wages that they would have received in town. Soon after, she started tracking down jobs for men as well. Part of the plan was to alleviate the gender imbalance caused by emigration: she hoped that by placing single women as respectable domestic hands in married families, bachelors in the area would soon catch on and consider them as potential wives. In 1846, she returned to England with hundreds of 'statements' from emigrants that she had collected during her stay in Sydney.[32] She published a sample of these in two pamphlets, *Comfort for the Poor!* (1847) and *Emigration and Transportation Relatively Considered* (1847). She also published a few of them in her advertisement for the Society in *Household Words*.[33] These 'statements' are Chisholm's interviews of emigrants to Australia, but with all the questions removed and the answers collected together in a paragraph. Strictly speaking, they are not 'letters', but they have much in common with them. As in the case of letters, the emigrants' voices in the statements are intended to be read by those 'back home': they contain similar news of prosperity, happiness and success that all emigrants shared, and, as we shall see below, they are similarly concerned with their status as authentic texts. Chisholm used these statements as evidence of the efficacy of emigration, to help set up the society. Like Sockett's *Sussex Emigrants*, Chisholm's statements narrate stories of success and a willingness to help those who are back home. Some aimed to encourage chain migration amongst already established social groups. For example, one emigrant tells his 'dear wife' that 'the best flour is only 20 shillings the sack and such quality that you cannot buy in England the bread is the best bread I ever eat in my life and the meat very fine [sic]'.[34] 'If you can emigrate out i [sic] shall be able to provide for you,'[35] offers another. Keen to help the men of the colonies settle into an established married life, Chisholm pitches her questions so that the answers also appeal to single women in Britain. One emigrant says that 'myself and brother Samuel live together; both are single; we make a good living'[36] and then goes on to list his possessions and what he earns. Another emigrant similarly highlights the fact that he is independent: 'I have been working for my own benefit about ten years in this colony, am single, – it's sharp work to meet with a wife here.'[37] Such advertisements of single, independent and well-earning men indicated to women in England that financial stability through good marriage prospects and stable jobs were available to them in the colonies.

The potency of the success narrative in Chisholm's pamphlets is generated through the accumulation of aggregate voices. The pamphlets are determined by what Leah Price calls the 'discontinuous structure of the anthology'.[38] In almost all the cases, there seems to be little logic as to the order of the statements: there is no overriding narrative to unify the disparate texts in the pamphlet. As we shall see, most collections of emigrants' letters were fragmentary, but Chisholm's collections of statements are far more so: they have no date and are not organised according to place or location. Instead, the 'collections of letters [or statements], like collections of anthology pieces, are strung together from self-contained texts signed by multiple authors':[39] the 'self-contained' nature of each individual statement challenges how we read across the gaps that simultaneously connect and separate them. The spaces between the letters are, in Barthes's words, both 'sequential' and 'agglomerative'.[40] Each emigrant's statement is patterned against another: each statement voices a unique set of experiences, fears and hopes, and yet shares the generic features of the surrounding ones. The notion of emigration as a positive move 'proliferates by [the] layering'[41] of these statements. Reading through the pamphlet, the impressions that one forms of emigration are a result of cumulative contact with the polyphony of the collection.

Even in edited collections where the letters are arranged chronologically, in the vast majority of cases the result is a loosely-structured text determined by the palimpsest of voices. For example, although Sockett writes that 'it will be seen that [in *Letters from Sussex*

Emigrants] the letters and extracts form a chronological series', the letters have no direct bearing upon the next (as in an epistolary novel, say), so the chronology in this case has little bearing upon the construction of a narrative. Instead, the collection gains its narrative charge because the emigrants refer to each other in their letters. For example, in one letter, Edward Boxall writes that, 'Wm. Cooper's land joins mine';[42] the very next letter is Cooper's, who writes that 'Edward Boxall, and his wife, and Wm. Phillips from Merston, and we, have built us a Shantee, and lives and works altogether on our own land [*sic*].'[43] Many pages later, William Phillips's letter appears: 'Dear father, William Cooper, and Edward Boxall, and his wife, and I lives together, and works on our own land.'[44] In the middle of all these letters is one from Edward's brother, George Boxall, who has emigrated with his wife and brother-in-law. The letters in Sockett's collection might be arranged chronologically, but the 'fleeting citations' of the names, and the 'surreptitious and discontinuous way' of stating them forms 'a galaxy of trifling data', which 'make sense only by coalescing': through this 'impressionistic' 'narrative technique',[45] the edited collection of printed letters network the emigrants into a narrative of a community moving over to Canada. The loose construction of the collection as a whole, coupled with the constant intra-textual references, project the idea that emigration is not the loss of familiar networks, but the transplantation of them into new surroundings. This effect is compounded when emigrants write of having met their friends in the colonies: Hasted writes, for example, to ask his friend to pass on the news that 'that I saw the two Whites, sawyers, from Arundel, they live near Hamilton and are well'.[46] The resulting structure of the collection was enormously beneficial to editors. Not only did it mean that such volumes could be quickly and easily prepared, it also meant that with relatively little effort the edited collection as a whole could be used to put to a wide range of uses.

Whereas Sockett's collection aimed to reassure readers that they would emigrate out within the safety net of a community, *Letters from Settlers & Labouring Emigrants in the New Zealand Company's Settlements of Wellington, Nelson & New Plymouth* (1843) uses the loose construction of the edited collection to project the idea of a community coming together, settling and developing in the colonies. The volume was published to encourage emigration and renew public trust at a time when the New Zealand Company was going through a particularly difficult time. The company was formed in 1839, following a merger between the New Zealand Colonisation

Company, the New Zealand Land Company and the New Zealand Company, in a plan for 'systematic colonization' spearheaded by Edward Gibbon Wakefield, but by 1843 it had declared itself insolvent and was suffering once again from tense relations with the Colonial Office.[47] Instead of being arranged into familial groups, the letters in *Settlers & Labouring Emigrants* are arranged according to the place: Wellington, Nelson and New Plymouth. Each section is arranged chronologically and thus the collection captures a snapshot of settlements undergoing rapid change. For example, in the Wellington section alone, one can trace the day-to-day events of the town. Writing to his parents on 12 March 1842, G. Fellingham comments that, '[s]ince the arrival of the last three emigrant vessels, our town has begun to look quite lively. Every person seems to have an inclination to build houses and fence in their ground; others are letting it, so that the town seems all life'.[48] Three weeks later, on 2 April, H. S. Tiffen writes that the 'Manewatu and other lands were opened for selection'.[49] But towards the end of the year, things suddenly changed. J. Philips writes home in December that the town is 'almost at a standstill at present': 'we have had a dreadful fire, upwards of sixty houses burnt, and a great many stores of all kinds'.[50] In the middle of an account of the 'first show' of the 'Horticultural Society' in which he proudly announces he 'got the four first prizes for vegetables', Joseph White also writes of the 'awful fire' they had about 'six weeks since' which 'burnt fifty-nine of the best houses in the town':

> the damage was reckoned to be £16,000; it happened about midnight; it was all burnt in less than half an hour. Many were obliged to catch their children in their arms, and escaped with nothing but their bed linen on. Some of the largest shopkeepers declared the next morning that they had not enough in the world to buy them a breakfast; fortunately no lives were lost.[51]

By January the next year, the town had righted itself. An officer of the 'Surveying Staff' wrote home that, 'We have a capital cricket club here, of which I am a member; we played a match for a dinner about a fortnight ago, and I had the good fortune to be on the winning side. There has been a great stir in Wellington, in consequence of the election of the first mayor.'[52] Cumulatively, the letters project an image of a young, thriving town with a mix of agricultural labourers and artisans, but which would welcome more affluent emigrants. This image is repeated over and over again in each letter: the collection thus projects New Zealand as an example of successful emigration.

On reading *Settlers & Labouring Emigrants*, one can see a narrative thread develop through the collection as one begins to trace changes that occur in a place and family over time. The sense of development and change that emerges is a result of the reader organising the disparate elements of various letters into a narrative. Publishing emigrants' letters had remunerative potential, and given that a volume could have as few or as many letters, and as little or as much organisation as desired, they were relatively quick and easy to put together. The letters build narratives of multiple successes: each letter voices the emigrant's satisfaction with food, employment, the possibility of marriage, and the benefits of an already-known community, and is corroborated by the surrounding voices. Thus edited collections of emigrants' letters project the colonies as places of opportunity and development.

Public Privacies: Intersecting Networks

In *Eighteenth-Century Letters and British Culture*, Clare Brant argues that 'the varied and often unpredictable circulation of letters confounds simple distinctions between public and private'. Rather than pitching a binary between the terms 'public' and 'private', it may be more useful to consider letters instead as operating 'within a third site, either a zone of overlap between public and private or a realm of more uncertain relations'.[53] Although Brant's argument is made with reference to the eighteenth century, it is particularly pertinent here. In 1832, Richard Neal, a bricklayer left his home in Sutton, Sussex to emigrate to Upper Canada. Arriving after a voyage of nearly two months, he travelled down the border to North America, eventually settling in Dundas, Canada. Writing home to his 'friends and relations' to reassure them of his arrival, he tells them:

> I never had one hour sickness all the time we were on the sea [. . .] Joseph Leggett and Elias were a little sick, but not much [. . .] When we landed at York, some went one way and some the other. I stopped there, Elias and Joseph Leggett went with Hilton, 180 miles further; they promised to write to me, but I have no letter from them [. . .] I promised to send you a state of the country: I will as soon as I can.[54]

Travelling out on the Petworth Emigration Scheme, Neal's letter is included in Sockett's *Sussex Emigrants*. His letter highlights the way in which printed emigrants' letters slip between the neat distinctions of 'public' and 'private'. His address to 'friends and relations' shows that the letter is originally meant for more than one person. There is nothing unusual in this: emigrants' letters were often collective and collaborative endeavours. To reduce the costs of paper, postage and receipt, emigrants often shared their pieces of paper: Sockett records as many as five people writing their letters on one sheet of paper.[55] Furthermore, as is likely to be the case with Neal's original letter, they were 'in some circumstances read aloud – to friends and neighbours grouped together, or by a literate person to an illiterate family'.[56] Edward Boxall, for example, instructs his mother to 'Copy this letter, and send it to my sisters'.[57] As such, they were 'often written to some extent for public consumption'.[58]

When the letter is circulated in networks of print, the body of people constituting the 'public' is considerably enlarged. In neither their manuscript nor their print forms do emigrants' letters conform to the notion of a sealed epistle between two correspondents. Neal's letter, containing information on the whereabouts and health of Joseph Leggett and Elias, would no doubt have brought reassuring news to those who knew these two men in the village. Print necessarily extends the kinship and friend networks that Neal's manuscript letter circulates in: the printed letter becomes dislocated from the reading community of Neal's village or family. Evidently, all answers to the question of how readers situated outside these local networks would have responded to such news are necessarily speculative, and we can in no way seek to understand or cover the range of ways in which the collection of letters would have been read. Nonetheless, one thing remains certain: printed letters provide glimpses into supposedly closed networks.

Unsurprisingly, when emigrants wrote home to their families, they wrote home not only with news of how they were faring, but also of their hopes, dreams and aspirations for the future. David Fitzpatrick picks up on the affective charge when he writes that the 'consolatory function of emigrant letters has been largely ignored by previous editors in the field':[59] letters 'reassured the reader' that even though the emigrants had departed, 'familial solidary was intact'.[60] The fear of loss of kinship ties over time and distance is more than apparent here. Sixteen-year-old John Luff writes to his aunt, 'I hope you will give yourself no more uneasiness about me at present; though the distance is far that we are from each other, I should like to see you once more, though I am resigned to the will of him that devises all things.'[61] 'You are there, and I am here,' writes another emigrant,

'I live in hopes (to) meet again where the Angels do also.'[62] Another seeks to reassure his parents with news of more immediate solace: 'Dear father and mother, we left you almost broken-hearted, but you may be satisfied that we have bettered our condition by coming here.'[63] The emotional charge that these letters carry is hugely important in determining the popularity of emigrants' letters as a genre. Such personal sentiments, openly circulating in print, allow the reader to understand the kinds of emotional risks that emigrants took when they decided to move, as well as the potential opportunities of emigration.

Benjamin Smith's *Twenty-Four Letters from Labourers in America to their Friends in England* (1829) is probably the best example of the interplay between personal sentiment and public readership. The collection is comprised of sequences of letters from a number families and a few miscellaneous letters from single emigrants. The first sequence of letters, from the Watson family, is by far the largest, covering the years 1819 to 1827. The earliest few letters are from John and Mary Watson to John's father. In 1823, John writes home, 'We wish very much to see brother William and Stephen: if they come they cannot be in a worse situation than we were when we landed, and for many months after; but then their prospects would be better than by remaining in England.'[64] Presumably, John receives news that Stephen will follow, for two years later (the next letter to appear in the sequence), he writes home anxiously: 'As for brother Stephen, we should like to know if he is gone back too; for we expected him this last winter, but have been disappointed; we are rather uneasy at not receiving a letter before this.'[65] After six letters from John and Mary, the first letter from Stephen and his wife Elizabeth appears being written back home to his parents. There appears to have been some miscommunication between members of the family as Stephen and Elizabeth had arrived in New York in 1823, with their children Thomas and their daughter Mary Jane Watson. Thomas has been 'taken' – presumably for an apprenticeship of some sort – by a certain 'Mr. William Fisher', while Mary Jane has been pseudo-adopted by a 'Quaker gentleman in Connecticut, who has taken her as his own' and will 'keep and clothe [her] and [. . .] send her to school'.[66] In 1825, Mary Jane sends her first letter home, signing it as 'Watson'; by 1827, she has married and become Mary Jane Coulson. By 1826, another Watson brother has arrived in America to settle – Mary Jane copies out his letter in her own letter to her grandmother in England. As the years go by, the collection of voices writing back from America grows: the Watson sequence is arranged chronologically – a seemingly neutral order – but the suggestion of change and progress is all the more powerful for it. The reader becomes privy to the changes in this family over eight years: circulating in the 'third site' between public and private, printed emigrants' letters straddle the overlapping networks between the intended recipients and a wider, unknown audience. As the rest of the chapter will show, beyond generating interest, the letters' interstitial position between personal and public spheres also shapes the ways in which they construct their own authenticities and make familiar the unfamiliar life of the colonies to a reading audience in Britain.

The Information Age

Despite being propaganda, printed emigrants' letters were sold and consumed as sources of information, providing a fresh alternative to the dull and dry lists of imperatives that at times dominated emigrant handbooks and guides.[67] As we have seen, they gave interested readers insight into the emotional investment required by emigration. However, they also provided a wealth of detail on the practicalities of emigration by relying on local colour and lively personal accounts. Emigrants were keen to share the newness of their experiences with their friends and family back in Britain: their letters are filled with accounts of the meticulous preparations for the voyage and of life in the colonies. Part of the task of the letters, therefore, is to negotiate the transfer of one reality – that of everyday life in the colonies – to another – the interested reader in Britain. Publishers and editors saw this transfer as one of the key selling points of their literature: over and again, the claim they make is that their collection offers 'information' on emigration. One guidebook, *Counsel for Emigrants*, says that its aim is to provide information that is 'useful and necessary to the emigrant'.[68] Another, S. H. Collins's *Emigrant's Guide to and Description of the United States of America*, gives 'a detailed account of all which is essential and really useful to the Emigrant' and aims to 'furnish him with such information as is absolutely necessary to enable him to judge rightly of the advantages or disadvantages attending a removal to that country'.[69] Smith & Elder publish *Settlers & Labouring Emigrants* in response to 'numerous applications [. . .] for information respecting New Zealand'.[70] As we shall see below, the 'information' in the letters is designed to assert a positive sense of difference and the idea that life in the colonies is like that in Britain, but better.

Having taken the journey to the colonies themselves, emigrants were in a good position to offer advice to those in Britain who wanted to follow. In 1829, James and Harriot Parks wrote to their father with an inventory of foodstuffs necessary for the voyage:

> Be sure to bring plenty of flour, some dried ham, and other bacon, plenty of potatoes, plenty of butter, sugar, tea, coffee, oatmeal, patent grots, rice, salt, vinegar, a few bottles of port wine to make sap, if you are ill. Take care your biscu'ts [sic] are good: be sure to bring plenty of flour and rice; don't be afraid of bringing too much, nor few. Great many in our vessel would give 3 times the value of a thing before they got over. Take ginger with you for your sap; plenty of rush candles: we had not near enough.[71]

'We had not near enough': the letter acts as a forewarning, advising those reading it how to avoid the pitfalls of emigration by learning from the experiences of those who have gone before. James and Harriot Parks emigrated with other members of their family: letters from John and Hester Parks are also included in the collection.[72] The latter two wrote home to their father, echoing the advice to 'bring plenty of flour to sea' but also exhorting him to 'not let Mr. Beck buy a parcel of salt beef 3 years old, as he did for us, and sea-biscuits not fit to eat'.[73] Swindling emigrants seems to have been something of an occupation for Mr. Beck. James and Harriot Parks continue the complaints against him in a poetic tirade:

> Be sure and don't let that infernal rogue lay in your provisions, nor anybody else; but see it all put up yourself [. . .] we had beef 2 years old not fit for a dog; our tea was not half tea; our oatmeal was half ground peas; our split peas, gray peas; our biscuits was the worst that could be got.[74]

Openly circulating in print, these accusations against Mr. Beck became a form of 'internationalised gossip':[75] they potentially damage his reputation and warn other emigrants against using his services.

Emigrants' letters were more than just a means of advising family members on how to organise the journey out, or what to expect from the settlement. They are frequently filled with requests for things to be sent over, such as the example below:

> It would be desirable if you could send or bring some seeds; an English pint of good potatoe [*sic*] oats, barley, a few seeds of the best kinds of potatoe, some yellow turnip seeds, early carrots, onions, caraway seed, some greens and cabbage seeds, a few roots of strawberries. We have wild gooseberries in the woods, but no garden gooseberries.[76]

Requests for seeds such as this are commonplace in emigrants' letters. John Plotz argues in *Portable Property* that in the context of migration, familiar everyday plants can become iconic signifiers of identity. He cites the example of Harriet Tytler, an Englishwoman, 'born, bred and married in India' who steals and first tastes strawberries at the age of eight. Plotz writes that 'Tytler cannot resist the chance literally to ingest England. That bit of strawberry theft exemplifies the cultural practices that allow self-styled exiles to think of England as a tangible alma mater, not a distant speck on the map'.[77] Familiar everyday plants carry symbolic weight for emigrants: the eagerness of the emigrant quoted earlier for '*English* potato oats' is not mere chance, but an assertion of identity. It speaks of a need to recreate the foreign landscape in the image of England. The planting of seeds from England in the colonies literalises the transplantation of 'home' in foreign landscapes. Francis Brady, emigrant to New Zealand, 'advise[s] all persons to take garden seeds with them, the sweetbriar and the hawthorn-berry in particular; though the country abounds with the most beautiful shrubs and myrtles, there is nothing so suitable for hedges'.[78]

Nostalgia is implicit within these requests, not only for the familiar sights of England, but also because of the domestic practices that centre around such plants, such as gooseberry- or strawberry-picking. However, as well as encoding a backward glance towards England, such requests can also be a glance to the future. One emigrant, for example, writes:

> We are very ill off here for clover to the cattle; it is not to be bought; I mean *red* clover, which is best. Will you therefore bring as much as sow two acres; the quantity will be about 16 lb. Could you also bring some rye grass seed, a little will do as we can raise more from it. We have Timothy grass here in its place, but we want to try it.[79]

Clearly, here the desire is not to recreate the familiar country hedgerows and gardens of England, but to find the right kind of fodder for cattle. The request speaks of labour and trade. Requests for seeds thus compact many different meanings into them. Although these personal requests in print may be worded the same as in the manuscript version, they take the form of implied advice when they circulate in public networks. The implication of such statements would have been apparent to potential readers: aware that emigrants before them had required these things, they would have been reminded or warned to pack these things themselves.

But if such requests speak of a lack in the colonies, there is plenty in the letters to show the colonies as a vibrant, thriving place:

> Do not distress yourself preparing great store of things, as if you could get nothing here. We can buy cotton prints, and cotton of all kinds, as cheap as at home. You may bring a few cuts of worsted for stockings, but we have far finer wool, and cheaper, than with you.[80]

The comment 'as if you could get nothing here' serves to allay potential fears back home that the colonies were undeveloped places marked by the absence of any society. Cumulatively, the image they build of the colonies is that of an already established way of life: by stressing the similarities between Britain and the colonies, the implicit reassurance is that the emigrant would not be travelling to the depths of wilderness, but to a place where the needs of everyday life could be readily sustained. This reading is supported by the lists of prices of everyday commodities in the colonies, a hallmark of the genre. The following, from George Boxall, is a typical example:

> This is the prices of this country. Barrel of flour, 196 lbs. price £1. 5s. Pork, 3d. per lb. Best green tea, 3s. 9d. Best butter, 7.5d. Sugar, 6d. Tobacco, 1s. a pound. Best mutton and beef, 2.5 a pound. We makes [sic] our own soap and candles. Price for work; sawyers, 10s. per hundred, single men about £20.[81]

Another emigrant writes:

> I will now state the prices of a few things in their money: you will mind that a dollar is equal to 4s. 2d. English money, and a cent is equal to one halfpenny, and no more [. . .] Whenever 'corn' is mentioned, it means 'Indian corn', all other kinds being called 'grain'. Shelled corn 45 cents per bushel; flour 4 dollars 62½ cents per barrel of 96 lb. or 14 English stones; sugar 9 cents to 10 cents per lb.; molasses 40 cents per gallon; window glass 1½ cents per foot; cast iron goods 5 cents per lb.[82]

These repetitive lists, that fill endless lines with seemingly trivial detail, have lost some of their relevance for us now.[83] Yet, as Cameron et al. argue, it is these small but important facts that would have attracted the most attention from interested readers: potential emigrants would have scoured these lists, anxious for any indications that they gave of what life in the colonies was like.[84] As Stephen Fender argues, the lists signify a particular political and moral code:

> Taken as a whole, the itemized lists imply a whole political economy – and a morality as well: the material richness of ordinary commodities as against the vain expectations of luxury; trade as against hoarded wealth; the potential for improvement as against instant gratification [. . .] there is something persuasive in the very poverty of their construction – their lack of adjectives, or other qualifiers, their simple paratactic compounding of one substantive after another, their minute qualification down to the last half-penny.[85]

Fender's reading is persuasive and nuanced: in addition to providing interested readers with information on the price of everyday products, these lists evoke visions for a future life that is based on trade and focused on an attainable level of wealth. But there is also an implicit comparison in these lists: rather than simply laying out the details of everyday colonial life, they also implicitly ask the reader to compare them to prices in England. These itemised lists encourage an oscillation between home and the colony, the colony and home, which allows potential emigrants to weigh up and measure where the more economic and efficient lifestyle can be.

The kinds of objects mentioned in the letters – lace, net, seeds – are all everyday, ordinary objects: the stress is on the *ordinariness* of everyday settler life. The information in the letters is meant to make the unfamiliar familiar, to stress the banality of the everyday and construct the image that life in the colonies is essentially the same as that in Britain, but the chances of attaining material success are greater. Asserting this positive difference has the effect of reducing the sense of distance between the colonies and Britain, as can be seen from the observations of one emigrant:

> I would not have you think that there are none here but pauper lunatics, for when we first reached Guelph, we were agreeably surprised to see a number of gentlemen dressed in white trousers, flannel jackets, and straw hats playing at cricket on the green, and they were quite adept at the game; they meet to play every Saturday.[86]

The image of men in white playing cricket on the village green constructs the colony – Canada – as the quintessential English village: by moving across the Atlantic and settling in Canada, one is not moving so far from home at all. Publishers were keen to establish that, far from being removed from the vicissitudes of life, the colony was another version of home, a place that is connected to England through its cultural practices, but also literally, a place of connections, where emigrants could bump into people they had known in England.

The Authenticity Effect

Whether emigrants were travelling across the Atlantic to North America and Canada, or around the world to Australia and New Zealand, the geographical distance made it hard to comprehend what far-off places were like. Lists of information stress the similarities between the colonies and Britain and the connections between them: this way of making familiar was one way to negotiate the distance between them. As Fender argues, lists of commodities emphasise the everydayness of emigrant life, and help construct the colony not as a mythological Eden, but as familiar, real terrain. They 'ground the settler's discourse in the solid materiality of everyday experience', and in doing so, 'convey an authentic sense of what was relatively unfamiliar to the writer, and absolutely unknown to the reader'. Focusing on the everyday 'deflect[s] the suspicion of fanciful exaggeration so often attaching to travel accounts of faraway places'.[87] Fender's argument that the platitudes of everyday life that these lists of commodities invoke are an authenticating strategy is persuasive: they evidence the fact of the migration *and* the facts of emigrant life. Emigrants were keen to assert that their letters were not the result of 'fanciful invention' or 'travel lying'. Hasted assures his readers that his account of Canada is 'a true picture'.[88] Collins states that 'he has drawn his information from sources so authentic as not to be refuted by any arguments, however specious; and his principal object has been, to give every possible information in his power, and that information to be TRUTH'.[89] In his letter, J. Tewsley, an emigrant from Dorking, 'promise[s]' to 'give [the reader] the truest information of this country'.[90] However, as we shall see below, emigrants and editors alike did not stop merely at stating that their letters contained true and original facts, but devised other strategies to overcome their readers' potential suspicion and assert the authenticity of the text.

The task of the printed letters was to make clear to the reader that the success stories they contained were not fabricated: hard facts of everyday life in the colonies were one way of ensuring this. But it is important to remember that letters were 'entangled'[91] in the transfer of information from the colonies to Britain: they did not simply *relay* information from emigrants to the colonies, but were imbricated in and constructed by this transfer of information. In *The Portable Bunyan*, Isabel Hofmeyr argues that, 'when books travel they change shape. They are excised, summarized, abridged, and bowdlerized by the new intellectual formations into which they migrate':[92] in other words, a text's geographical migration is simultaneously a migration of form. This is particularly apposite in the case of emigrants' letters as they are caught up by the print market when they arrive in England. Benjamin Smith, the editor of *Twenty-Four Letters* describes how he sent out 'two persons in opposite directions, with orders to call at all the cottages where they had reason to think that letters had been lately received from America' and prints the 'first 24' that are collected.[93] Printed emigrants' letters were therefore doubly migrant: they moved both geographically and in form. The migration of the letter from manuscript to print was a site of particular anxiety: how were readers to know whether editors had changed anything? Recognising this potential source of worry, editors offered viewings of the manuscript letters in their offices. Interested readers would be able to come in and compare the printed edition of letters to the manuscript originals. In his *Emigrant's Guide*, the radical figure William Cobbett republishes the letters that appear in *Twenty-Four Letters*. He writes that as he 'did not know' Benjamin Smith, he 'thought it necessary to go to the parties themselves, and obtain the originals':

> The *originals* will be deposited at Fleet Street, for one week after the publication of this book; and, when that week is passed, I shall return them to the parties from whom I have received them. I shall lodge them at Fleet Street, for the purpose of being inspected by any gentleman who may have the curiosity to do it; and I do it also to the honour of the parties who have written the letters.[94]

Other editors offered viewings of the manuscript letters. Sockett kept original letters in his office, and newspaper editors also mentioned that the originals were available at their offices.[95] It is difficult to determine whether the opportunity to check the published letter would have been taken up, or how often, but the offers of viewings indicate, not so much that *seeing* is believing, but that the *possibility* of seeing is believing: this is an authenticating strategy where the veracity of the published letter is endorsed by the *possibility* of a sensory engagement with the text.

Such viewings were a means of reassuring readers that the letter's migration of form had not compromised its authenticity. This system of authenticating the printed letter does not take into account the fact that both emigrants and their families were hugely anxious that the manuscript letter's authenticity was compromised by its mobility, as it travelled through the postal system in Britain and abroad. As Cameron et al. point out, for 'many assisted emigrants, the facts and rumours associated with emigration became the more sinister in the light of their own mistrust of the motives of their sponsors'. In the case of the Petworth emigrants, '[w]ord was spread that Egremont and Sockett supported emigration only to reduce the expense of the poor rate and were therefore circulating false letters'.[96] The letters in *Letters from Sussex Emigrants* counter such suspicions. In 1832 Mary Holden, for example, a Petworth emigrant, added a postscript to her letter to inform her family that she has 'enquired about the letters, to know the fact and truth about their being opened by the head gentlemen' and are 'sure now that they are not opened until you receives [sic] them'. The significance of this postscript may be understood with reference to a comment she had made earlier in her letter: 'you may understand that all the letters be all opened, before they go out of this Country, to see that there is not any falsehood sent; and if there is anything in them, against the country, they are kept back'.[97] It is unclear how well-grounded these fears were, but Holden is not alone in reassuring sceptical readers in England that her letters are not tampered with. John Watson, for example, asks his mother to '[t]ell William we are astonished at him doubting the truths of our letters: we can assure him the letters don't get altered before they reach him. America is as good as we have stated before; and he would find it so if he had heart enough to come'.[98] The opening of letters addressed to another person was against the law, so it is unlikely that emigrants' letters would have been opened by either emigration agents, land company officials, or postmasters. However, the anxiety seems to have been prevalent. In his introduction, Sockett details the precautions people took to 'guard against the possibility of imposition' and prove that their letters were not 'deceitful fabrications':

> Reports having circulated by persons unfriendly to emigration, that the very favourable accounts which had been received from preceding emigrants, were deceitful fabrications: many curious devices were practised,

by the friends of those who went from Sussex, to guard against the possibility of imposition. The paper on which letters from Canada were written, was prepared in England, either by a heading in the name of a friend, a name written across, certain mystical holes pricked with a pin, or, what was more general, a sort of tally, formed by a corner of the paper being scrawled upon, and then torn off, the piece torn away being carefully preserved at home. In one instance, a very small, and peculiarly shaped, crooked pin, placed under the seal, came back from the 'far west'; with especial directions, that this infallible proof should be again returned thither. These directions have been complied with, and the crooked pin, is now once more on its voyage.[99]

To show that letters were originally marked, Sockett put introductory lines above the relevant letters. For example, above a couple of letters, he writes that, 'The two following letters were both written on a sheet of paper, from which a corner had been torn, and left with a relation in England.'[100] The two letters are Edward Boxall's and William Cooper's, which indicates that the practice of marking letters was spread across the community of Petworth emigrants. If the letter from America returned with a torn corner that fitted the piece left behind, readers at home would know that the letter was indeed genuine. Emigrants also marked the writing paper in different ways. Mary Holden writes at the top of the letter with instructions to her brother: 'When you are in Canada, fill this up, and send it to me; send all the news you can: say the truth and nothing but the truth' (Figure 1).[101]

Above another letter, Sockett writes, 'From Thomas Adsett, who went from North Chapel, Sussex, to the Rev. Robert Ridsdale, Rector of that parish. [Written on a sheet of paper, which Mr Ridsdale had directed to himself, and given to the man when he went away].'[102] Again, if the letter returns with the respective lines written across the top, the readers at home can be assured that it has not been tampered with.

Sockett's use of emigrants' tokens is not new: they had long been an integral part of the history of convict transportation. As Michele Field and Timothy Millett have demonstrated, tokens were important gestures of kinship and affection between convicts and their loved ones.[103] In the 1840s, Caroline Chisholm also used emigrants' tokens extensively in her pamphlets. Sometimes these were intangible, in the form of memories, as in the case of the emigrant who cites '[a]s a token', a memory of him 'stood crying over my sleeping child, and thought I could not leave it; as a further token, a snowstorm came on'.[104] More often than not, though, tokens were solid,

43

From Mary, the daughter of Thomas Holden, Widower, who went from Kirdford, Sussex, with 7 children. To Serjt. Holden, 2nd. Regt. Tower Hamlets Militia.

The heading was written on the paper, before it left England.

DEAR BROTHER,—*When you are in Canada, fill this up, and send it to me; send all the news you can; say the truth, and nothing but the truth. Sarah Holden, Slinfold near Horsham, Sussex, England.*

DEAR FRIENDS,

This comes with our kind love to you all, hoping to find you all in good health, as, thank God, it leaves us alive, and well at present. We were all very sea sick, and had a very long and rough voyage. On the 2nd. of May, about half past 4 in the morning, the sea was very rough, and the ship was tossed, so that the berths, on our side, fell from one end of the ship to the other, but no one was hurt a great deal. We were driven so much towards the north, we had very hard frosts and snow, and it was very cold, and we often thought that we should go to the bottom; but our heavenly father, that awful Protector of persons, brought us safe to land at last. We were six weeks getting to Quebec: we did not go a shore there; we landed at Montreal, and we were then towed up the river by Durham boats to Prescot, and then in steam packets to York, and from York, 350 miles, in schooner vessels to Kettle Creek. And we were then carried in waggons up the country, 66 miles. It was the 22nd. of July, when we got to where we are settled. Father has got 100 acres of land, and has to pay for it two dollars per acre, in six years time. Father thinks of getting in two acres of wheat this year. We have got a cow. Father gave 30 dollars for her. We expect to find very hard times this winter. We have ten miles to go for flour, and all our provisions, but I hope, please God will help us through it this winter. The Gentleman is going to have a log house put up for us. Ann, and Harriet, and Ruth, have got places 40 miles from us. Father says, he can see a good prospect of doing well after a few years. It is good land. Father sends his kind love to all of you, and hopes that you will make up your minds, and take a good resolution and come here, for here is a good prospect of doing well, and getting a good living. Father says he would not come back to England again for no respects. Dear

F 2

Figure 1 Sockett's Introductory Lines for Mary Holden's Letter, King's College London, Foyle Special Collections Library

material objects: another emigrant says that 'as a token [that] he [the family friend in England] may know you [Chisholm] have seen my own self, he gave me at parting the half of his pledge ticket, the part that has the medal'.[105] Again, any friends or family members reading these statements in England would know the accounts were true if the memory or the object tallied with what they knew. As she explains, each statement is

> attested [to] by the relators, by some little family token or incident known to their relatives at home, with the design that this should stand as a guarantee to those here that the statements in question are not fictitious, and that their friends might place confidence in my opinion or advice, should they wish to emigrate.[106]

These tokens played an important part in the printed letter's performance of authenticity. The marking of letters, the accompanying object and the mention of shared histories, worked as a kind of code, a guarantee of authenticity amongst a closed group of people. As mentioned previously, editors needed to gain the public's trust if their collection of letters was to sell and to successfully promote emigration. But while print replicates the text of the letter, it cannot replicate any accompanying token – and indeed, to do so would defeat the objective. Instead, the letter retains the textual traces of the object under question to produce its own 'authenticity effect'. I am borrowing here from Roland Barthes's work on the 'Reality Effect'. He argues that all too often, we overlook the significance of concrete objects in novels and assume that they require no further interrogation beyond an acknowledgement of their presence within the text.[107] Rather than 'corresponding to a kind of narrative *luxury*', these textual objects help establish the 'effect' of being in the real world. At first, to make the connection between the reality effect and emigrants' tokens seems a little counter-intuitive. The 'reality effect', the illusion that we are in the real world when we read the story, is produced by the presence of such 'meaningless' detail. On the other hand, emigrant tokens are filled with meaning: they strive to fit into a connected world, or rather, to make apparent the connections in a world where people are moving further and further away from each other.

The seminal word in Barthes's argument, however, is not 'reality', but 'effect'. Mentioning in the printed text the ways in which the letter or statement was authenticated makes the reader aware of the once-present authenticating token. Though the reader of the printed letter may never experience a sensory engagement with the authenticating object, Sockett and Chisholm leave the textual traces in the letters because they show that the manuscript letter *was* once authenticated – and this thus validates the authority of the published letter. In the same way that for Barthes, the reality effect is something more than a gesture to the world outside the novel, the illusion of authenticity that emigrant tokens produce is constituted in successfully creating the sense of a history to the text, in the sense of a pin or the piece of coal originally *having-been-there*. In *Illuminations*, Walter Benjamin similarly argues that the 'authenticity of a thing is the essence of all that is transmissible from its beginning, ranging from its substantive duration to its testimony *to the history which it has experienced*'.[108] Just as textual objects help establish the effect of reality within the novel for Barthes, so too the presence of the material world in emigrants' letters, whether they be in the form of lists of everyday commodities or emigrants' objects, help establish the effect of its authenticity. Offering viewings of the original manuscript worked by asserting that a manuscript letter once existed; the authenticity effect produced by these tokens similarly works by asserting that the emigrant token once existed.

In effect, then, collections of emigrants' letters sell a version of the authentic, just as much as they are selling information on how to emigrate, or curious tales of private lives. In *Consuming Traditions*, Elizabeth Outka argues that 'we usually perceive the selling of authenticity as fraud, as the inauthentic masquerading as the authentic'.[109] What is at stake in the anxiety over the authenticity of the emigrants' letters is the affective history encoded in these emigrants' tokens. As emigrants moved away from their families, they feared that their kinship ties were being tampered with, that someone was interfering from outside of their personal networks of circulation. Sitting alongside these fears was the hope that despite being separated by time and distance – most likely for the rest of their lives – they would not lose contact with all whom they had once known. Emigrants' tokens became necessary because of the dislocation from place – because people move away from each other and because letters circulate in different networks. As much as letters stressed the possibilities of new beginnings in the colonies, they simultaneously stressed that emigration did not necessarily entail a clean break from their old lives. One of the emigrants Chisholm interviewed, John H----, sends a piece of coal with his name 'engraved' on it back home. His brother's reply is printed below his statement:

The person you mention, John H------, is my father's son, and brother to me. If you have any news to communicate from John, should feel very much obliged if you will do so. I am the brother you mention who engraved his name on a piece of coal; he emigrated from Liverpool about six years ago, and have had only two letters from him during that time.[110]

The shared nature of the pin under the seal or the piece of paper with lines written on it that is passed back and forth opens up the opportunity for an affective discourse based on an imagined realm of touch. Similarly, given as a gift and returned as a token, the piece of coal is the material artefact through which these two brothers trace themselves back to each other after a period of six years. Though the printed letter or statement itself takes no part in the consolidation of affect between family members, the tokens in them show that the dislocation from their homes is not necessarily a shedding of history, or a shedding of relations and family ties. They act as a reassurance that not only are the places to which emigrants are going similar to Britain, but that the affective networks in which they are enmeshed *can* be extended across time and space. In effect, then, through their evocations of the material world, printed emigrants' letters sell not just a version of authenticity, but also the affective histories which the tokens evoke.

Thus, printed emigrants' letters are a particular subset of booster literature that engage with the complexity of their own authenticity, even while they aim to provide practical information on emigration. Carrying the traces of their manuscript origins, printed emigrants' letters oscillate between the personal and public networks that form the conditions of their circulation. In a curious act of doubling, they become implicated in these networks of circulation, so that wherever they arrive – whether in the hands of village members, or in the hands of the reader – they do so as contested texts, negotiating the facts of their authenticity. They do not fit into the model of a one-way backward glance to the 'motherland'. Instead, by affirming the similarity between Britain and her colonies, and that kinship ties *can* be extended over time and space, the letters disrupt that sense of distance between emigrants and Britain.

In this chapter, I have considered how print is in thrall to its manuscript origins, constantly trying to evoke what was once there. In the next chapter, I explore what it means for this relationship between manuscript and print to be inverted: both the manuscript shipboard periodicals that I look at mimic print newspapers. The conditions of being mobile make printed emigrants' letters suspect, but how do the conditions of being mobile affect newspapers that are actually produced on the move? What kinds of communities are they produced by, what kinds of communities do they reach and what kinds of communities do they produce in turn? If printed emigrants' letters disrupt the sense of distance between Britain and the colonies, how do shipboard periodicals engage with this sense of distance, given that they are produced in the supposedly liminal space of the sea?

Notes

1. Wendy Cameron and Mary McDougall Maude, *Assisting Emigration to Upper Canada: The Petworth Project, 1832–1837* (Montreal: McGill-Queen's University Press, 2000), p. 26.
2. Not all relationships were congenial, however, and Hasted was sometimes forced to move because of disruptive neighbours. See Wendy Cameron, Sheila Haines and Mary McDougall Maude (eds), *English Immigrant Voices: Labourers' Letters from Upper Canada in the 1830s* (Montreal: McGill-Queen's University Press, 2000), pp. 151, 255, 274, 281 and 381.
3. *Letters from Settlers in Upper Canada*, p. 1 (7 February 1834).
4. Ibid. p. 6 (7 February 1834).
5. See Cameron et al., *English Immigrant Voices*, p. 382 (7 February 1834).
6. Ibid. p. 390 (15 December 1839).
7. Ibid. p. 384 (25 January 1841).
8. *Letters from Settlers in Upper Canada*, p. 6 (7 February 1834).
9. Cameron et al., *English Immigrant Voices*, p. 384 (7 February 1834; 25 January 1841).
10. Charles Heaphy, *Narrative of a Residence in Various Parts of New Zealand: Together with a Description of the Present State of the Company's Settlements* (London: Smith & Elder, 1842), p. vii.
11. See *Illustrations to 'Adventure in New Zealand' by Edward Jerningham Wakefield. Lithographed from Original Drawings Taken on the Spot by Mrs Wicksteed, Miss King, Mrs Fox, Mr John Saxton, Mr Charles Heaphy, Mr S. C. Brees and Captain W. Mein Smith, R.A.* (London: Smith & Elder, 1845).
12. Heaphy, *Narrative of a Residence*, p. vii.
13. Ibid. p. viii.
14. Charlotte Erickson, *Invisible Immigrants: The Adaptation of English and Scottish Immigrants in Nineteenth-Century America* (London: Weidenfeld and Nicolson, 1972), p. 2.
15. William D. Jones, 'Going into Print: Published Immigrant Letters, Webs of Personal Relations, and the Emergence of the Welsh Public Sphere',

in *Letters Across Borders: The Epistolary Practices of International Migrants*, ed. Bruce S. Elliott, David A. Gerber and Suzanne M. Sinke (Basingstoke: Palgrave Macmillan, 2006), pp. 175–99 (p. 176).
16. David A. Gerber, *Authors of their Lives: The Personal Correspondence of British Immigrants to North America in the Nineteenth Century* (New York: New York University Press, 2006), p. 11.
17. Ibid. p. 10.
18. Cameron et al, *English Immigrant Voices*, p. xxi. Emphasis added. Examples of edited collections of printed letters include Erickson *Invisible Immigrants*; Gerber *Authors of their Lives*; David Fitzpatrick, *Oceans of Consolation: Personal Accounts of Irish Migration to Australia* (Cork: Cork University Press, 1994); and Patrick O'Farrell and Brian Trainor (eds), *Letters from Irish Australia, 1825–1929* (Sydney: New South Wales University Press; Belfast: Ulster Historical Foundation, 1984).
19. Cameron et al., *English Immigrant Voices*, p. xxi.
20. Erickson, *Invisible Immigrants*, p. 4. As David Gerber argues in *Authors of their Lives*, it is no less difficult to judge the motives behind the writing of manuscript letters than printed ones. Success stories may have been 'honest lies', a form of face-saving for the emigrants who had left England against the advice of their families. We have no way of reading beyond or even perceiving any 'strategic silence[s]' (p. 99), nor can we answer the questions that arise from the existence of the letters that survive. This problem of verifying original intent in the manuscript letters is similar to that of verifying inaccurate editorial intervention in printed letters.
21. Jones, 'Going into Print', p. 176.
22. Eric Richards, 'Voices of British and Irish Migrants in Nineteenth-Century Australia', in Colin G. Pooley and Ian D. Whyte (eds), *Migrants, Emigrants and Immigrants: A Social History of Migration* (London: Routledge, 1991), pp. 19–41 (p. 22).
23. Thomas Sockett (ed.), *Emigration: Letters from Sussex Emigrants who sailed from Portsmouth, in April 1832, on Board the Ships,* Lord Melville *and* Eveline, *for Upper Canada: Extracts from Various Writers on Emigration to Canada, and from Canadian Newspapers, with Reference to the Letters: Capt. Hale's Instructions to Emigrants and a Gazetteer of the Places Named in the Letters* (London: John Phillips, 1833), p. 8. Volume hereafter referred to as *Sussex Emigrants*.
24. Sockett, *Sussex Emigrants*, p. 47.
25. Ibid. p. 8.
26. Ibid. p. 47.
27. Cameron and Maude, *Assisting Emigration*, p. 48.
28. Thomas Sockett (ed.), *Canada: Letters from Persons who have Emigrated to Upper Canada under the Management of the Petworth Emigration Committee* (Petworth: John Phillips, 1834); James Marr Brydone,

Narrative of a Voyage, with a Party of Emigrants, Sent out from Sussex, in 1834, by the Petworth Emigration Committee (Petworth: John Phillips, 1834); Thomas Sockett (ed.), *Continuation of Letters from Sussex Emigrants in Upper Canada* (Petworth: John Phillips, 1836).
29. Dudley Baines, *Migration in a Mature Economy*, p. 53.
30. Cameron et al., *English Immigrant Voices*, p. xvii.
31. Caroline Chisholm, 'A Bundle of Emigrants' Letters', *Household Words* (30 March 1850), pp. 19–24 (p. 19).
32. This short account has been drawn from Caroline Chisholm, *The Story of the Life of Mrs Caroline Chisholm, the Emigrants' Friend, and her Adventures in Australia* (London: Trelawny Saunders, 1852).
33. See also Julie M. Barst, 'Pushing the Envelope: Caroline Chisholm, Colonial Australia, and the Transformative Power of Postal Networks', *Prose Studies: History, Theory, Criticism* 33 (2011), pp. 200–16, for a discussion on Chisholm's reliance on a global postal service.
34. Chisholm, 'A Bundle', p. 21.
35. Ibid. p. 20.
36. Caroline Chisholm, *Comfort for the Poor! Meat Three Times a Day!! Voluntary Information from the People of New South Wales, Collected in that Colony by Mrs. Chisholm in 1845–46* (London: John Ollivier, 1847), p. 3.
37. Caroline Chisholm, *Emigration and Transportation Relatively Considered in a Letter Dedicated, by Permission, to Earl Grey*, 3rd edn (London: John Ollivier, 1847), p. 24.
38. Leah Price, *The Anthology and the Rise of the Novel: From Richardson to George Eliot* (Cambridge: Cambridge University Press, 2000), p. 91.
39. Ibid. p. 14.
40. Roland Barthes, *S/Z*, trans. Richard Miller (London: Cape, 1975), p. 8.
41. Ibid. p. 8.
42. Sockett, *Sussex Emigrants*, p. 8.
43. Ibid. p. 9.
44. Ibid. p. 47.
45. Barthes, *S/Z*, p. 22.
46. *Letters from Settlers in Upper Canada*, p. 3.
47. For more information on the history of the company, see Patricia Burns, *Fatal Success: A History of the New Zealand Company*, ed. Henry Richardson (London: Heinemann Reed, 1989).
48. *Letters from Settlers & Labouring Emigrants, in the New Zealand Company's Settlements of Wellington, Nelson, & New Plymouth, from February 1842 to January 1843* (London: Smith & Elder, 1843), p. 8. Volume hereafter referred to as *Settlers & Labouring Emigrants*.
49. *Settlers & Labouring Emigrants*, p. 10.
50. Ibid. p. 27.
51. Ibid. p. 57.
52. Ibid. pp. 62–3.

53. Clare Brant, *Eighteenth-Century Letters and British Culture* (Basingstoke: Palgrave Macmillan, 2006), p. 5.
54. Sockett, *Sussex Emigrants*, pp. 6–7.
55. Ibid. pp. 37–41.
56. O'Farrell and Trainor, *Letters from Irish Australia*, p. 3. Erickson has a different opinion from this mode of thought. In *Invisible Immigrants*, she argues that the 'picture of the widely circulated letter [. . .] was probably an inaccurate one', as the majority of emigrants 'wrote private letters, not intended for oral "publication" in the village' (p. 36). The intended audience varied from letter to letter: while some may have contained strict instructions to let no one outside the family read it, others were written with the thought of publication in mind.
57. Sockett, *Sussex Emigrants*, p. 8.
58. O'Farrell and Trainor, *Letters from Irish Australia*, p. 3.
59. Fitzpatrick, *Oceans of Consolation*, p. 20.
60. Ibid. p. 22.
61. Sockett, *Sussex Emigrants*, p. 10.
62. Ibid. p. 15.
63. Ibid. p. 11.
64. Benjamin Smith (ed.), *Twenty-Four Letters from Labourers in America to their Friends in England*, 2nd edn (London: Edward Rainford, 1829), p. 13. Volume hereafter referred to as *Twenty-Four Letters*.
65. Smith, *Twenty-Four Letters*, p. 14.
66. Ibid. p. 19 and p. 17.
67. A. C. Buchanan's *For the Information of Emigrants arriving at New York, and Who Are Desirous of Settling in Canada* (Quebec: Office of His Majesty's Chief Agent for the Superintendance of Emigrants in Upper and Lower Canada, 1834), for example, is a leaflet filled with dense text and dry imperatives.
68. *Counsel for Emigrants, and Interesting Information from Numerous Sources; With Original Letters from Canada and the United States* (Aberdeen: John Mathison, 1834), p. xi. Volume hereafter referred to as *Counsel*.
69. S. H. Collins, *The Emigrant's Guide to and Description of the United States of America: Including Several Authentic and Highly Important Letters from English Emigrants now in America, to their Friends in England*, 4th edn (Hull: Joseph Noble, 1830), Preface, n.p.
70. *Settlers & Labouring Emigrants*, p. 1.
71. Smith, *Twenty-Four Letters*, p. 31.
72. The letters do not make clear how James and Harriot are related to John and Hester. They could be two siblings and their partners.
73. Smith, *Twenty-Four Letters*, pp. 28–9.
74. Ibid. p. 31.
75. See Gerber, *Authors of their Lives*, pp. 98–109 (p. 99).
76. *Counsel*, p. 34.

77. John Plotz, *Portable Property*, p. 45.
78. *Settlers & Labouring Emigrants*, p. 3.
79. *Counsel*, p. 58.
80. Ibid. p. 59.
81. Sockett, *Sussex Emigrants*, p. 25.
82. Collins, *The Emigrant's Guide*, p. 135.
83. This is demonstrated by the fact that Erickson decides to edit them out of most of her letters in her collection *Invisible Immigrants*. See p. 9: 'In the rather unpleasant task of cutting, I have omitted references to letters, to health, and messages from other immigrants and to other persons, once the network of friends and acquaintances of the immigrant has been established in the early letters. I have also cut most accounts of ocean voyages, most lists of American prices and some rather shallow descriptions. This material is not without interest, but is not central to the themes of the book.' As Fitzpatrick notes, such editorial decisions mean that the affective quality of the letters is lost. See *Oceans of Consolation*, pp. 20–1.
84. Cameron et al., *English Immigrant Voices*, p. xli.
85. Stephen Fender, *Sea Changes: British Emigration and American Literature* (Cambridge: Cambridge University Press, 1992), p. 50.
86. *Copies and Extracts of Letters from Settlers*, p. 9.
87. Fender, *Sea Changes*, pp. 50–1.
88. *Letters from Settlers in Upper Canada*, p. 5.
89. Collins, *The Emigrant's Guide*, 'Preface', n.p.
90. Charles Barclay (ed.), *Letters from the Dorking Emigrants who went to Upper Canada in the Spring of 1832* (Dorking: Robert Best Ede, 1832), p. 28.
91. Nicholas Thomas, *Entangled Objects: Exchange, Material Culture, and Colonialism in the Pacific* (London: Harvard University Press, 1991).
92. Isabel Hofmeyr, *The Portable Bunyan: A Transnational History of The Pilgrim's Progress* (Princeton: Princeton University Press, 2004), pp. 2–3.
93. Smith, *Twenty-Four Letters*, p. 2.
94. William Cobbett, *The Emigrant's Guide: In Ten Letters Addressed to the Tax-Payers of England Containing Information of Every Kind, Necessary to Persons who are About to Emigrate including Several Authentic and Most Interesting Letters from English Emigrants, Now in America to their Relations in England* (London: the author, 1829), p. 43; p. 44, original emphasis. See Richard Ingrams, *The Life and Adventures of William Cobbett* (London: Harper, 2005), p. 145 for a discussion of Cobbett's radical politics and his encouragement to people to emigrate to America, and James Grande, *William Cobbett, the Press and Rural England: Radicalism and the Fourth Estate, 1792–1835* (Basingstoke: Palgrave Macmillan, 2014.

95. Cameron et al., *English Immigrant Voices*, p. xxxi.
96. Ibid. p. xxxi.
97. Sockett, *Sussex Emigrants*, p. 44; p. 43.
98. Smith, *Twenty-Four Letters*, p. 24.
99. Sockett, *Sussex Emigrants*, p. viii.
100. Ibid. p. 8.
101. Ibid. p. 43.
102. Ibid. p. 45.
103. Timothy Millett, 'Leaden Hearts', in Michele Field and Timothy Millett, *Convict Love Tokens: The Leaden Hearts the Convicts Left Behind* (Kent Town: Wakefield Press, 1998), pp. 5–30.
104. Chisholm, *Comfort for the Poor!*, p. 10.
105. Ibid. p. 8.
106. Chisholm, *Emigration and Transportation*, pp. 18–19.
107. Roland Barthes, 'The Reality Effect', in *The Rustle of Language*, trans. Richard Howard (Oxford: Basil Blackwell, 1986), pp. 141–8.
108. Walter Benjamin, *Illuminations*, ed. and intro. Hannah Arendt, trans. Harry Zorn (London: Pimlico, 1999), p. 215. Emphasis added.
109. Elizabeth Outka, *Consuming Traditions: Modernity, Modernism, and the Commodified Authentic* (Oxford: Oxford University Press, 2009), p. 5.
110. Chisholm, *Comfort for the Poor!*, p. 7.

Chapter 2

Emigrant Shipboard Newspapers: Provisional Settlement at Sea

Writing in her shipboard diary in 1839, the nineteen-year-old Eliza Darvall notes the appearance of the first issue of a shipboard newspaper. 'The first paper was published today,' she writes, 'and received with great applause, Mr. Docker's leading article being excellent.'[1] Her sister, Emily Darvall, who was older than her by two years, makes a similar note in *her* diary: 'This morning appeared at breakfast the first number of the "Alfred" edited by Mr. Docker, and it created much interest. Although we had only two days [sic] notice, everybody had contributed and indeed, many papers were omitted for want of room.'[2] The shipboard newspaper that the Darvall sisters write of, the *Alfred*, is named after the ship on which they and their family were sailing out to Sydney. The extent of the textual legacy of the voyage, in the form of the two Darvall sisters' shipboard diaries, the shipboard newspaper and the passenger list, is an extremely rare occurrence. It may be due to the social prominence of the Darvall family. The sisters' father, Major Edward Darvall, had connections with the East India Company; their elder brother, John, became a very important barrister and politician in New South Wales and was granted a knighthood; and Emily herself became a poet of some importance in her later years.[3] Emily's comment on submissions being omitted for want of room speaks of the enthusiasm that people on board the ship had for making the periodical. This would be sustained over the next twelve weeks, as emigrants produced an issue of the *Alfred* each Saturday during the voyage.

In 1868, another ship by the name of *True Briton* set sail from Kent for Melbourne. Unlike the voyage of the *Alfred*, no supporting material in the form of diaries, passenger lists or other official documentation relating to the voyage survives. The lone document that *has* survived is the eleven weekly runs of the shipboard newspaper, the *Open Sea*, from which we can surmise the minimum length of voyage.[4] As with the *Alfred*, the *Open Sea* was a collaborative endeavour, produced by emigrants during the journey. The production of shipboard newspapers was a popular form of entertainment on the long voyage to the Antipodes. Yet despite their popularity *during* the voyages, they seem to have had little function once they were over: carrying neither the official weight of surgeon superintendent diaries and captain log-books, nor the affective pull of emigrant diaries and letters, a vast number of them have not survived for posterity. Although emigrants frequently refer to shipboard newspapers in their diaries, a search for them in both online and card library catalogues yields no results. Emigrant brothers, William and Laurence Kennaway, for example, write in their diary that, 'A newspaper called the Sea Pie has been started to releive [sic] the monotony of the voyage; it comes out every Saturday.'[5] John Clapham, an emigrant to Sydney in 1861, notes in his diary that, 'The Tiptree Times was sent for us to read & I read it out for the benefit of us all, it was full of fun. Sporting, Commercial, Domestic, Police Report, etc. etc.'[6] In his shipboard diary to his way to New Zealand, Edward Jerningham Wakefield, Edward Gibbon Wakefield's only son, writes that they have 'established during the voyage a weekly manuscript paper and a debating society'.[7] None of these three papers has survived. Those newspapers which *have* survived now do so in print, either because they were printed on board the ship (mainly from the 1870s onwards) or because local printers in their destinations printed and sold them as souvenirs. What makes the *Alfred* and the *Open Sea* truly remarkable is that both survive in manuscript: they were produced by hand on the voyage and seem never to have been printed upon arrival.

Using the *Alfred* and the *Open Sea* as case studies of manuscript periodicals produced during the voyage out, this chapter argues that shipboard periodicals aspired to produce a provisional culture of settlement on board the ship as a preparatory step to the real task of settlement in the colonies. Through their mimicry of print periodicals, the *Alfred* and the *Open Sea* aimed to transform the voyage out into a useful and productive period that would enable them to learn how to live better lives in the colonies. As Katherine Foxhall argues, '[v]oyages did not just deliver emigrants and convicts, they made them into colonists'.[8] The transition that Foxhall argues occurs during the voyage is a shift in emphasis, from the diffusion of working-class people (emigration) to a determined act of middle-class settlement in new lands (colonisation). Attending to the cultural moment of emigrant shipboard periodicals' production shapes our understanding of social formations during the voyage and the importance of this during the settler process. More than just 'prevent[ing] boredom and restlessness'[9] or giving 'rhythm to undifferentiated periods of [time]',[10] shipboard periodicals played an important part in producing social formations during the voyage. As Bill Bell argues, the 'very existence' of shipboard newspapers 'indicates the extent to which a contemporary press had become by the mid-nineteenth century a necessity for the organisation of social life'.[11] Critics have previously understood the voyage out and the space of the ship as detached and distinct from the lands of departure and arrival. Janet C. Myers, for example, writes that the ship is a 'liminal'[12] space, while Michel Foucault describes the ship as 'a floating piece of space, a place without a place, that exists by itself, that is closed in on itself and at the same time is given over to the infinity of the sea'.[13] Attending to the textual activity of the voyage, however, allows a very different spatial politics to emerge. In *Atlas of the European Novel*, Franco Moretti proposes the idea of a 'literary geography': a form of reading novels that involves mapping the locations of a novel and seeking to understand what the resulting map might tell us about spatial relations.[14] Moretti's modes of mapping are what Emma Christopher, Cassandra Pybus and Marcus Rediker call '"terra-centric" narratives'.[15] In the maps that Moretti draws for us, the ocean is merely distance to be crossed: his lines skim over its surface without pausing to consider the kinds of knotted entanglements that crossing the immense expanse of water poses. Rather than connecting the colonies and the metropole in a continuum of geographical distance, emigrant shipboard periodicals upset that sense of distance, merging the spaces of the ship, Britain and the colonies together. This chapter shows that, through their enactment of a provisional culture of settlement on board the ship, shipboard periodicals such as the *Alfred* and the *Open Sea* aim to produce a provisional culture while at sea. In so doing, they disrupt the sense of geographical distance between the metropole and the colony and thus expose how the colonial ideology of settlement is at work in the supposedly liminal space of the sea.[16]

Performing Print

The *Alfred* and the *Open Sea* were produced nearly three decades apart: between them, they cover a span of time during which the idea of emigration to Australia consolidated itself as a valid and legitimate move. The opening up of free emigration to Australia, the gold rush of 1851 and the work of philanthropists, such as Caroline

Chisholm, had all cumulatively helped to erode the negative image of the country as a penal colony and instead set in place a more positive way of thinking about it. Mainstream periodicals, such as *Household Words*, *Blackwood's Magazine*, *Sharpe's London Journal* and *Chambers's Edinburgh Journal*, teemed with news from the colonies, letters from emigrants, updates on emigration policy, as well as fictional and non-fictional accounts of emigration. The sheer number of stories set in the Australian bush that circulated in land-based periodicals reflected the hold Australia had over the public imagination: although a few portrayed the negative aspects of emigration, by far the most were positive stories of settlement.[17] Magazines dedicated to providing information for intending emigrants, such as the *Colonist*, *Sidney's Emigrant Journal* and *Sidney's Emigrant's Journal and Traveller's Magazine* were also set up.[18]

Given the prominence of emigration-related material in print periodical culture at the time, it is unsurprising that emigrants aboard the *Alfred* and the *True Briton* drew upon the visual characteristics of print periodicals in the *Alfred* and the *Open Sea* respectively. The *Alfred* uses a two-column format, and the front page of each issue has a masthead, motto and the date and issue number (Figures 2 and 3).

Whereas each issue of the *Alfred* is meticulously consistent in layout throughout its twelve-week run, the *Open Sea* is looser in construction. The front page of each issue has the title of the journal, the issue number and the date, but rather than dividing the text into

Figure 2 Close-Up of Mast of the *Alfred*, State Library of New South Wales, Mitchell Library, A1680

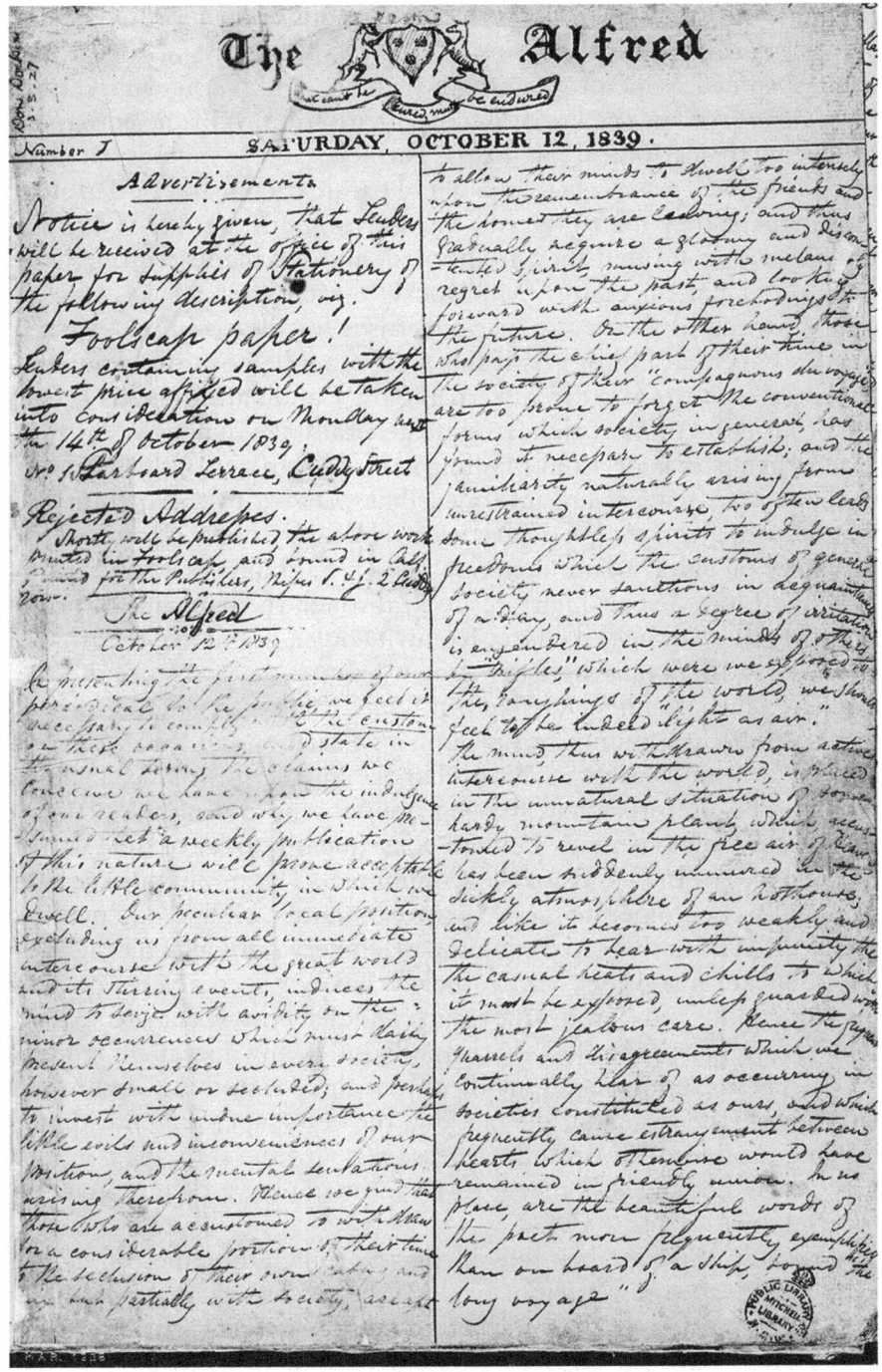

Figure 3 Sample First Page of an Issue of the *Alfred*, State Library of New South Wales, Mitchell Library, A1680

columns, the *Open Sea* follows the conventions of the more expensive periodicals that were appearing during the 1860s by having a one-column spread, which reflects both the changing literary markets of the time, as well as the literary and class aspirations of the emigrants producing the periodical (Figure 4). The newspapers' mimicry of print extends beyond their visual layout and paratextual features. Through the language they use to refer to themselves, both the *Alfred* and the *Open Sea* pretend that they are printed, and not manuscript, papers. The *Alfred* has an editor, 'Mr. Docker'. After four weeks, Docker steps down, and the newspaper advertises for his position: 'Wanted for this paper, an Editor.' As if this were a public position, the newspaper goes on to state, 'In advertising for Candidates for this office, the proprietors think it right to state generally the qualifications they require in a person desirous of filling it' (1, 5).[19] In one of the 'Notices' in the *Alfred*, readers are informed that, 'Owing to the quantity of matter *already printed*, we have been reluctantly obliged to defer the "Chapter on Hats" to our next number' (1, 5. Emphasis added). Similarly, the *Open Sea* also narrates itself through the language of print. Like the *Alfred*, it has an editor, Jeremy Diddler, but unlike the *Alfred*, Diddler is a fictional character drawn from a character in an 1803 farce by James Kenney, *Raising the Wind*, that was being performed in the 1860s in a number of prominent East London theatres, such as the Pavilion Theatre in Whitechapel.[20] In the fifth issue, Diddler writes in his editorial that, 'having been absent' during the production of the previous issue, he 'had consequently to leave the control of the paper in the hands of the Committee'. The resulting issue was a 'stupidly conglomerate mess' as the Committee blundered, 'making pie of the type and disarranging the machinery until alas the sight of the publication so upset Mr. D. that he has not been able to recover his full equilibrium', and as a result, Diddler now wishes to extend 'on his own behalf [and] solely to apologise' to any distraught readers (5, 1). These comments are made in jest: there is nothing apparently wrong with the issue, but the fact that the newspaper pretends that it is being produced by a printing press on board the ship when in fact it is clearly not suggests that it revels in imagining an alternative life for itself.

Crucially, through their referencing of print culture, the *Alfred* and the *Open Sea* do not attempt to dupe the reader into believing that they *are* print newspapers. Rather, the shipboard newspapers' materiality constantly ruptures its performances of print in playful and subversive ways. Unlike land-based periodicals, shipboard periodicals are produced *on the move*: the fact of mobility underpins every aspect

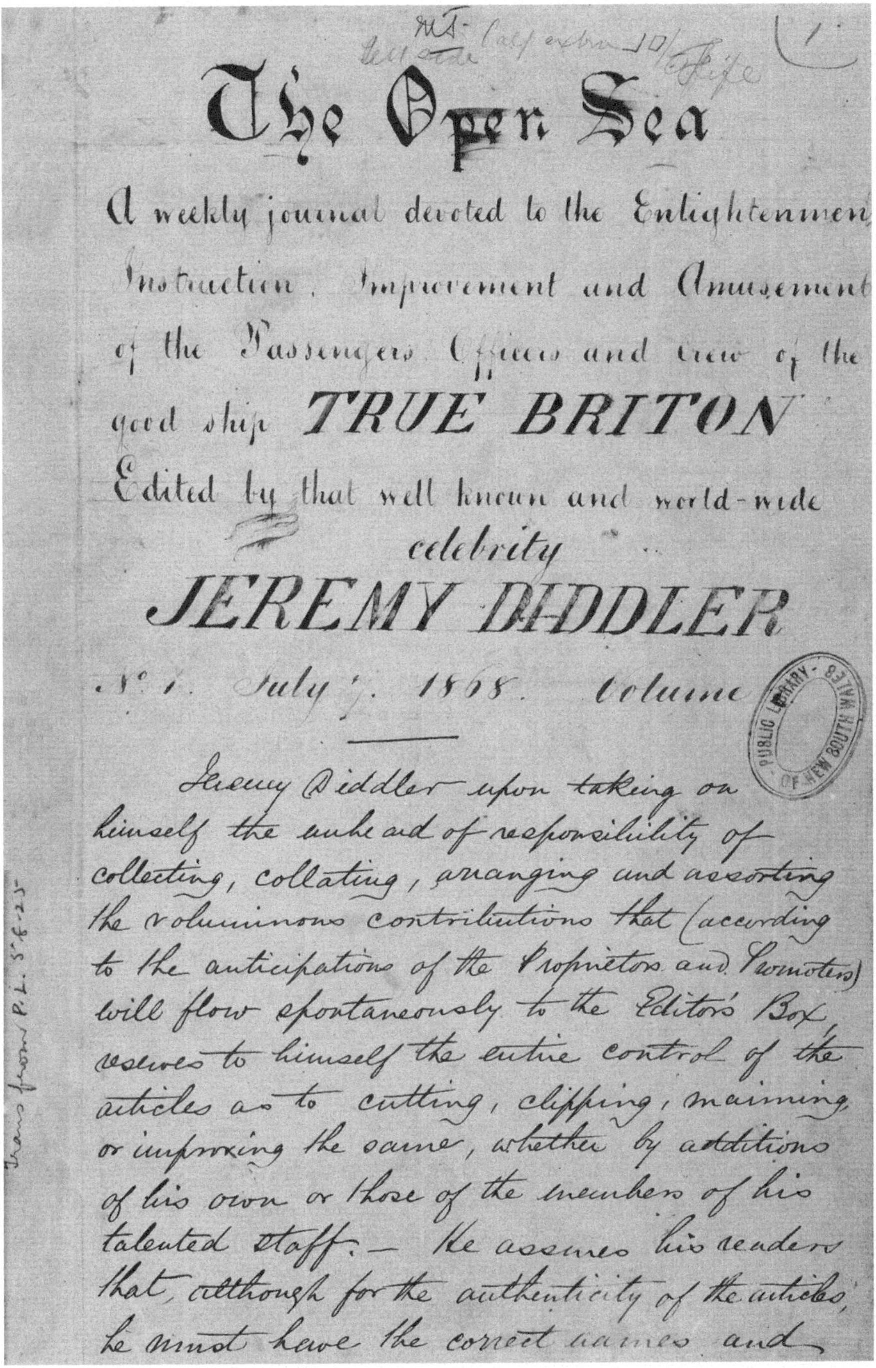

The Open Sea

A weekly journal devoted to the Enlightenment, Instruction, Improvement and Amusement of the Passengers, Officers and crew of the good ship **TRUE BRITON**

Edited by that well known and world-wide celebrity

JEREMY DIDDLER

Nº 1.   July 9. 1868.   Volume

Jeremy Diddler upon taking on himself the onerous of responsibility of collecting, collating, arranging and assorting the voluminous contributions that (according to the anticipations of the Proprietors and Promoters) will flow spontaneously to the Editor's Box, reserves to himself the entire control of the articles as to cutting, clipping, maiming, or improving the same, whether by additions of his own or those of the members of his talented staff. — He assures his readers that, although for the authenticity of the articles, he must have the correct names and

Figure 4 Front Page of First Issue of the *Open Sea*, State Library of New South Wales, Mitchell Library, A1645

of their being, from their material production to the kinds of 'news' they related. The availability of paper seems to have been a predominant anxiety. The very first item in the *Alfred* is an advertisement asking readers for 'supplies of Stationary [*sic*]' including 'Foolscap Paper!' (1, 1). The *Open Sea* advertises for paper in its second issue. To ensure 'the publication of future numbers', any emigrant possessing a 'supply of Foolscap paper' should 'immediately' present it to the 'Proprietors of this Journal' who will pay a 'liberal' sum for it (2, 16). Such advertisements suggest that the decision to produce shipboard periodicals was not a premeditated act, but was often spontaneous and made after the voyage was under way. The physicality of these periodicals and the constant sourcing of paper, ink and labour to ensure their full runs speaks of their potentially precarious existence. The *Open Sea* is made from various papers, all of different colours and sizes. The *Alfred* is made from paper all of a uniform size, but the tiny, cramped handwriting in it suggests an effort to be as economical with the space as possible.

Any attempt to mimic print periodicals is automatically undercut with irony. The *Open Sea*, for example, sets out its terms of subscription in the very first number, as any printed publication might. It requires 'One article from all contributors', and somewhat unorthodoxly, 'Good nature' from the 'Ladies', and 'One glass of Punch' from the 'Gentlemen'. The last two will 'be impartially divided amongst the contributors by the Editor in his good-natured manner' (1, 2). More often than not, a printed paper takes for granted that it will have a team of editors, that it has terms of subscription, and that it is printed. In stark contrast, the manuscript periodicals playfully draw attention to these aspects of print, and in so doing, highlight and emphasise the fact of their manuscript production.

On Land? Or at Sea?

Through their partial mimicry of printed newspapers, the *Alfred* and the *Open Sea* open up a space of subversive playfulness. Their performance of print allows them to live a fiction in more ways than one. Emigrants aboard both the *Alfred* and the *True Briton* radically realigned the spatial imaginaries in their newspapers, conceiving of themselves as part of land-based communities, not as a travelling community at sea. The *Alfred* sets itself up as the newspaper of 'Alfredstown', which needs a team of correspondents steadily recounting the news as it develops. The newspaper refers to the town's 'Cuddy Square', 'Poop Terrace', 'Poop Square' and 'Middlemast' (3, 1).[21] As can be expected from a newspaper covering a small country town, the *Alfred* has a number of reporters. In an announcement on 'Public Amusements', it reports that although the 'Theatres are closed', the editors have 'heard that a rehearsal took place [. . .] on Thursday evening': 'we have directed our reporter to attend' (1, 5). The 'Foreign Intelligence' section is 'from our own Correspondent' (1, 2). The metaphor of the *Alfred* as a town is used throughout the entire run of the paper. The *Open Sea* similarly draws on the images and tropes of a land-based community to narrate itself, although it does not sustain this trope with the same level of consistency that the *Alfred* does. In the first issue of the *Open Sea*, for example, the item on 'Local News' includes the following report:

> Village Sports. – On Thursday afternoon a grand athlete display took place on our village green. – The games were keenly contested by some of our most accomplished gymnasts. – By far the most elegant display was made in the perilous game of Spanish Fly[22] [. . .] There were many ladies on the ground and their wreathed smiles, gave zest and animation to the competitors. – The toilettes of the ladies were exceedingly handsome, and the whole presented a gay and animated spectacle. (1, 5)

The above passage could be mistaken as coming from a provincial newspaper, reporting perhaps on a weekend fête. It is only because we know its original context that it is apparent to us that the article is in fact writing of shipboard entertainment through the language of a village fête. In doing so, the newspaper nostalgically recalls a comfortable, happy village life. As if to reinforce this metaphor, it often refers to the ship as a village: 'We think this [playing of games on deck] is a step in the right direction, as, in our village, too little attention has been paid to physical education' (1, 5). Erika Elce argues that emigrants used shipboard newspapers to 'articulate not only their sense of physical distance from England but also, in spite of this distance, their emotional and cultural proximity'.[23] As we can see, one of the ways in which the manuscript shipboard newspapers achieve this cultural proximity is by overlaying the spatial imaginary of the ship with land-based communities. The periodical, whether land- or sea-based, was one of the main arenas in which the practice of settlement was performed. As the *Somersetshire News*, a periodical that emigrants produced during their voyage from Plymouth to Melbourne in 1869 points out, one of the most important aspects of settlement was simply having a periodical itself:

> Considering that now-a-days not only every principality and power, but almost every petty parish and municipality possesses its official gazette – and that the butcher, the baker, the candlestick-maker, and almost every other artificer or tradesman has his own organ – it is matter for surprise that so important a community as that dwelling on board the *S. S. Somersetshire* should have remained so long without a representative journal.[24]

Here, the editors assert that producing a periodical is an inherent part of settlement. Not only do they draw on various categorisations of settlement – 'principalities', 'parishes' and 'municipalities' – they also draw on the trades that are necessary for any established settlement. In other words, it was simply inconceivable to the editors of this paper that a community, however small and however far removed from the vicissitudes of everyday life on land, would not have their own periodical providing entertainment and recounting the news as it developed.[25]

Yet, land-based communities in the nineteenth century were by no means fixed and stable. As Josephine McDonagh argues, the nineteenth century was characterised by great internal migration as people moved from the countryside into the cities in search of employment, yet the periodical culture of land-based communities frequently fantasised about being stable.[26] Thus, when shipboard periodicals use land-based communities as metaphors to describe the ship, they share with land-based periodicals the fantasy of supposedly settled, contained communities such as the country town or village. Talking of the emigrant ship as a 'home' or 'village' was common rhetoric in the nineteenth century. In his emigrant guide, *Out at Sea* (1862), P. B. Chadfield, for example, asserts that an '"emigrant ship at sea" is a floating home for the many families on board; partaking in a great measure of the character of a house'.[27] Throughout his shipboard diary, the emigrant James Hopkins refers to the ship as his 'wooden house'.[28] This chapter does not assert that just because the *Alfred* and the *Open Sea* invoked a similar rhetoric, this immediately produced a feeling of settlement on board the ship.[29] It does, however, assert that through their production and consumption, the *Alfred* and the *Open Sea* aspired to create a community of readers out of the body of emigrants on the ship. As the following section shows, however, the lines of inclusion for each periodical's network of readers were distinctly different.

Producing the Shipboard Community

For most of the century, the question of how the voyage out was to be managed so that it remained economically profitable and took into consideration the health and safety of the emigrants remained a hot topic of debate in Parliament. Aside from the very real problems of food rations, shipwrecking, fires and sanitation, there was also the question of ensuring relations were kept cordial between large numbers of people who were at close quarters for extended periods of time. Those in government knew that tempers among passengers could run high in the confined space of the ship on a journey that could, at times, seem interminable. In order to prevent accidents and arguments from occurring, ships had detailed rules for everyday shipboard life set out in documents such as 'Instructions to Emigrants of Emigrant Ships Sailing under Government Superintendence'. The surgeon superintendent, the medical doctor who was in charge of the health of all those on board the ship, was in charge of enforcing the rules of the instructions on the emigrants. Various editions of these rules were printed throughout the century; while small changes were made, the core regulations remained the same. The instructions stipulated the amount of food and water that could be allocated to men, women and children. They set out the number of items of clothing emigrants were allowed in their berths, and the amount of luggage they were allowed in stowage; what time emigrants were to get up in the morning and what time they were to go to bed. Emigrants were required to carry out daily duties, such as cleaning the deck before and after breakfast each morning, rolling the beds up, doing the washing and hanging it out on dry days. The rules for emigrants at the back of the instructions were to be 'hung up in at least one conspicuous place between decks', in clear view of the emigrants.[30]

The regulations set out a timetable to which emigrants were required to adhere. It is easy to read this public display of the timetable as a Foucauldian means of 'disciplining' emigrants,[31] but it is also true that the majority of emigrants were new to travel by ship. Such a timetable shaped their day and regulated their activities and thus provided them with a framework for habitation on board the ship. In an attempt to minimise the disruption of being at sea, the Colonial Land and Emigration Commission required the superintendent to keep emigrants in the same social groups that they were in when they were on land:

> The people ought to be berthed according to their natural connections, and so as to place in the neighbourhood of one another those whose relative circumstances and habits render it most likely that they will agree.[32]

While the notion that placing emigrants from the same village next to each other would lessen the likelihood of fights breaking out is somewhat simplistic, the wish to produce the ship as a miniature version of the communities that emigrants had left behind manifests itself in the commission's instructions. The desire to assign emigrants their berths in a manner that retains their 'natural connections' with those from their own 'neighbourhoods' is an attempt to place people in familiar, recognisable social communities, in the hope that this would ease tensions during the voyage.

In much the same way as the government's instructions, shipboard periodicals such as the *Alfred* and the *Open Sea* sought to regulate the voyage out by producing the ship as a legitimate environment for habitation. In his first address to the *Alfred*'s audience, the editor, Mr. Docker writes:

> Introducing the first number of our periodical to the people, we feel it necessary to comply with the custom of these occasions, and state [. . .] why we have presumed that a weekly publication of this nature will prove acceptable in the little community in which we dwell. Our peculiar local position, excluding us from all immediate intercourse with the great world and its stirring events, induces the mind to [comment?] with avidity on the minor occurrences which must daily present themselves in every society, however small or secluded; and perhaps to invest with undue importance the little evils and inconveniences of our position, and the mental [sensations?] arising therefrom. (1, 1)

Shipboard life can result in two extremes of behaviour. There are those

> who are accustomed to withdraw for a considerable portion of their time to the seclusion of their own cabins [and] allow their minds to dwell too intensely upon the remembrance of their friends and the homes they are leaving and thus gradually acquire a gloomy and discontented spirit, musing with melancholy regret upon the past and looking forward with anxious forebodings of the future. (1, 1)

The other extreme are those who

pass the chief part of their time in the society of their 'compagnes du voyage' [and] are too prone to forget the conventional forms which society in general has found necessary to establish; and the familiarity naturally arising from unrestrained intercourse too often lead[s] some thoughtless spirits to indulge in flirtations which the customs of general society never sanctions. (1, 1)[33]

As Mr Docker points out:

> It is with a view to prevent the occurrence of these evils [as stated above], that the present publication has been projected; to endeavour [. . .] to lead the minds of our 'hermits' to take an interest in passing events, trivial as they are [that] the present publication has been projected. (1, 2)

Mr Docker's deference to the 'custom of these occasions' shows that the *Alfred* draws on certain generic conventions of print periodicals. However, this sits in tension with the kind of community reading and producing the periodical. Over and again, Docker draws attention to the 'little community' of shipboard emigrants, their 'peculiar local position' and 'small' and 'secluded' nature. Both size and location increase the possibility of social tensions: without the influence of the 'great stirring world' as a distraction, emigrants on board the ship are prone to become absorbed in the 'little evils and inconveniences' of the voyage. Through their performances of print, shipboard periodicals such as the *Alfred* attempt to mitigate this. The opening editorial of the *Open Sea* states that 'no abuse or grievance will be aired' in the paper (1, 2). The *Alfred* makes a similar assertion:

> Enthroned in our editorial chair we therefore [. . .] invite all the members of our community to grace our tournament of pens [. . .] we venture to express a hope that we have secured the pens of many fair and lovely writers, who will lead our readers over the delightful fields of thought. (1, 2)

It is difficult to determine the extent to which these editorial claims translated into reality. Evidence from emigrants' diaries, and even other shipboard newspapers, suggests that day-to-day shipboard life involved fights, petty theft and illicit liaisons.[34] As Bill Bell argues, shipboard periodicals were put together by strangers, 'for whom the preservation of a modest distance was important to the maintenance of a private life'. Their 'mimicry of the public sphere, allowed for the tangible expression of sociability, while still creating a rhetorical distance between those involved in its production and circulation'.[35] Through the weekly reportage of events, the *Alfred* aimed to provide a rhetorical distance between emigrants that was conducive for convivial relations – but, at the same time, to produce a sense of community.

However, the *Alfred* aims to create this sense of community among a very circumscribed group of people. The spatial imaginary of Alfredstown – 'Cuddy Square', 'Poop Terrace', 'Poop Square' and 'Middlemast' (3, 1) – is produced from the places of the ship that were reserved for first-class passengers. 'Cuddy' is another word for the cabins of first-class passengers, and the 'poop' is the uppermost deck of the ship, where only cabin-passengers and the captain were allowed. Alfredstown was not the only place in the newspaper. In an article entitled 'Foreign Intelligence', Alfredstown's 'Correspondent' reports from the steerage quarters of the ship: 'Steeragio, Oct. 9th – The present state of affairs in the Kingdom of Muckiana continues to be highly satisfactory. Perfect content appears to reign over all the provinces, each family revelling in those enjoyments, so peculiarly gratifying to their habits' (1, 2). In the second issue, however, the Foreign Intelligence Correspondent, reports a 'dreadful affray' between two 'natives' of Steeragio. One

> of these Visages, conscious of the powers of endurance possessed by her olfactory nerves had been induced to undertake the cleansing out [. . .] the office of Scavenger for that beautiful town, a task far surpassing the immortal labours of the demigod Hercules, whose achievements in the Augean Stables, it appears to have been her ambition to excel. (2, 1)

The reporter's distaste here for the stench of steerage berths was not unfounded. As Robin F. Haines notes, '[a]t sea the emigrants' senses were assaulted on every front [. . .] one needs little imagination to conjure up the smells in the married quarters in steerage, where often one-third of emigrants were children, many of them untrained babies and toddlers'. The 'horrendous smells created by a combination of vomit, faulty water closets and diarrhoea below decks' turned the steerage accommodation into 'a vile and stinking purgatory'.[36] Despite the historical accuracy of the *Alfred*'s reporter, the disparaging tones and the clear spatial demarcation between Alfredstown and Steeragio highlights the extent to which class politics influence the content and tone of the shipboard periodical.[37]

It should come as little surprise, then, that steerage passengers had little to do with the production of the *Alfred*. The periodical was produced and consumed by a small group of cabin passengers. From their diaries, it is clear that Emily and Eliza Darvall took great delight in it, and Emily and her mother regularly contributed to it. The feeling of class snobbery may have been heightened on this particular voyage as the *Alfred* was also carrying out a number of 'assisted' emigrant passengers, who had had help in paying for their journey: first-class passengers could distance themselves as much as possible from steerage passengers by reporting news from there as though it were an entirely different country. Emily notes in her diary of one particular Saturday when 'she has been 'reading [the paper] aloud' in the 'Cuddy' 'ever since breakfast' and 'listening to the strange guesses made on all sides'.[38] Reading the paper aloud seems to have been a common practice: on another Saturday, Eliza writes that 'Mr Docker has just read the whole paper aloud and it is better even than the last'.[39] The image of cabin passengers sitting in the small enclosed space of their cabins reading aloud stories from the 'Steeragio' and 'Muckiana' highlights that shipboard periodicals did not necessarily always aim to produce all-inclusive communities. Thus, although the *Alfred* frequently addresses its audience with 'public announcements' (1, 5), the sense of what constitutes this 'public' body is limited by class.

If the *Alfred* – both the ship and the paper – worked on the basis of an exclusionary spatial politics, the *Open Sea* uses its pages to establish and organise a more inclusive community. An article entitled, 'Our Medical Review' appeared in the first issue of the *Open Sea*. The author informs their reader that, while they take 'much pleasure' from the fact that 'the health of the ship "True Briton" has been, on the whole, very good', they also 'desire to impress, *on all classes of passengers*, the necessity, which there is for them, to pass as much of their time upon deck, in the fresh air, as they conveniently can' (1, 11. Emphasis added). Taking a walk on the deck reduced the amount of time steerage emigrants spent in overcrowded berths, and thus reduced the risk of contamination and spread of disease. While the desire in the *Open Sea* to maintain a healthy environment stems in part from the advances in maritime healthcare and medical understanding more generally by the 1860s,[40] the advice is in line with the paper's more inclusive attitude towards different classes.

Various other instances of this can be found in the *Open Sea*. For example, the paper reports on a meeting held by the editorial committee: the members' 'astonishment' at 'finding class feeling so predominant' is 'not to be expressed in words' (2, 4). Accordingly, the decision is taken at the end of the meeting that 'the perusal of the Cabin library be if possible extended to all on board' (2, 15). This gesture of good-will may have translated into reality in multiple ways. When Edward Cornell, an emigrant on board the *Red Jacket* to Melbourne in 1856, goes down into the steerage berths to distribute a few religious tracts, he sees that although 'by far the greater number [of emigrants] were playing at cards or dominos', it 'was pleasing to see so many carefully reading their Bible, a matter of which is by no means easy below the Deck for want of good light'.[41] Francis Gosling, an emigrant to Australia in 1836, writes that he has been gifted a small 'library' by his father – the diary provides a useful insight into the young man's regular and steady reading.[42] Edward Jerningham Wakefield writes that there is 'an ample supply of useful and interesting books' on the journey, which 'caused the time to pass cheerfully enough'.[43] Yet not all emigrants were this fortunate. Clapham, for example, writes in his diary that, 'you certainly have heaps of time' on board the ship, 'but take a book and the variety of noises around & first one & then another talking by & to you, so that after reading a sentence 6 or 8 times over you give it up'. To think that 'Shipboard is the place for reading', is a 'great mistake'.[44] His sentiment is echoed by the journalist Alexander Mackay, who warns prospective emigrants that the notion that the emigrant ship is 'the place for reading or study' is but a 'dream': 'It is either too cold, when there is the slightest breeze, or too hot when it is calm: it is too noisy at all times. Happy is he who, under such circumstances, has a resource against ennui in his own reflections.'[45] Despite this, however, shipboard reading was encouraged as a means of self-improvement. The *Open Sea*'s measure to encourage more reading is part of a larger phenomenon. From at least the 1850s, if not before, government-assisted emigrant ships had a library on board, with a large selection of religious and educational reading matter, as well as fictional material.[46] In his *Emigrant Voyager's Manual* (1850), William Henry Giles Kingston encourages his readers to 'make as much use' of the books provided by the ship,

> remembering that you may never again have so excellent an opportunity of improving yourselves as you now enjoy. Those who can read the best should teach their companions who cannot. While some are occupied with manual works, others may read to them, and this is a very pleasant way of gaining knowledge.[47]

The decision of the 'Diddling Committee' of the *Open Sea* to open up the 'Cabin library' for those in the lower accommodations would most likely have been made by cabin passengers, which suggests that the class politics on board the ship was more inclusive than that of the *Alfred*.[48]

This reading is supported by the fact that the periodical was kept on the deck, one of the few places on the ship where all passengers of all classes were able to mingle freely. A 'Lost, Stolen, or Strayed' notice in the second issue informs readers that the previous week, 'One of the Numbers of "the *Open Sea*" [. . .] disappeared from the deck, in an unaccountable manner, the person in whose possession it now is, will oblige by leaving where he found it' (2,16).[49] This suggests that the newspaper aspires to make itself available to all on board the ship.

In their different ways, then, the *Alfred* and the *Open Sea* sought to regulate the space of the ship. As we have seen, however, the periodical's regulation of the space of the ship was also a regulation of class: through their modes of consumption and production, the shipboard periodicals either reinforced class segregation, or attempted to overcome it. In *Serials and their Readers*, Bill Bell argues that serials disrupt a 'linear' production of literature where 'the author [. . .] produces a text' which a 'mass readership [. . .] consumes [. . .] with a convenient passivity'. Serials operate on a 'simultaneous production and consumption', where 'readers and reviewers' freely offered advice on the latest work-in-progress in letters and review articles which appeared at the same time as the works themselves were appearing.[50] Shipboard periodicals are evidently produced out of this non-linear mode of production, but importantly, this mode of production is imbricated in a network of power relations. Steerage passengers, for example, presumably had little opportunity to read what was written about them in the *Alfred*. As a natural consequence, they were automatically excluded from writing in to the editor. The editors of both the *Alfred* and the *Open Sea* mention that they have not been able to publish all contributions on account of there being so many: whose voice was taken on board to shape the next issue? Whose was ignored?

Space was thus essential to the shipboard periodical in more ways than one. Through its production and consumption, it aimed to produce communities of readers on board the ship, but at the same time, the communities that it shaped affected the spatial politics of the periodical page.[51] Unlike the eager ladies travelling first class on the *Alfred* who submitted articles unsolicited, the women of *True Briton* seem to have been more reluctant to contribute pieces. A sense of relief is clearly evident when the editor writes in the third issue of the *Open Sea* that they have 'at last enlisted the ladies' to provide 'two of the short pieces': 'We cannot adequately express how welcome their handwriting is. A little voluntary help and encouragement from them is like a little holiday to our hard worked staff' (3, 11). That the majority of submissions were from men is clearly evident even in light-hearted sections, such as the regular column, 'Little Things For Little Minds', which was filled with puns that referenced typically male amusements: 'Two Ruling Kings. – Jo-king and Smo-king' (1, 12). 'How to kill time – Shoot every day' (2, 12). 'Wanted to know – if two hogsheads make a pipe, how many will make a cigar' (2, 13). The first submissions from women throw this androcentric bias into sharp relief. One of the pieces in question is a letter of complaint, placed under the section, 'Local News' and signed with the name 'Rosina':

> Sir, Who shot the dog? The canine butchers who have been parading the deck and monopolizing the space which in my humble opinion ought to be devoted to the perambulations of the ladies are requested to cease their murderous intentions towards the dogs, and also to consider that the spars upon which we are obliged to sit and look on are not beds of roses. – The gentler sex deserves more consideration at the hands of those who display such pretentious bravery. (3, 11)

Rosina's mention of 'canine butchery' is most likely a metaphorical contextual reference to a shipboard event. Ships would have carried livestock on board as food which gave rise to unpleasant odours. In the medical review, the editors write that they look forward to the time when 'our livestock is diminished, and there are fewer dirty animals tainting the atmosphere with foul smells' (1, 11). What is much more interesting, however, is the fact that the first women's article to find space in the newspaper is simultaneously an article that demands the rights to equal access of space on deck.

The emigrants on board the *Alfred* and *True Briton* used their periodicals to either maintain class and gender structures and spatial segregation, or to break them down. If the periodical's fantasy of print allows for the merging of the spatial imaginary of land-based communities and the ship, then the periodical's regulation of space allows for the merging of its textual space and the spatial politics of the ship. The *Alfred* and the *Open Sea* thus use their textual space to influence the spatial politics of the ship and to provide a discourse of feeling as well.

Narrating the News

In 'Floating Worlds', Jason Rudy argues that Benedict Anderson's argument that print made it possible for people across vast distances to imagine themselves in synchrony 'applies' in the case of shipboard communities 'in microcosm'. He states that the 'anonymity of most contributors lends to the newspapers' sense of shared purpose [...] In most circumstances, we cannot know whether their authors were male or female, privileged or poor'.[52] Although the paucity of historical facts may now prevent us from coming to conclusions about authors of particular articles in newspapers, communal reading practices as discussed above suggest that items were not anonymous to the emigrants themselves. Furthermore, while the production of shipboard newspapers allowed emigrants to imagine themselves in synchrony with their friends and families in Britain and the colonies, the very fact of the microcosm of the ship shapes the formation of news and the imagined community on board the ship in important ways. In a letter to the editor of the *Open Sea*, an emigrant on board the *True Briton* presents what appears to be an ideal version of life on board the ship:

> Taking the plethora of daily newspapers in England as the standard of what you may mean by seriously-useful writing I find that their subjects are chiefly political, legal and criminal. – It would be idle to enter upon such discussions here as in our little community we have no politics. – No foreign telegrams and no boreing [sic] letters from foreign correspondents cause your readers to turn impatiently from the well packed page. – We have no squabbles but what are decided easily and promptly; the laws' delay is utterly unknown to us, and we are without the luxury of contemplating the careful and deliberate way in which justice is administered in courts. – We are equally without crime, so that the usual topics of the journalist are all denied us. – This however, goes to show that life on shipboard has a social aspect so gratifying that many of its results would be desirable in large communities. (3, 5)

It is unlikely that this is an accurate representation of life on board the ship. Far from being a safe haven from the legal and judicial world, the voyage out was a heavily regulated process. The passing and repeal of various Passenger Acts throughout the nineteenth century are testament to the contested nature of the voyage out. As Helen Woolcock argues, 'by mid-century [...] the British vessel became a floating welfare state with reciprocal rights and privileges' for the emigrants.[53] The central assertion of this passage in the open sea is that life on board the ship is organised differently from that on land – *and therefore requires a different narration of news*. 'Denied' the 'usual topics of the journalist' – 'legal, political, criminal' news – shipboard emigrants must turn to other topics of interest to narrate, or construct new modes of narration.

The first issue of the *Alfred* contains a poem on the death of an Irish emigrant girl in the section on 'Original Poetry':

> She came from her mountain home
>   In that far isle of the west. –
> Bright dreams of hope were filling
>   Her simple – joyous breast.
> Lured by the voice of kindness
>   To leave her native shore [. . .]
> The bark still keeps her onward course
>   But she – is with the dead! [. . .]
> And the Irish girl with all her hopes
>   Sleeps in the deep – deep sea!

Poems on emigrants and their emotional upheavals as they left their homes were staple features in both land-based and shipboard periodicals at the time, and the verse in the *Alfred* reads like a generic poem lamenting the death of an unfortunate emigrant. In fact, it actually relates to a genuine incident on board the ship. On Thursday 10 October, Emily writes in her diary, 'I fear poor Biddy Malone is dying. I saw her the other day and she looked very wretched, lying in a small berth in a very small hospital, close and dirty, but I hope she is well attended, as Mr. Docker visits her as well as the Doctor.'[54] Biddy died the following day. Eliza, Emily's younger sister, writes, 'We have just buried poor Biddy Malone, who has been dying of consumption ever since she came on board [. . .] The ceremony was very melancholy, and when the splash was heard, her sisters and friends raised a mournful wailing which they continued for some time.'[55] Evidently, by the time that Biddy's death appears in the *Alfred* on 12 October, it is no longer 'news'; everyone knows of it. The case of the Biddy Malone poem illustrates the different form of narration effectively: as there seems to be little of any novelty to relate in shipboard communities, the point of interest lies not so much in *what* is reported as in *how*. Thus, while emigrants may already know of Biddy Malone's death, the poem itself provides the element of novelty and a moment of shared reflection. Biddy has no name in the poem and instead the figure of the 'Irish girl' who now forever 'Sleeps in the deep – deep sea' could be any of the working-class emigrants who died during any voyage out as a result of previous ill health or poor living conditions during the voyage. While the poem attempts to raise sympathy for her through its sentimental tone, any sense of pathos is abstracted. In essence, then, the *Alfred* uses shipboard events as the source of its 'news', but it does not participate in a conventional mode of reportage. Rather, through its fictionalised (or, more accurately in this case, poeticised) retelling of its events, it provides its readers with an affective field in which they can all participate.

The *Open Sea* similarly takes full advantage of the 'continuum'[56] of fact and fiction and blurs the boundaries between them through the character of the editor, Jeremy Diddler. As the *Open Sea* continues to run, Diddler begins to feature more and more in the 'news' reported. Issue Three, for example, announces that a 'portrait' of Jeremy 'painted for presentation to the Museum' will be 'engraved for publication in the ensuing weeks [sic] issue of our journal' (3, 1). Accordingly, the fourth issue appears with an illustration of the presumed 'painting', along with an article reporting the 'gymnastics, and the irrepressible desire' of the committee members on the occasion of the unveiling of the painting: their frivolities were such that it 'made the atmosphere so intensely hot that catalepsy set in' (Figure 5). When 'The Diddling Committee awoke from their trance' they saw the 'untamable [sic] and unconquerable Jeremy looking at the Portrait presented him midst such glorious festivity' (4, 2). In an article in the fifth issue, 'Crossing the Line', Jeremy Diddler not only becomes an emigrant on the ship as she 'crosses the line' (the nautical phrase for crossing the equator) but actually a character in a fictional story where he visits 'the banquetting [sic] hall where was seated in submarine glory the venerable monarch of the main [Neptune] – rubicund and jolly he looked, his pleasant smile diffusing gladness and light to all around him' (4, 11). The modes of reportage in the *Open Sea* slide between various forms of fictionality: while Diddler himself may be a figment of imagination, the stories in which he appears that relate to shipboard life range from being 'just' a story, to being fantastical.

The size of the community on board the ship necessitates this fictionalised form of reportage: in small communities, where the production of a weekly newspaper cannot keep up with oral circulation, it must create other forms of reportage in order to maintain that sense of novelty. In short, the shipboard periodical becomes its own source of news. Each of the instances that we have looked at so far – the Biddy Malone poem, the hanging of the painting and the story of Neptune – are all related to shipboard events. While both the *Alfred*

Figure 5 'Engraving' of Jeremy Diddler in the *Open Sea*, State Library of New South Wales, Mitchell Library, A1645

and the *Open Sea* share some of the features of conventional reportage of print newspapers, the kinds of news they relate and the semi-fictionalised ways in which they relate them suggest that they aim to network their community of readers into the present moment, not by providing a weekly account of the events on board the ship, but by providing a space of shared reflection and entertainment. By providing this discourse of feeling, the shipboard periodical also hoped to regulate it: emphasising a light joviality would go some way towards preventing social tensions from arising.

Spatial Hybridity

It is impossible to determine the extent to which the *Alfred* and the *Open Sea* actually produced a culture of settlement on board the ship, but it is evident that, through the very production of a periodical and through the periodicals' vocabulary of print and land-based communities, this was one of their aspirations. The shipboard periodical thus regulated the voyage out by overlapping and merging different spatial imaginaries – the spaces of the town or village with that of the ship, the space of the ship with that of the periodical and vice versa. As we shall see, this imagined merging of different spaces is integral to how the periodical projects the provisional culture of settlement on board the ship onto life in the colonies.

Countless handbooks and manuals urged emigrants to see the voyage, not as an empty period of waiting until they reached the colonies, but as a chance to improve themselves and prepare for life in the colonies. Kingston's *Emigrant Voyager's Manual*, for example, is filled with advice that is centred around life in the colonies. He recommends emigrants spend time making models of 'wagons and carts, and Wheelbarrows' because 'up the country it will be important to know how to make a wheelbarrow [. . .] when, perhaps, no regular carpenter is to be found within twenty, or even fifty miles of you'.[57] He advises his readers that 'one should learn how to cobble shoes and mend clothes', 'for it is very probable that you will settle a long way from either a tailor or a cobbler'.[58] On the other hand, in the section on model-making, the reader is told that 'well-made models' of ships are 'very pretty ornaments or they may serve as toys for boys; but as they can be of no use to you, I do not recommend you to employ much of your time on them'.[59] Kingston urges upon his reader the importance of the voyage, as the emigrant 'will never again, probably, have so much leisure in the whole course of your lives; never such an opportunity in every respect of improving yourselves'.[60]

Shipboard periodicals also stressed this rhetoric of improvement that dominated emigrant guides such as Kingston's. In doing so, they also attempted to produce a transformation from emigrant to colonist during the voyage. In the fifth issue of the *Open Sea*, a chant appeared, which emigrants presumably marched to on deck for exercise. It consisted of four stanzas of four lines, with a repeated chorus:

> March, march, ladies and gentlemen,
>   March for the health and strength of our party
> Suppertime by and bye, soon will show reason why
>   All the 'True Britons' should take a long breath.

The emphasis on breathing well and staying strong and healthy is evidently a reference to specifically maritime health: as mentioned previously, staying below the decks in the often rank air and poor ventilation was discouraged. Nonetheless, the military tone of the chant and the emphasis on strong, healthy bodies inevitably shades into a nationalistic discourse on settler emigration that views young, healthy single men and women as ideal colonists.

Tellingly, the last sermon of the *Open Sea* is on 'Earnestness': 'No! No! Young man,' cries Diddler, 'it cannot last that you shall be out late night after night and at your business all right in the morning. You will be there, but you will not be there in earnest.'; 'No! Ladies,' he cries, 'it will not do, – you cannot gossip with your neighbours day after day, you cannot dawdle about shipping; you cannot lounge a forenoon over a novel, and trust your nimble fingers to make up for the lost time' (11, 2–3). A 'man in earnest is a grand study': 'without bragging, often without show he pursues his object, waits when Fortune frowns, and almost infallibly succeeds'. While such a man may not 'compare favourably' 'amongst the ladies' because he does not 'shine in drawing rooms [and] rarely in dining rooms', nevertheless, 'he shines eclipsing all else' 'in the pulpit, at the press, on the battlefield, amidst the raging storms, on the Exchange, at the fireside' (11, 3). Diddler insists that women 'are more earnest than men', and their 'task' is 'to fan the flame of earnestness where it is likely to flag in the bosom of husband, brother, son or lover' (11, 4).[61] The sermon makes no overt reference to settlement, but the stress on diligence, patience and, in the case of women, supporting their men, fits in with the colonial ideology of emigration. As we shall see in the next chapter, emigrant manuals and periodicals sometimes sought to disabuse potential emigrants of any notions of easy success in the colonies. They made it clear that hard work and patience and the ability to rise above sometimes multiple failures was an inevitable and integral part of settlement: success came only to those who worked and waited for it.

Fundamentally, however, the emphasis on settlement, first on board the ship and then in the colonies, was not a means of forgetting Britain and wholeheartedly embracing a new life in the Antipodes. The newspapers posit a more complicated relationship between Britain and Australia than the simple uni-directional flow of people, goods and cultural practices to the colonies. They recognise that the relationship may not be a simple binary, but in fact may be a messier, entangled knottiness of spatial and textual relations. A poem looking back on the voyage appears in the last issue of the *Alfred*, in which the poet recalls the moments as the ship leaves the harbour, and 'Albion's receding cliffs are seen no more': 'My aching eyes now vainly seek the shore / The kind farewell no longer meets my ear.' A renewed sense of community mitigates this sense of loss: on board the ship, the poet finds a group of 'friends – let them not go – / They came like truth, they should not fade like dreams' (12, 11). These concerns with loss, continuity and formations of new communities echo throughout the periodical. In the column 'Intercepted Despatches', there is a letter that purports to be from 'Alfred Thomas' to 'Mrs Sophie Blueyedbrown', resident of 'Rabbitburrow Park' in 'New South Wales'. As the previous chapter has shown, whether manuscript or print, whether circulating in personal or public networks, emigrants' letters acted as a point of connection between people in their new settings, and the homes they had left behind. For this reason, the letter in the *Alfred* is particularly interesting. Both the names 'Blueyedbrown' and 'Rabbitburrow Park' indicate that the letter is fictional. As an imaginary letter, it quite evidently plays little part in actually maintaining a connection between beloved family members over time and space. Alfred Thomas appears to be a person who went out with Sophie Blueyedbrown and, having left Sophie to settle in New South Wales, is returning to England with his 'fellow passengers some of whom are well known to you'. The last comment suggests that Alfred Thomas's fellow passengers also travelled out with Sophie and are now travelling back to England. This spatial dynamic where would-be emigrants are returning home to England, but are writing to their friends in New South Wales, complicates a one-way flow between metropole and colony. The figure of Alfred Thomas highlights the multi-faceted and complex ways in which emigrants are situated. Whereas emigrant guidebooks and manuals were written with an eye to homes in the future colonies, produced in the 'in-between' space of the voyage, shipboard periodicals offered a space in which emigrants could articulate that sense of being between places, of being both homed and unhomed at the same time. Displaced from home and travelling 'to a soil that is not mine' (12, 11) and yet constantly looking back home and producing new communities during the voyage, they write of themselves as placed in the messy, complex junctures of being between places.

In their diaries, emigrants frequently write of the huge expanse of the ocean and how the voyage often feels like a huge temporal and spatial expanse. Edward Charlwood, for example, writes in his diary,

> We don't seem to have energy enough to talk to one another, we can't settle down to read, and one soon gets tired of walking about so we lounge and eat and drink and smoke and sleep the day away somehow but I often think what a shocking waste of time it is.[62]

In his diary, Henry Curr records his awe of the ship which 'is in an immense circle of water; the wide canopy of the sky is resting upon its outer edge in the far distant horizon'.[63] With their stress on their 'isolated' position, and on being a 'little' community marked by the 'passing' of 'trivial events', shipboard periodicals seem, in part, to share this sentiment of the ship as separated from the rest of the world by the vast immenseness of the ocean. At the same time, however, the emigrants who produced these shipboard periodicals recognise that they are imbricated in a wider network of social relations. It is by now widely acknowledged that print culture, through novels and newspapers, enabled people who had never seen each other before to imagine themselves as a community simultaneously moving forward through homogeneous empty time: this is what makes it possible for the nation to imagine itself as a collective entity.[64] Evidently, as the discussion of the production and dissemination of the periodicals in this chapter shows, these little shipboard periodicals reproduce ideas of nationhood and colonisation even though they do not make an 'imagined community' in the same way that a print periodical does. Instead, the periodicals produce a 'spatial synchronicity'. Through their factual fictions, they imagine the emigrant ship through a multiplicity of spatial configurations all overlaid onto that of the ship. This geographical hybridity is one of the fundamental points of the ideology of settler emigration: the ability to carry the affect of places elsewhere, and to encourage a flow between the metropolis and the colony is the task that, to a greater or lesser extent, all texts of emigration literature participate in.

Thus, produced during the liminal space of the voyage, shipboard periodicals place themselves at the interfaces of fact and fiction, manuscript and print, and novelty and the news, drawing upon and subverting generic expectations and conventions of print periodicals. They offer a fresh understanding of the cultural conditions of settler emigration: against emigration literature's preoccupations of loss, anxiety and despair, they exhibit a subversive playfulness, in both their form and content. In the previous chapter, I looked at how the public sphere of print untethered letters from their network of personal associations and that this circulation in the public sphere of print created a culture of suspicion. In this chapter, I have looked at how manuscript shipboard newspapers created a fantasy of print precisely because it allowed them to participate in imagining themselves as operating within a wider geographical scope than the one in which they were currently located. While the manuscript newspaper draws on aspects of print periodicals in order to invest itself with some of its attributes, nonetheless it does so in order to subvert some of the claims of print periodicals and to articulate for themselves what the experience of emigration might entail. In the next chapter, I look at another example of how emigrants write back to booster literature. Focusing on the work of Susanna Moodie and Catharine Parr Traill, I look at the ways in which they wrote back to the print culture of emigration to voice alternative gendered narratives of emigration that represent the female experience of emigration.

Notes

1. Eliza Charlotte Darvall, *Diary, 8 Sept.–29 Dec. 1839, with biographical note 1968*. Sydney, Mitchell Library, MLMSS 1547: microfilm CY 2978, frames 93–149. Jeremy Long has transcribed Eliza Darvall's diary in Jeremy Long, *Strugglers and Settlers: Darvall Family Letters 1839–1849* (Springwood: Butterfly Books, 1994), pp. 43–80. In the interests of accessibility, I have quoted from Long's book throughout this chapter when using Eliza Darvall's diary, unless otherwise stated. This quotation is from p. 47. All further references to Eliza Darvall's *Diary* will take the form 'Long, *Diary*', followed by the page number.
2. Emily Darvall, *Typescript Extract of Diary of Miss Emily Darvall, Kept during the Voyage of the 'Alfred' from England to Australia in 1839*, in *Thomas Lodge Murray-Prior papers, 1843–1889, together with Miscellaneous Family Papers, 1837, 1893*, p. 13. Sydney, Mitchell Library, MLMSS 3117/Box 11/ Item 2: microfilm CY 4336, frames 1–151. All further references to this text will take the form 'Darvall, *Typescript Extract*', followed by the page number.
3. John Darvall had sailed out on a previous voyage with his new wife a few months earlier. The Darvall sisters were travelling with the rest of the family: their father, Major Darvall, their mother, another sister, Rose, and two brothers, Fred and Horace, to meet them.
4. A voyage of around eleven weeks is not unlikely: despite the three-decade gap between the voyages of the *Alfred* and the *True Briton*, the length and possible routes of the two ships were quite similar. By the 1860s, steamships were becoming more popular than sail only on shorter, transatlantic routes: with a few exceptions, sailing ships were the dominant mode of transport to Australia. The most notable exception was the celebrated steamship, *SS Great Britain*, which made thirty-two trips to Australia between 1852 and 1876. See Adrian Ball and Diana Wright, *SS Great Britain* (Newton Abbot: David & Charles, 1981), p. 39. It was only in the 1880s that steamship travel to the Antipodes began to take over from sail. See Andrew Hassam, *Sailing to Australia: Shipboard Diaries by Nineteenth-Century British Emigrants*

(Manchester: Manchester University Press, 1994), p. 7. For details of the route to Australia, see Jack Loney and Peter Stone, *The Australia Run*, Series: Australian Shipwrecks, VI (Benalla: Marine History Publications, 2000), pp. 5–48.
5. R. C. Lamb and R. S. Gormack (eds), *Biscuit and Butter: A Colonist's Shipboard Fare, the Journal Kept by William & Laurence Kennaway on the Emigrant Ship* Canterbury, *London to Lyttelton, 1851* (Christchurch: Nag's Head Press, 1973), p. 45.
6. John Clapham, *Diary of his Voyage to Sydney, 1860–1861, with Transcription by Margaret Kentley, 1975*. Sydney, Mitchell Library, MLMSS 6944: microfilm CY 4319, p. 10.
7. Quoted in Paul Bloomfield, *Edward Gibbon Wakefield: Builder of the British Commonwealth* (London: Longmans, 1961), p. 212.
8. Katherine Foxhall, *Health, Medicine, and the Sea: Australian Voyages, c.1815–1860* (Manchester: Manchester University Press, 2012), p. 1.
9. Elizabeth Leane, 'The *Adelie Blizzard*: The Australasian Antarctic Expedition's Neglected Newspaper', *Polar Record* 41 (2005), pp. 11–20 (p. 11).
10. David H. Stam and Deirdre C. Stam, 'Bending Time: The Function of Periodicals in Nineteenth-Century Polar Naval Expeditions', *Victorian Periodicals Review* 41 (2008), pp. 301–22 (p. 302).
11. Bill Bell, 'Bound for Australia: Shipboard Reading in the Nineteenth Century', *Journal of Australian Studies* 25 (2001), pp. 5–18 (p. 18).
12. Janet C. Myers, *Antipodal England: Emigration and Portable Domesticity in the Victorian Imagination* (Albany: State University of New York Press, 2009), p. 13.
13. Michel Foucault, 'Of Other Spaces', trans. Jay Miskowiec, *Diacritics* 16 (1986), pp. 22–7 (p. 27).
14. Franco Moretti, *Atlas of the European Novel, 1800–1900* (London: Verso, 1998), p. 3.
15. Emma Christopher, Cassandra Pybus and Marcus Rediker, 'Introduction', in Emma Christopher, Cassandra Pybus and Marcus Rediker (eds), *Many Middle Passages: Forced Migrations and the Making of the Modern World* (Berkeley: University of California Press, 2007), pp. 1–19 (p. 1).
16. Philip E. Steinberg, *The Social Construction of the Ocean* (Cambridge: Cambridge University Press, 2001), p. 6.
17. The number of stories of emigration and the colonies in periodicals is so many that it would serve little purpose even to attempt to provide a selection here. E. M. Palmegiano's *The British Empire in the Victorian Press, 1832–1867: A Bibliography* (London: Garland Publishing, 1987) is a very good bibliography for stories relating to empire and the colonies, as a starting point. See the Introduction, pp. xxx for a general account of empire and periodicals and pp. xxx for an account of Australia, New Zealand and British North America in the periodicals.

18. *Open Sea: Weekly Journal No. 1–11, 7 July–Sept. 1868, on the ship True Briton*. Sydney, Mitchell Library, A1645: microfilm CY 2072, frames 177–249. As explained above, '1, 5' refers to the fifth page of the first issue.
19. Interestingly, although emigration was a popular feature in periodicals, periodicals that were dedicated specifically to emigration often fared poorly. *The Colonist*, edited by William Henry Giles Kingston, went through only two issues. Samuel Sidney (pseudonym of Samuel Solomon) and his brother John set up *Sidney's Emigrant Journal* as a weekly periodical in 1848. It ran from 5 October 1848 to 12 July 1849. Samuel set up *Sidney's Emigrant's Journal and Traveller's Magazine* in 1849 by himself, but it had only six issues. See Stanley Tick, 'Sidney, Samuel (1813–1883)', *Australian Dictionary of Biography*, <http://adb.anu.edu.au/biography/sidney-samuel-2662/text3599> [accessed 21 September 2017].
20. See *Mixed Playbill for Gil Blas!; Mr. Eden Clarke; Willy Reilly and his Own Dear Cooleen Bawn; The Vokes Family; Raising the Wind, Pavilion Theatre* (n.p.: n.pub., 26 July 1861).
21. *Alfred: Weekly Magazine of the Emigrant Ship, Alfred, No. 1–2, 12 Oct.–28 Dec. 1839*. Sydney, Mitchell Library, A1680: microfilm CY 2072, frames 1–70. All quotations from the *Alfred* and the *Open Sea* are referenced in-text and refer to the issue number, followed by the page number. Thus here, '3, 1' refers to the first page of the third issue (*not* the first issue of the third volume). Furthermore, as it is clear in the chapter which newspaper I am quoting from, I have omitted their titles in in-text references.
22. A game of leapfrog in which the first person to leap over becomes the leader and sets feats for the others to perform as they leap over. Any player who fails takes the place of the back.
23. Erika Behrisch Elce, '"One of the Bright Objects that Solace Us in these Regions": Labour, Leisure, and the Arctic Shipboard Periodical, 1820–1852', *Victorian Periodicals Review* 46 (2013), pp. 343–67 (p. 345).
24. *Somersetshire News: A Ship Newspaper, Issued on Board the S.S. Somersetshire, on her Passage from Plymouth to Melbourne* (Melbourne: Sands and McDougall, 1869), p. 1.
25. D. H. Borchardt, 'Printing Comes to Australia', in D. H. Borchardt and W. Kirsop (eds), *The Book in Australia: Essays Towards a Cultural and Social History* (Melbourne: Australian Reference Publications, in association with the Centre for Bibliographical and Textual Studies, Monash University, 1988), pp. 1–15 cites the example of the First Fleet carrying on board 'an old wooden screw press, a small selection of used type and some paper and ink' (p. 2). While it would be some time before a proper printing press was established in the country, the fact that the British government thought it necessary to send the convicts away with a printing press on board points to the integral relationship between settlement and print.

26. Josephine McDonagh, 'Urban Migration and Mobility', in Sally Ledger and Holly Furneaux (eds), *Charles Dickens in Context* (Cambridge: Cambridge University Press, 2011), pp. 268–75 (pp. 268–9).
27. Philip B. Chadfield, *Out at Sea; Or, the Emigrant Afloat, Being a Hand Book of Practical Information for the Use of Passengers on a Long Sea Voyage* (Derby: Chadfield & Son, 1862), p. 30.
28. James Hopkins, *Journal of Passenger on the* Schomberg *on her Last Voyage from Liverpool bound to Melbourne, 6 Oct.–26 Dec. 1855*. London, National Maritime Museum, XJOD/1.
29. The realities of shipboard life for labouring classes may not have been too dissimilar from life at home. Cf. Robin F. Haines, who asserts in *Life and Death in the Age of Sail: The Passage to Australia* (Sydney: University of New South Wales Press, 2006) that 'For many labouring families, life at sea was, perhaps, not so very different from the domestic situations that they had left behind' (p. 36) and that the 'ship, in reality, constituted a tenement block of two or five hundred people or more' (p. 80).
30. Stephen Walcott, 'Instructions to Surgeons of Emigrant Ships Sailing under Government Superintendence' (London: William Clowes, 1843).
31. Michel Foucault, *Discipline and Punish: The Birth of the Prison*, trans. Alan Sheridan (London: Allen Lane, 1977), p.149.
32. Walcott, 'Instructions', p. 9.
33. The irony of this is that Emily Darvall met her future husband, Robert Barton, on board the *Alfred* and married him a few weeks after their arrival in Sydney. They went on to have ten children.
34. As many good historical accounts of nineteenth-century life at sea already exist, I have not gone into more depth here than is necessary. See for example, Don Charlwood, *Settlers under Sail*, 3rd edn (Melbourne: Burgewood Books, 1999); Ann Giffard and Basil Greenhill, *Travelling by Sea in the Nineteenth Century: Interior Design in Victorian Passenger Ships* (London: A. and C. Black, 1972); Haines, *Life and Death* (2006).
35. Bell, 'Bound for Australia', p. 17.
36. Haines, *Life and Death*, p. 75; p. 77.
37. See Andrew Hassam, '"Our Floating Home": Social Space and Group Identity on Board the Emigrant Ship' (London: Sir Robert Menzies Centre for Australian Studies, 1992), p. 1 for a description of how heavily demarcated by class the spatial organisation of the ship was. Steerage passengers were not allowed in intermediate berths or first-class cabins, intermediate passengers were allowed in steerage but not in cabins, and first-class passengers were free to go anywhere – if they chose to do so.
38. Darvall, *Typescript Extract*, p. 17. It is not clear from Emily's diary what her fellow emigrants are guessing.
39. Long, Diary, p. 59.
40. See Foxhall, *Health, Medicine, and the Sea* and Robin F. Haines, *Doctors at Sea: Emigrant Voyages to Colonial Australia* (Basingstoke: Palgrave Macmillan, 2005) for accounts of maritime healthcare, especially pp. 67–76.

41. Cornell, Edward, *Journal Kept on Board the Royal Mail Clipper* Red Jacket *from Liverpool to Melbourne, May to Aug. 1856*. London, National Maritime Museum, TRN/20, p. 2 [24 May 1856].
42. Francis Alexander Gosling, *Journal of a Voyage from London to Sydney on Board the* Alexander *in 1836*. Sydney, Australian National Maritime Museum, 00001689.
43. Quoted in Bloomfield, *Edward Gibbon Wakefield*, p. 212.
44. Clapham, *Diary of his Voyage to Sydney*, p. 18.
45. Alexander Mackay, 'An Emigrant Afloat', *Household Words* (31 August 1850), pp. 534–9 (p. 537).
46. See *Instructions to Surgeon Superintendents of Government Emigrant Ships* (London: George Eyre and Andrew Spottiswode, 1858), pp. 70–2.
47. William Henry Giles Kingston, *The Emigrant Voyager's Manual* (London: Trelawney Saunders, 1850), p. 38.
48. For an account of shipboard reading, see Bill Bell, 'Crusoe's Books: The Scottish Emigrant Reader in the Nineteenth Century', in Bill Bell, Philip Bennett and Jonquil Bevan (eds), *Across Boundaries: The Book in Culture and Commerce* (Winchester: St Paul's Bibliographies, 2000), pp. 116–129. For an account of shipboard reading as a means of moral improvement in a slightly different context, see Rosalind Crone, 'Attempts to (Re)shape Common Reading Habits: Bible Reading on the Nineteenth-Century Convict Ship', in Beth Palmer and Adelene Buckland (eds), *A Return to the Common Reader: Print Culture and the Novel, 1850–1900* (Surrey: Ashgate, 2011), pp. 103–20.
49. I am assuming that, as the editors are asking for it to be returned to the deck, this is the usual place where the paper was kept. This request appears in the second issue of the periodical. It asks for the issue of the previous week (the first week's) to be returned. The fact that 'one' of the first issues has been taken from the deck suggests that more than one copy was made: the lack of available statistics makes it difficult to say whether this was a common practice (and I have not been able to trace if another copy of the newspaper is extant) but there is evidence to suggest that it was not unheard of. In 1875, small numbers of manuscript copies of *The Sobraon Occasional* were produced and circulated between passengers during the voyage, and when the ship reached Melbourne, copies were printed by Mason, Firth & M'Cutcheon as souvenirs. See *The Sobraon Occasional Published on Board the* Sobraon *during her Outward Voyage to Melbourne, 7 October–26 December 1875*. Sydney, Mitchell Library, MLMSS 7715/Item 1 and the library catalogue records for details of the newspaper's transition from manuscript to print: <http://www.acmssearch.sl.nsw.gov.au/search/itemDetailPaged.cgi?itemID=991987> [accessed 21 September 2017].
50. Bill Bell, 'Fiction in the Marketplace: Towards a Study of the Victorian Serial', in Michael Harris and Robin Myers (eds), *Serials and Their Readers, 1620–1914* (Winchester: St Paul's Bibliographies, 1993), pp. 125–44 (p. 129). For a very good discussion of how correspondence columns shaped a magazine's reading community, see Lynne Warren,

'"Women in Conference": Reading the Correspondence Columns in *Woman* 1890–1910', in Laurel Brake, Bill Bell and David Finkelstein (eds), *Nineteenth-Century Media and the Construction of Identities* (Basingstoke: Palgrave, 2000), pp. 122–34.
51. See Rebecca Steinitz, *Time, Space, and Gender in the Nineteenth-Century British Diary* (Basingstoke: Palgrave Macmillan, 2011), p. 44 for a reading of textual space.
52. Jason R. Rudy, 'Floating Worlds: Emigre Poetry and British Culture', *ELH* 81 (2014), pp. 325-50 (p. 328).
53. Helen R. Woolcock, *Rights of Passage: Emigration to Australia in the Nineteenth Century* (London: Tavistock, 1986), p. 65. See pp. 64–5 of this book for information on the various Passenger Acts of the mid-century; and Cameron and Maude, *Assisting Emigration to Upper Canada*, pp. 60–1 for a brief history of Passenger Acts in the early 1830s.
54. Darvall, *Typescript Extract*, p. 11.
55. Long, *Diary*, p. 47.
56. See Lennard J. Davis, *Factual Fictions: The Origins of the English Novel* (New York: Columbia University Press, 1983), p. 9. See also Chapter 3, 'News/Novels: The Undifferentiated Matrix', pp. 42–70. I am also drawing on the work of Matt Rubery here to construct my argument on the shared discourses of news and fiction. See Matthew Rubery, *The Novelty of Newspapers: Victorian Fiction after the Invention of the News* (Oxford: Oxford University Press, 2009).
57. Kingston, *Emigrant Voyager's Manual*, p. 30.
58. Ibid. p. 40.
59. Ibid. p. 29.
60. Ibid. p. 4.
61. The role of women in the context of nineteenth-century settler emigration is a complex and fraught one. The next chapter will look at the relationships between gender, emigration and literature.
62. *The 1863 Shipboard Diary of Edward Charlwood: From England to Australia*, facsim. edn (Warrandyte: Burgewood Books, 2003) [15 July 1863].
63. Henry Curr, *Diary: Covering the First Six Weeks of his Voyage from England to Australia on the Full-Rigged Ship* Morning Light *in 1856*. Sydney, Vaughan Evans Library, 3 0001 00014741 5, p. 12 [12 July 1856].
64. Benedict Anderson, *Imagined Communities: Reflections on the Origin and Spread of Nationalism*, rev. edn (London: Verso, 2006), especially chapter 3, 'The Origins of National Consciousness', pp. 37–46.

Chapter 3

Fragmentary Aesthetics: Susanna Moodie and Catharine Parr Traill in the Canadian Bush

For sisters Susanna Moodie and Catharine Parr Traill, marriage and emigration were two sides of the same coin. Emigration was Moodie's 'husband's call'.[1] When she cried for her life in England, she consoled herself with the fact that 'my children round me play, / My husband's smiles approve' (75). Parr Traill asks herself rhetorically, '[H]ave I not a right to be cheerful and contented for the sake of my beloved partner? [. . .] if for his sake I have voluntarily left home, and friends, and country, shall I therefore sadden him by useless regrets?'[2] Confirming the news of her marriage to her friends, James and Emma Bird, she writes that 'the waves of the Atlantic will soon roll between' them, but despite this, she is still 'willing to lose all for the sake of one dear valued friend and husband to share with him all the changes and chances of a settlers [sic] life'.[3] Before the sisters met their respective husbands, they had both resigned themselves to spinsterhood, hoping to use their literary ambitions to secure themselves financially. Their childhood had been filled with literary endeavours. Later, Parr Traill would liken themselves to the other, more famous, literary sisterhood of the Brontës: '[W]ere I to write a history of the childhood of the Strickland family,' she muses in her journal, 'how many things there would be that would remind the reader of the early days of the Brontës.'[4] As they grew older, these endeavours began to take on a professional form, as they sought out publishing opportunities in London.[5] In between the years 1818, when her father died, to 1832, when she left for Canada, Parr Traill published at least a dozen books and made many more contributions to periodicals.[6] By 1830, Moodie too had 'published several books of entertainment and moral instruction', and 'contributed numerous stories and poems to [. . .] popular annuals and gift books'. Additionally, she had begun to gain recognition as 'a writer of promise in literary circles such as those in which [the abolitionist]

Thomas Pringle moved'.⁷ It was in London, in Pringle's house, that Moodie first met her future husband, John Dunbar Moodie, and then through John, that Parr Traill met hers, Thomas Traill. John Moodie had recently returned to England, with the 'threefold intention' of writing an account of his adventures in South Africa, where he had emigrated to in 1819, finding a wife, and returning to 'Groote Valley', his South African farm.⁸ Her fear of wild animals, coupled with her distaste for slavery, however, caused her to break off an initial engagement to John. In a letter explaining to her friends, she declared, 'I have changed my mind. You may call me a jilt or a flirt or what you please [. . .] I will neither marry a soldier nor leave my country for ever.'⁹ Within a few weeks, however, she had changed her mind again and they were married on 4 April 1831. Parr Traill married a little over a year later, on 13 May 1832. Early into the Moodies' marriage, it became apparent that they could not maintain their social status on John's income of a half-pay officer.¹⁰ John decided to emigrate to Canada, and Thomas Traill followed suit: their wives had little choice but to acquiesce.

In addition to emigration propaganda, there were many other personal stories to persuade John and Thomas in favour of Canada. Moodie and Parr Traill's brother, Samuel Strickland, had been offered a job by John Galt, secretary to the Canada Company, in 1828.¹¹ The company, a London-based organisation, had bought vast areas of Crown land in the Huron Tract to sell on to prospective emigrants. Samuel's father-in-law, Robert Reid, returned to England – and arrived unexpectedly on the Moodies' doorstep, with tales of his own, and of Samuel's, success.¹² One of Parr Traill's friends, James Black, had emigrated to Canada in 1821 with his wife and children. Their letters were a mine of information which Parr Traill drew on to write a story about emigration, *The Young Emigrants; Or, Pictures of Canada; Calculated to Amuse and Instruct the Minds of Youth* (1826), even before she had met Traill.¹³ Marriage – and then emigration – seemed a viable escape from poverty for the sisters, although as Charlotte Gray notes, 'it was the genteel poverty of the marginal middle-class rather than the grinding poverty of industrial slums and rural hardship'.¹⁴ A literary sensibility had drawn Moodie and John together when they first met, but Moodie feared that marriage and emigration would precipitate an abrupt end to her literary endeavours. In her letters, she writes that her 'blue stockings, since I have become a wife, have turned so pale that I think they will soon be quite white',¹⁵ and Tom Wilson, her neighbour in England, warns her that there is no place in Canada for literary-minded people such as herself. As she was to find out, however, emigration opened a set of new literary opportunities and challenges across the Atlantic for herself, and for Parr Traill.

In this chapter, I examine two of the most important texts in this rich corpus of trans-Atlantic literary publishing: Susanna Moodie's *Roughing It in the Bush* (1852) and Catharine Parr Traill's *The Backwoods of Canada* (1836). Both of these texts are now firmly regarded as Canadian classics, foundational texts that have simultaneously set in place a standard of Canadian literature and, particularly in the case of *Roughing It*, generated many other texts in the forms of editions and imaginative responses throughout the nineteenth and twentieth centuries.[16] However, to take them as solely Canadian texts risks overshadowing the fact that they were read and reviewed in Britain before they were pirated in North America or published in Canada. Both *Roughing It* and *Backwoods* were initially published in their volume formats in London, for a British audience. Of the two, *Roughing It* by far enjoyed the most international acclaim. In the same year that it was published in Britain, the American publisher, George Putnam, produced an excised edition catering to a North American audience. It was only in 1871 that *Roughing It* was published in Canada.[17] Rather than considering the British editions of these texts as stable entities confidently acting as a record of pioneer life, I wish to reconsider them in this chapter in the light of their original claim: that of inventing distinctively different narratives of emigration from those circulating in booster literature for a readership in Britain. Convinced that the female experience of emigration was fundamentally different from that of the male experience, and frustrated that the difficulties encountered by women were not adequately represented in the narratives of success circulating in booster literature, Moodie and Parr Traill turned to writing *Roughing It* and *Backwoods* to narrate in semi-autobiographical form their own experiences of settlement.

Both sisters referred to their works as 'sketches'. This chapter seeks to understand the critical work of the sketch in the context of narrating gendered experiences of nineteenth-century emigration and settlement. The sketch, in both its visual and verbal forms, has traditionally been understood as a preliminary endeavour, a preparatory stage for the finished novel or painting. However, as Richard Sha argues, an emerging body of artists and novelists from the late eighteenth century onwards began to celebrate the incompleteness of the sketch, and its roughness of finish, as part of its aesthetic appeal.[18] As Alison

Byerly notes, the sketch conveyed a sense of immediacy through its supposedly 'spontaneous' and 'impromptu nature', and its 'apparent arbitrariness'.[19] Amanpal Garcha, in his incisive book *From Sketch to Novel*, argues that sketches capture these fleeting moments of time, but are simultaneously characterised by their 'aesthetic stasis': in focusing on a particular temporal moment, the sketch defies narrative progression. This sense of being held in a temporal limbo is a key response to modernity: through their apparent stability, sketches 'offer readers an alternative to modernity's rushed time'.[20] The sketch's emphasis on a particular moment in time and place makes it particularly suitable for narrating what Sandra Zagarell calls 'narrative of community', that is, works that 'take as their subject the life of a community' and the 'minute and quite ordinary processes through which a community maintains itself as an entity'.[21] Mary Russell Mitford made the sketch and its association with the narrative of a community immensely popular through her long series of 'Village Stories' published in *Lady's Magazine* between 1822 and 1824.[22] Although there is no historical evidence for any connection between Parr Traill and Mitford, four of Moodie's surviving letters to Mitford show that she corresponded with her (at least while Moodie was in England) and greatly admired her work.[23] Indeed, the parallel between the two authors has been highlighted by Carl Ballstadt, who argues that Mitford's *Our Village* offered a narrative model for Moodie's *Roughing It*.[24]

This chapter draws on the current critical work on the sketch, but it situates Moodie's and Parr Traill's works firmly within the context of emigration literature. It argues that, at the same time as hoping to invest their work with the themes of tradition and stability that the sketch was immersed in, the sisters' use of the sketch reflects the disaggregated sense of community and the jumble of people and experiences that emigration necessarily entailed. The sisters reclaimed the fragmentary aesthetics of the sketch, pointing out that life in the bush as emigrant wives and mothers allowed for little time to write more than short pieces. Their narratives of emigration were firmly grounded in the domestic arts of home-making: the difficulties of making bread, making a house a home, raising children in foreign places – and *not* on accounts of the soil or climate – and thus spoke to the 'truth' of a woman's experience of emigration. Simultaneously, they asserted that the sketch involved observation of close detail, rather than a panoramic gaze – in short, a fundamentally different way of seeing – and this allowed the sisters to write a different, gendered 'truth' of emigration to that circulating in booster literature.

Form, Gender and Authenticity

Early on in *Roughing It in the Bush*, Moodie mentions that John is going to 'Yoxford' with their neighbour Tom Wilson to hear a certain 'Mr. Cattermole lecture upon emigration to Canada' (42).[25] Moodie has little positive to say about Cattermole. Unequivocal in her 'uncharitable dislike' for the man (47), she hopes that 'Mr. Cattermole, with the unpronounceable name, will disgust [his audience] with his eloquence for [. . .] he is a coarse, vulgar fellow, and quite lacks the dignity of a bear' (43). It is difficult to point to the source of Moodie's vehemence against Cattermole even before she has emigrated. Cattermole was a speaker for the Canada Company and a part-time agent for the Crown Lands Department. He promoted emigration to Canada during a sixteen-month tour that took him across Norfolk, Essex, Kent and Suffolk, where the Moodies and Parr Traills lived.[26] It was in Cattermole's interests to persuade as many people to emigrate as he could through his lectures and pamphlets: for each emigrant he recruited, he received a financial bonus.[27] Cattermole received £190 for his tour, an amount that he claimed to be less than what the tour had cost him. He claimed to have directly influenced the decision of over 6,000 people to emigrate.[28] Like the multitude of other pro-emigration narratives circulating in print, Cattermole's lectures and literature stressed the benefits of settler life. In his pamphlet, *Emigration: The Advantages of Emigration to Canada* (1831), he aimed to refute the notion held by 'many otherwise well-informed persons' that Canada is a 'country covered with eternal snows, and scarcely fit for the habitation of a civilized being'. He asserts that with regard to 'climate, soil, and capability for an advantageous settlement, it is not exceeded, if equalled by any country in the world'.[29] He continues, '[I]t would be difficult, perhaps impossible, to find in any other region of the globe, a tract of country of the same magnitude, with so many natural advantages, as that part which lies between lakes Ontario, Erie, Huron, and the Ottawa river.' He describes Canada as a place where '[d]eer abound in the woods', 'lakes teem with white fish', and the 'society in York is equal to any provincial town in Britain'.[30] These are not merely 'vague assertions' he assures his reader, for he can provide 'well authenticated proofs'.[31] He drew a careful veil over the gloom of the forests, the lack of an established social order, and the amount of hard labour needed to maintain an emigrant settlement.

Both sisters were familiar with Cattermole's pro-emigration stance: when John and Tom Wilson left to attend Cattermole's lecture at Yoxford, Parr Traill was present and she would have heard

Moodie talk about it later. Crucially, however, in both their works, the sisters connect Cattermole to failed emigration. Enthused by Cattermole's speech, Moodie's neighbour Tom Wilson calculates that 'if the Canadian soil yields half only what Mr Cattermole says it does, I need not starve' and he emigrates (48). Four months later, he returns to England, weak with prolonged illness and 'with barely enough to pay for his passage home' (82). Similarly, the only mention of Cattermole in *Backwoods* is in connection with a young man on his way back to England, who 'had been induced, by reading Cattermole's pamphlet on the subject of Emigration, to quit a good farm, and gathering together what property he possessed, to embark for Canada', where he found that he 'had been vilely deceived' for the 'discomforts are unbearable' (43).

Beyond these singular brief instances, the sisters never mention Cattermole again, but the desire to correct exaggerated stories of success in the colonies shapes both their narratives. Interspersed throughout *Backwoods* are frequent references to how Parr Traill's experience of what she has read fails to live up to the reality that confronts her. She is 'greatly disappointed' by her first time in Montreal, 'a place of which travellers had said so much': it was comparable to 'the fruits of the Dead sea, which are said to be fair and tempting to look upon, but yield only ashes and bitterness when tasted by the thirsty traveller' (38). When she hears of 'a whole family having had no better supply of flour than what could be daily ground by a small hand-mill, and for weeks being destitute of every necessary, not even excepting bread', she 'could not help expressing some surprise, never having met with any account in the works I had read concerning emigration that at all prepared one for such evils' (85). The Indian summer, of which she had read 'such delightful descriptions', falls 'far below' her expectations (108).

Moodie opens *Roughing It* with a direct attack on booster literature. She writes critically that interest in emigration was

> industriously kept alive by pamphlets, published by interested parties, which prominently set forth all the *good* to be derived from a settlement in the Backwoods of Canada; while they carefully concealed the toil and hardship to be endured in order to procure these advantages. They told of lands yielding forty bushels to the acre, but they said nothing of the years when these lands, with the most careful cultivation, would barely return fifteen [. . .] They talked of log houses to be raised in a single day [. . .] but they never ventured upon a picture of the disgusting scenes of riot and low debauchery exhibited during the raising. (10)

Both *Roughing It* and *Backwoods* frame themselves as a corrective to booster literature's silence on the difficulties of life in Canada. Parr Traill writes irritably of travellers who

> generally make a hasty journey through the long settled and prosperous portions of the country; they see a tract of fertile, well-cultivated land, the result of many years of labour; they see comfortable dwellings, abounding with all the substantial necessities of life [. . .] He concludes, therefore, that Canada is a land of Canaan, and writes a book setting forth these advantages [. . .] He forgets that these advantages are the result of long years of unremitting and patient labour; that these things are the crown, not the first-fruits of the settler's toil; and that during the interval many and great privations must be submitted to by almost every class of emigrants. (85)

Arguing that it is 'cruel to write in flattering terms calculated to deceive emigrants into the belief that the land to which they are transferring their families, their capital, and their hopes, [is] a land flowing with milk and honey, where comforts and affluence may be obtained with little exertion', Parr Traill insists that '[t]ruth has been conscientiously her object in the work' (9). Moodie makes a similar claim to truth, in her epigraph to *Roughing It*, where she writes:

> I sketch from Nature, and the picture's true;
> Whatever the subject, whether grave or gay,
> Painful experience in a distant land,
> Made it my own. (n.p.)

In sharp distinction to the concerns of authenticity of printed emigrants' letters explored in the first chapter, the two sisters' concerns with authenticity are not tied up with ensuring the commodity status of the text. Instead, both are tied up with correctly conveying a *gendered* experience of bush life. Parr Traill justified the production of *Backwoods* by pointing to the fact that men and women experienced emigration in diametrically opposing ways:

> Young men soon become reconciled to this country which offers to them that chief attraction to youth, – great personal liberty. Their employments are of a cheerful and healthy nature and their amusements such as hunting, shooting, fishing and boating are peculiarly fascinating. But in none of these can their sisters share. The hardships and difficulties of the settler's life therefore are felt peculiarly by the female part of the family. (5)

Reading booster literature that was currently in print would be of little use to women who were emigrating with their families, for 'a woman's pen alone can describe half that is requisite to be told of the internal management of a domicile in the backwoods' (9). Later, Parr Traill would write *The Female Emigrant's Guide and Hints on Canadian Housekeeping*, a guide completely dedicated to managing domestic life in the bush.[32] A lack of female writing about colonial life is a prevalent theme in women's emigration literature. In Catherine Helen Spence's second novel, *Tender and True* (1856), Mary's husband is filled with 'such a desire' to emigrate having read his friend Marshall's 'account of his life and doings in Adelaide', but to Mary, the letter 'seemed so distant, so vague; and as is the case with all men's letters, he only described what he was doing, and not the kind of people he was living with' and she wonders what 'a lady's account of the colony' looks like.[33] In order to convey correctly the gendered 'truths' of bush life, both Parr Traill and Moodie turn to the sketch.

The sisters' use of the term 'sketch' to describe both *Roughing It* and *Backwoods* may initially appear surprising: while *Roughing It* readily lends itself to this description, *Backwoods* might be more appropriately and overtly understood through the lens of a collection of printed emigrants' letters. There is little attempt to present a fluent narrative in *Backwoods*: although each letter is headed by a date, any sense of temporal drive – the feeling that one is progressing through narrative time – is undercut by the presence of numerous lengthy descriptions of the flora and fauna she finds in the woods and near her home. The text opens with the ship's departure from England, but it ends abruptly: one could be forgiven for thinking that there is another letter yet to come after the last one. *Roughing It* has a more overt temporal framework: the text begins with the ship's arrival in Canada, and ends with their departure from the backwoods – a period of seven years. However, neither of the two texts has the narrative coherence of a novel or anything that can be called a 'plot' – there is no climactic moment, or narrative complication or resolution. Instead, both are characterised by a loose diachronic structure, a patchwork-like quality that Garcha identifies as one of the constituent features of the sketch genre. Garcha argues that, with their emphasis on quickness, rapid change and incompleteness, sketches 'acknowledged modernity through their fragmentary nature and offered respite from this changeability through their stasis'.[34] He continues:

as economic and social changes intensified and the reading public's sense of those changes' potentially disintegrating effects reached a peak, fiction responded by emphasizing aesthetic fragmentation and coherence, the two contradictory but interrelated principles sketches foreground.[35]

According to Garcha, on the one hand, the plotless description of sketches provides a sense of stasis and a respite from the fast-paced life of modernity; on the other, their fragmentary nature produces the sense of constant change which is characteristic of modernity. Emigration was a constituent feature of the 'economic and social changes' in the nineteenth century, and the two 'contradictory but interrelated principles' of fragmentation and coherence that Garcha identifies can be seen in Moodie's and Parr Traill's work. As the rest of the chapter will show, the sisters narrate the confusion of emigration through their sketches, but they simultaneously use their sketches to build a sense of community in their new environments.

In addition to this, however, the sketches in *Roughing It* and *Backwoods* are caught up in the task of relating one reality – that of economic hardships and social difficulties of settling in Canada – to another – the desires and expectations of eager emigrants in Britain. Fragmentation and stasis have always been constituent features of the genre of the sketch, from its late-Romantic beginnings through its development in the nineteenth century, but it gains a new currency within the context of emigration. Moodie's and Parr Traill's sketches produce the complementary aesthetics of fragmentation and coherence, but throughout, they harness these aesthetic formations to bolster their claims of authenticity.

Once in Canada, Moodie becomes extremely depressed. Lonely, without the company of friends, family, or a literary circle, she

> would sit for hours at the window [of her house] as the shades of evening deepened round me, watching the massy foliage of the forests pictured in the waters, till fancy transported me back to England. It was long, very long, before I could discipline my mind to learn and practise all the menial employments which are necessary in a good settler's wife. (205)

Yet, when she tries to be a 'good settler's wife', her efforts are hampered by her lack of experience: her genteel and literary upbringing had not equipped her to manage a household from scratch – and certainly not an emigrant household – and her failure to bake bread, fear of the woods and fear of milking cows make an already difficult life even more so. Additionally, her ignorance of social customs, coupled with her snobbery, make her an easy target for her neighbours. An example of this is the sketch 'Our First Settlement', a good part of which details the practice of 'borrowing', an episode which almost every nineteenth-century reviewer chose to quote. Moodie is forced into accepting an empty whisky decanter which she does not want by her neighbour. Upon returning to claim the decanter, the girl demands that it be filled with whisky as an expression of gratitude. Having 'borrowed' the decanter, Moodie proves herself easy prey: the sketch is filled with incident after incident of borrowing, and Moodie's constant inability to outwit her neighbours. Judging the correct mode of behaviour is confusing. She says, 'When we came to the Canadas, society was composed of elements which did not always amalgamate in the best possible manner' (134). Of course it is not the case that society has become more coherent, but that her grasp of Canadian etiquette has developed with time. As the years go by, she acquires the skills necessary for bush life so much so that she assures her reader, 'you will soon learn to love Canada as I love it, who once viewed it with a hatred so intense that I longed to die' (26). To read *Roughing It* is to be confronted with a jumble of disaggregated experiences. The sketches reproduce for the reader Moodie's initial understanding of emigrant life, an understanding which is incomplete and fragmentary. They mimic the continual setbacks and disappointments that a new emigrant must be prepared to encounter: these slow, incremental steps towards progress are the other face of the frenetic change and accelerated pace of modernity.

The fragmentary aesthetics of *Roughing It* is doubly inscribed: in addition to mimicking the uneven experiences of emigration, it also acts as an implicit comment on the economic difficulties of the bush. The origins of *Roughing It* lie in a series of eight sketches published in the late 1830s in two Montreal-based literary periodicals – the *Literary Garland* (1838-51), edited by James Lovell, and *Victoria Magazine* (1847-8), edited by the Moodies themselves. When Lovell invites her to contribute a few sketches, she puts aside the fact that 'the mind is in no condition for mental occupation' when 'the body is fatigued with labour, unwonted and beyond its strength' and instead works hard into the late hours of the night:

> I no longer retired to bed when the labours of the day were over. I sat up, and wrote by the light of a strange sort of candle, that Jenny called 'sluts', and which the old woman manufactured out of pieces of old rags, twisted together and dipped in pork lard, and stuck in a bottle. They did not give a bad light, but it took a great many of them to last me for a few hours. (281)

Roughing It is produced in the snatched moments of time stolen from Moodie's sleep. In the context of the bold claims of booster literature, the irony of this passage is doublefold: firstly that Moodie should have to turn to writing at all in order to supplement the meagre income from her farm, and secondly that her financial circumstances are so strained that she lacks even the most basic necessities to write her sketches. In her letters, Moodie writes a lot about the 'spirit of Poesy', the 'first flight of [her] muse'[36] and the 'spontaneous outpourings of [her] mind, vividly alive to the beauties of Nature',[37] but this passage in *Roughing It* materialises her writing, placing it within a stringent economy where she has to make the best use of the tiniest fragment of small opportunities. Moodie's tacit admission that she cannot afford to buy candles, and that even when she makes her own, she needs to keep a careful eye on their efficiency is a comment on the physical privations of bush life. In her article 'Effortless Art', Byerly notes that the narrators of Dickens's and Thackeray's sketches adopt an artful carelessness in their narration that 'disguise[s] the economic necessity that engendered the production of these pieces'. She continues,

> Beneath the smooth surface created by the casual style of Dickens's sketches, we can sense an uneasy preoccupation with issues of money, work, and social class that reflects the financial burden that led to their creation.[38]

By contrast, Moodie *forges* a relationship between her sketches and the economic imperative that brings them into being. Unlike Parr Traill, who rarely writes of bush poverty in personal terms, Moodie makes it clear that literary ambition and accolade are secondary to the money that writing brings in. When she receives her first payment for her first sketch in the *Literary Garland*, she 'actually shed tears of joy': 'It was my own. I had earned it with my own hand; and it seemed to my delighted fancy to form the nucleus out of which a future independence for my family might arise' (281). Moodie redrafted the preliminary sketches in the *Literary Garland* and *Victoria Magazine* to bring *Roughing It* to the full form that we have today. She gathered them together, split some, supplemented others, and wrote eleven completely new ones. Though the book was published in two volumes in 1852 by the London publisher, Richard Bentley, Moodie maintains the initial roughness of composition: there are few, if any, narrative points fluidly connecting one event to the next. Thus, Moodie authenticates her claim that life is indeed difficult in the bush through her choice of form. Short, fragmented pieces that can be fitted in at the end of a physically tiring day's work better convey the realities of emigration than a long fluent essay, for example. In order to convince her audience that what she says about the hardships of life in Canada is really true, Moodie's form matches up to its content.

Where is Here?

'Where is here?'[39] Northrop Frye famously asks of Canada in his concluding remarks on country's literary history. This, he argues, is a much more pertinent question than 'Who am I?', as few other 'national consciousness[es] [have] had so large an amount of the unknown, the unrealized, the humanly digested, so built into it': 'To feel "Canadian" was to feel part of a no-man's-land with huge rivers, lakes, and islands that very few Canadians had ever seen.'[40] For Frye, the geographical scope of Canada complicates the question of belonging. For the nineteenth-century female emigrant, however, it was not the immensity of the land that posed problems, but the fact of its perceived novelty. Any sense of belonging was impeded by the lack of a powerful, mythic sense of history connected to Canada's landscape. According to an unnamed friend of Parr Traill's, Canada is

> the most unpoetical of all lands; there is no scope for the imagination; here all is new – the very soil seems newly formed; there is no hoary ancient grandeur in these woods; no recollections of former deeds connected with the country. (128)

Although geological discoveries were revealing Canada as an ancient place at the time that these women were writing,[41] scientific fact could not act as a substitute for the lived experience of the land. But if the lack of a cultural memory of Canada and its absence within a collective consciousness prevented any sense of ownership over or belonging to the land, for Moodie and Parr Traill writing about the landscape and the natural environment was one way in which to overcome the sense of the unknown and make familiar the unfamiliar.

Moodie was keenly aware of the power that a literary rendering of Canada could play in creating affective ties and transforming the 'country of [. . .] exile' (32) to a new home. She lamented the lack of an established literary circle to support and enable young writers in Canada and almost from the moment of her arrival there, began to publish in Canadian and North American periodicals, such as the *Albion*, the *Emigrant and Old Countryman*, the *Cobourg Star*, the *Canadian Literary Magazine*, and of course, the *Literary Garland*. She and John also contributed to the *Anglo-American Magazine*, *The Maple Leaf*, the *Family Herald* and the *British American Magazine*. Moodie's contributions included poems and sketches, which remembered life in England with nostalgia, as well as pieces that displayed a more practical approach to settlement in Canada.[42]

Many critics have argued that new emigrants such as Moodie and Parr Traill were confronted with the difficulties of using old literary forms to narrate the particularities of the Canadian environment. Some critics have been more disparaging of the emigrant sisters' efforts than is warranted. Diane Bessai, for example, condemns the 'unthinking dependence of the emigré'[43] on older literary forms, whilst Sandra Djwa writes of the supposed lack of originality of emigrant writers.[44] As Susan Glickman archly points out, however, it is unreasonable to expect 'new ways of seeing and describing the world to have sprung magically from the foam as European ships sailed the St. Lawrence'.[45] Parr Traill's difficulty in trying to find 'forms and language to accommodate a distinctive environment of landscape, climate, flora and fauna',[46] can be seen in the passage below:

> A very beautiful plant of the lily tribe abounds both in our woods and clearings; for want of a better name, I call it the douri-lily, though it is widely spread over a great portion of the continent [. . .] The flower consists of three petals, the calix three; it belongs to the class and order Hexandria monogynia; style, three cleft; seed-vessel of three valves; soil, dry woods and cleared lands; leaves growing in three, springing from the joints, large round, but a little pointed at the extremities. (203)

Parr Traill's ability to provide the botanical name of the flower – 'Hexandria monogynia' – stems from her amateur training in botany, an interest that she had taken up as a young woman when in Britain and which she continued for most of her life after she came to Canada. Michael Peterman argues that Parr Traill's work on botany – both in *Backwoods* and in her later guides – is marked by a 'splendid anachronism': she was a 'nineteenth-century woman given an eighteenth-century education to prepare her [. . .] for emigration and isolation'.[47] Parr Traill was fully aware that her approach to botany was unconventional. She writes, 'our scientific botanists in Britain would consider me very impertinent in bestowing names on the flowers and plants I meet with in these wild woods' (120). She feels the burden of a male audience weighing upon her: the body of 'scientific botanists' in Britain was predominantly male, not female. In *Studies of Plant Life in Canada*, the later guide that she produced with her niece Agnes Chamberlin, she writes that 'modern botanists' have a tendency to fill their scientific manuals with 'harsh-sounding, unmeaning' names; she throws her lot in with the 'more gallant' ' florists and herbalists of older times' who gave 'pretty names' to flowers.[48] Parr Traill's decision to mix the Latinate name of the flower, with an amateurish description and her own name for it – 'douri-lily' – is more than just an outdated style and disregard for modern convention. Her vocabulary cuts across a number of different genres in an effort to narrate an unfamiliar landscape. As she moves from one mode of naming to another, we see her struggling to make her existing language fit an alien context.

In *The Idea of Landscape*, John Barrell writes of the poets John Clare and Robert Bloomfield both finding themselves in places 'out of [their] knowledge' in their wanderings around their local parish.[49] Barrell writes that within the locality of Helpston, Clare recognises the area around him from the 'simple habit of knowing': 'the names he knew for the flowers were the right names as long as the flowers were in Helpston. But once out of the parish, his knowledge ceased to be knowledge; what he knew as fact was only fact'.[50] Barrell is not alone in making this distinction between an affective and instinctual 'knowledge' of one's surroundings and an objective, factual engagement with it. Wallace Stegner argues that an affective engagement with a 'place' is a 'kind of knowing that involves the senses, the memory, the history of a family or a tribe'; a proper 'knowledge of place'

> comes from working in it in all weathers, making a living from it, suffering from its catastrophes, loving its mornings or evenings or hot noons, valuing it for the profound investment of labor and feeling that you, your parents and grandparents, your all-but-unknown ancestors have put into it.[51]

Taken out of the familiar environs of Suffolk, Parr Traill's uneven language suggests that she is trying to move away from scientific fact – objective, rational knowledge – to create her own way of 'knowing' the Canadian landscape. Jovially, she refers to herself as a 'floral godmother' giving 'names of my own choosing' to flowers where the Indian or Canadian names are not known to her (120). The act of naming here is an assertion of dominance over her unfamiliar environment, but it is also a way of making the unfamiliar terrain familiar, referable and inhabitable. Even though she recognises that the lily is in fact widespread, she names it 'douri-lily' after her town 'Douro', creating an area that is within her own, personal 'knowledge'. It suggests that she is trying to recreate the comforting sense of 'place' that enveloped her when she was in England.

Although 'douri-lily' may not reach the heights of poetic fancy, it is nonetheless an act of imaginative engagement with her environment, which settler women viewed as integral to developing any sense of place. Parr Traill's naming of the flora around her is the beginning of this slow accrual of lived experience. In *Roughing It*, on her trip to Stony Lake, Moodie writes of another act of naming:

> The Indians call this lake *Bessikákoon*, but I do not know the exact meaning of the word. Some say that it means 'the Indian's grave', others 'the lake of the one island'. It is certain that an Indian girl is buried beneath that blighted tree; but I never could learn the particulars of her story, and perhaps there was no tale connected with it. She might have fallen a victim to disease during the wanderings of her tribe, and been buried on that spot; or she might have been drowned. (221, original emphasis)

Moodie's awareness of the fictions associated with places is evident through her use of words such as 'story' and 'tale'. The fiction-making potential here arises out of Moodie's failure to ask indigenous elders about oral traditions. But it also arises out of the confusion of translation: presumably the language differences between the Chippewa tribes and the English settlers have prevented a clear direct translation of *Bessikákoon* and given rise to a multiplicity of stories surrounding the lake. Predictably, Moodie uses an English name, 'Stony Lake', rather than the Indian *Bessikákoon*, to refer to the lake. The English name is a reference to 'the rocky pavement that forms the bank' of the lake and its 'pebbly bottom' (220). Similar to Parr Traill, Moodie fiercely claims a proud ownership over her surroundings: Stony Lake may be 'a mere pond [. . .] when compared with the [. . .] inland seas of Canada', '[b]ut it was *our* lake, and, consequently, it had ten thousand beauties in our eyes' (220, original emphasis). While Stony Lake describes the lake accurately, in no way does it carry the historical charge of *Bessikákoon*.

Although intrigued by the myths surrounding the lake, the actual story is of little consequence to Moodie: the sense of ownership is a lot more important.

As well as being an act of colonial dominance, naming the environment is a means of producing an affective engagement with it. As Barrell points out through his examples of Clare and Bloomfield, taking regular trips outside was also an important part of producing this knowledge. In his analysis, mobility can be threatening for Clare and Bloomfield: it takes them out of their environs to the places with which they have no affective connection when their walks and trips supersede the boundaries of their known, familiar locale. But as Moodie and Parr Traill show, in an environment which is completely unfamiliar, mobility is necessary for – one might even say, essential to – *creating* that knowledge of a place. To 'know' a place completely in the context of emigration is to cease the constant comparisons to the landscape they have left behind and overcome their nostalgia by learning to inhabit Canada without the constant backward glance to the past. Upon arriving in Canada, Parr Traill finds that the 'outline of the country reminded me of the hilly part of Gloucestershire' and that she looks 'in vain for the rich hedge-rows of my native country' (55). Tellingly, it is when Parr Traill finds herself lost in the woods surrounded by a 'profound stillness of that vast leafy wilderness', that her 'thoughts gradually wandered back across the Atlantic to my dear mother and to my old home' (100): her physical sense of being lost is compounded by her psychological disconnection with her surroundings.

For both sisters, the key to overcoming this nostalgia for the past and generating a closer and more affective relationship with their environments lies in taking trips around the bush. It is here that their literary debt to Mitford's *Our Village* can be most perceptibly felt. At various moments in *Our Village*, Mitford invites her readers to step outside and leads them through the village, noting the lay of the land and the people around her as she does so. As Josephine McDonagh argues, these country walks have a 'locality-making function': amongst other things, they produce a distinct and recognisable sense of place. It is not unsurprising, she argues, that for this reason, Mitford's style is 'appropriated by writers of [. . .] new settlements'.[52] In the same way that Mitford takes her readers on country walks through the village, so too Moodie and Parr Traill take their readers through the Canadian bush. These trips help their readers to imagine Canada as a place that is traversable and knowable through the bodily experience of moving through it. Parr Traill writes that the 'sources of enjoyment' she encounters when she 'walk[s] abroad' 'keeps [her] from being dull' and indeed, many of the static sketches of *Backwoods* are contextualised in walks that she takes in the woods (90). For example, when she went walking with Thomas, her husband, on a frozen lake, she 'was struck by the appearance of some splendid berries on the leafless bushes that hung over the margin of the lake' (121); in the summer she can 'walk for some way along the flat shores' of the bank of the lake, and observe the 'different strata of limestone, full of fossil remains' (122); she wishes her friend were with her on her 'rambles among the woods and clearings' as she discovers various 'floral treasures' (180–90). When Moodie goes on this trip to Stony Lake, she stumbles across a 'tuft of blue harebells', which 'flooded' her 'soul with remembrances of the past', gathering them up, she 'placed them in [her] bosom, and kept them for many a day; they had become holy, when connected with sacred home recollections' (227). Although she seems to have wandered at a place that might be within her 'knowledge', it is an emotionally jarring experience. Musing in the boat back from Stony Lake, as she 'floated past scenes so wild and lonely', Moodie feels that, 'filled with the love of Nature, my heart forgot for the time the love of home' (229). Forgetting her love for England makes space for her affections for the Canadian landscape to emerge. Writing about the landscape and the act of traversing through it is not just a 'record'[53] of pioneer experience. It is also an experiment in finding a language through which the alien environment can be narrated, and the unfamiliar made familiar and inhabitable.

Knowable Communities

So far, I have argued that the works of Moodie and Parr Traill help them to create a 'sense of place' and thus overcome the feeling of alienation that the unfamiliar Canadian landscape generates. This sense of place, however, is also rooted in notions of community: the landscape described in their works is not vast and unpopulated, but peopled. Although Moodie and Parr Traill kept in touch through letters and these literary exchanges after they emigrated, they never saw their family or their friends in England again. Both agreed that it was the loss of this society and the bonds of family and friendship that proved most difficult for the settler's wife. Moodie laments 'the loss of society in which I had moved, the want of congenial minds, of persons engaged in congenial pursuits' (130), while Parr Traill notices that of the emigrant middle-class women, '[f]ew enter their whole heart into a settler's life' as they 'miss the domestic comforts they had been used to enjoy; they regret the friends and relations they left in the old country; and they cannot endure the loneliness of the backwoods' (90). In *The Country and the City*, Raymond Williams coins and defines the phrase 'knowable community' in novels. He writes:

> Neighbours in Jane Austen are not the people actually living nearby; they are the people living a little less nearby who, in social recognition, can be visited. What she sees across the land is a network of propertied houses and families, and through the holes of this tightly drawn mesh most actual people are simply not seen. To be face-to-face in this world is already to belong to a class. No other community, in physical presence or in social reality, is by any means knowable.[54]

Frye's argument that Moodie is 'a British army of occupation in herself, a one-woman garrison', 'surrounded by a half-comic, half-sinister rabble that she thinks of indifferently as Yankee, Irish, native, republican, and lower class',[55] has to a certain extent over-determined critics' readings of her attitudes to the settler community she finds herself in.[56] The image of the garrison suggests that Moodie exists in isolation from the 'rabble' surrounding her, but in actual fact, Moodie's problem when she arrives in Canada is that she no longer has control over the selection of her 'knowable community'. This is in the physical sense: she writes irritably about the fact that people just open the door and walk into her house without her leave. But it is in the literary sense as well. William New writes that, in the 'hierarchy of taste', 'certain genres held higher status than others', and so '[t]he novel [. . .] was in turn deemed more significant than the short story and sketch'.[57] *Roughing It*'s autobiographical nature, coupled with the fact that it aims to provide an account of emigration through its narrative means that Moodie has to dispense with the novel's cast of classed characters. The result is much richer for it. Much of *Roughing It*'s vibrancy seems to come from the number of eccentric characters that she meets that spill onto the pages – Brian, the still-hunter, Malcolm, the 'little stumpy man', and Old Woodruff with his three wives, for example. Nonetheless, Moodie cannot shy away from representing the working classes. She remarks sarcastically that the 'sight of the Canadian shores had changed [the steerage passengers] into persons of great consequence' (27), and mocks their boasts that 'we shall a' be lairds here [. . .] and ye mun wait a muckle tiem before they wad think aucht of you at home' (26). She notices with irritation that servants in the bush have little respect for their masters: 'let them once emigrate, the clog which fettered them is suddenly removed [. . .] they are free [. . .] to wreak upon their superiors the long-locked-up hatred of their hearts' (132).[58] However, one senses a shift in her attitude in this, as she writes '[y]ou must become poor yourself before you can sympathise with them, and fully recognise them as your brethren in the flesh' (285). Grappling with an uncertain social hierarchy means that it is initially difficult to be 'selective' in her representation of this knowable community in the bush. Her sense of 'community' is thus both shaken and enlarged.

It was not only people of a different class who entered her sphere, but people of a different colour too. Moodie's abolitionist stance meant that she had sympathies with people of other races, although it is a sympathy of her time and, at times, unrecognisable to a modern audience.[59] Parr Traill shared Moodie's perspective. In 1826, she wrote a short story for children, *Prejudice Reproved; Or The History of the Negro Toy-Seller*, in which a young boy is taught to overcome his fear and distaste for a black toy-seller. The aim, as Parr Traill makes clear, is to remind children that 'dispised [sic] and neglected negroes are beings of the same order as ourselves, alike endowed with reason and immortality'.[60] Carole Gerson notes that in other travel and emigrant writings at this time, the 'Indian' is 'visible as a generalization but usually invisible as an individual human being',[61] but in the sisters' works, they are 'nam[ed] and describe[ed]' as 'distinct individuals',[62] as detailed as the white settler population. In fact, Moodie oscillates between these two modes. Her sketch, 'The Wilderness, and Our Indian Friends', is filled with the names of First Nation people: Susan Moore, Peter and Tom Nogan, Peter's son John Nogan, John, of Rice Lake, Old Snow-storm, indicating that many of her anecdotes are about *real* people and *real* events. First Nation people are evidently also a part of Moodie's 'knowable community'. 'It was not long,' she writes, 'before we received visits from the Indians, a people whose beauty, talents and good qualities have been somewhat overrated, and invested with a poetical interest which they scarcely deserve' (186). Her anecdotes reveal the extent to which First Nation people mingled with her and her family on a social level: 'Scarcely a week passed away without my being visited by the dark strangers'. John Moodie 'never allowed them to eat with the servants', but 'bought them to his own table' (187). She seems to have had mixed gatherings as well: she describes one incident when her brother comes round and calls the chief, Nogan, 'ugly' without realising that the latter is both present and understands English. 'Never shall I forget,' she writes, 'the red flash of that fierce dark eye as it glared upon my unconscious brother' (189). Gerson argues that the 'meeting in the "contact zone" [. . .] is as much a woman-to-woman connection as a European/Native contrast'[63] which 'underscores the importance of woman-to-woman engagement in European-First Nations interaction'.[64] This is to a certain extent true: Moodie comments on the 'affection of Indian parents to their children', and is extremely sympathetic to the Indian woman who comes to her with her child dying of consumption: 'Think what this woman's love must have been for that dying son, when she had carried a lad of his age six miles, through the deep snow, upon her back, on such a day, in the hope of my being able to do him some good. Poor heart-broken mother!' (193).

Thus, while there is no doubt that at times Moodie is generous and sympathetic to First Nation peoples, nonetheless, there is also a definite sense that she is 'writing in and of her own time'. Her work is often filled with generalised statements such as 'They are a highly imaginative people'; 'They believe in supernatural appearances'; 'The Indians are often made a prey of and cheated by the unprincipled white settlers' (199–200). She writes of a young, adolescent girl being 'a beautiful child of nature' and her prelude to the chapter, 'Man of strange race! Stern dweller of the wild! / Nature's free-born, untamed, and daring child!' shows that she employs a late eighteenth-century rhetoric for talking about indigenous peoples 'by denying them a place in modernity'.[65] While it is true that the 'elegaic tone sometimes adopted by both sisters invests First Nation Canadians, as remnants of the past, with a romantic quality',[66] Moodie was keenly aware that this was not just a literary technique, but that the fact of white settlement was turning it into a reality. She writes, 'Often have I grieved that people with such generous impulses should be degraded and corrupted by civilised men; that a mysterious destiny involves and hangs over them, pressing them back into the wilderness, and slowly and surely sweeping them from the earth' (200). The fact that Moodie often writes of the indigenous peoples as though she were presenting an unknown artefact to her readers, and the fact that her husband 'was anxious to *collect* some of their native Indian airs' (191. Emphasis added), suggests that it is almost as though she were trying to forestall any sense of loss. The irony, of course, is that she does not see herself as playing an active role in the erosion of culture and people.

The sketch of the bush is thus peopled with all kinds of characters: Moodie and Parr Traill must negotiate their everyday life across the criss-crossing networks of race, class and gender. Writing about the networks of people which form their community thus produces an affective engagement with their environment, and hence, a sense of settlement that is true to their middle-class, gendered experiences of emigration.

Trifling Matters

The sketch was integral to being able to narrate correctly the landscape and the people who inhabited it. It required an observant eye, attuned to fine detail, to narrate all the small goings-on. The ability to be able to construct this different way of viewing was also linked to being able to tell a certain kind of truth. As Moodie writes, the 'real character of a people can be more truly gathered from such seemingly trifling incidents than from any ideas we may form of them from the great facts in their history and this is my reason for detailing events which might otherwise appear insignificant and unimportant' (194). For both Moodie and Parr Trail, writing and publishing their experiences of settlement was both an economic imperative and a means of producing the feeling of being settled in a community. Renaming the landscape was an act of colonial dominance and ownership. But this was also a gendered inscription: the sisters were acutely aware of the fact that they saw the environment through female eyes, experienced it through the female body and wrote about it through the female pen. Though their choice of form – the sketch – allowed them to explore and present their experiences of bush life authentically, at the same time, they were aware that, writing as women, it was also a choice that was open to much criticism.

Like many other examples of nineteenth-century women's travel writing, their work is often 'contextual[ised] in apology', as women writers 'confess throughout to "faults" such as scrappiness, unstructured narrative, the substitution of trivia or domestic gossip for "serious" or intellectual material'.[67] Whereas sketches by men are marked by an anticipatory quality that holds the promise of the full form of the novel or painting,[68] sketches by women were, more often than not, considered *the* finished product: the ostensibly slight form was 'often attributed to female mental deficiencies'.[69] As Richard Sha argues, the 'purportedly limited capacities of the female mind made the sketch's lack of completion uniquely suitable for women writers [. . .] these pronouncements marked women as [. . .] capable only of fragmentary works'.[70]

Backwoods is filled with apologetic remarks on the fragmentary, inconsequential nature of the content, suggesting that Parr Traill falls into the category of women writers who express unease with their form. She warns the reader to '[p]repare your patience [. . .] for a long and rambling epistle' (207), worries that she 'shall tire [them] with my ornithological sketches' (185) and fears that her 'only resources are domestic details and the natural history of the country' (240). However, she is also careful to overturn these apologies by accompanying them with assertions that what she narrates *is* interesting and *is* of consequence. Although she tells the reader, 'You must bear with me if I occasionally weary you with dwelling on trifles,' she immediately follows this up with the statement that 'To me nothing that bears the stamp of novelty is devoid of interest' (13). She asserts that 'we draw the greatest pleasure from the most trifling sources' (19): 'objects that are deemed by many unworthy of attention' present to her 'an inexhaustible fund of interest' (23). Although there is 'certainly a monotony in the long and unbroken line of woods', 'there are objects to charm and delight the close observer of nature' (63).

Thus, rather than subscribing to the view that women writers are *incapable* of writing a coherent piece larger than a sketch, Parr Traill argues that to observe the supposedly 'inconsequential trifles' that fill her 'ramblings' constitutes a different way of perceiving the landscape. She argues that women writers *embrace* the small things, and that these constitute the majority of her work because they contain a wealth of interest and information. In this, she shares '[o]ne of the great gifts of poets in the later eighteenth and early nineteenth centuries', which was 'their courageous creation of works that drew unapologetically and sympathetically on the tiniest features of their immediate surroundings'.[71] This attention to detail 'testified to the significance of the small and unassuming and, in the process, demonstrated the extraordinary potential of the apparently ordinary' and 'offered special inspiration to those who had been conditioned to think of themselves as ignorant and powerless'.[72] Parr Traill's keen and observant eye to the Canadian environs creates a different Canada from those portrayed in emigrant guidebooks aimed at men. One such example is when she notices that there are 'clay-built ovens stuck upon four legs at a little distance from the houses':

When there is not the convenience of one of these ovens outside the dwellings, the bread is baked in large iron pots – 'bake kettles' they are termed. I have already seen a loaf as big as a peck measure baking on the hearth in one of these kettles, and tasted of it too; but I think the confined steam rather imparts a peculiar taste to the bread, which you do not perceive in the loaves baked in brick or clay ovens [. . .] Besides the oven every house has a draw-well near it, which differed in the contrivance for raising the water from those I had seen in the old country. The plan is very simple: – a long pole, supported by a post, acts as a lever to raise the bucket, and the water can be raised by a child with very trifling exertion. (49)

Parr Traill asserts that narrating such details are worth recounting because of their 'novelty': a different kind of knowledge is as valuable as descriptions of the soil and climate, and is available to all who wanted to see and experience their landscape differently. Her observation of the 'bake kettles' and 'draw-wells' reinscribes the landscape so that it is shaped by the female labour of settlement; not just in terms of the masculine labour of clearing the forests, but also through the domestic labours of home-making. Thus, what might be perceived as 'faults' of 'feminine writing' – the seemingly inconsequential details, the loosely connected sketches – are in fact highly stylised and nuanced ways of observing the Canadian environment closely. This keen attention to detail allows the sisters to see beyond the ostensibly mundane veneer of everyday colonial life in ways that allow an affective engagement with the environment.

A Gendered Landscape

Moodie and Parr Traill wrote to counter the sometimes wild tales of success that circulated in booster literature, but as they did so, they simultaneously asserted the centrality of the emigrant mother in the process of emigration. Emigrating within the presumed safe haven of the family structure, married women were almost always considered an accessory to their husband's initiatives and schemes in the nineteenth century. Although there was plenty of fear and anxiety over the numbers and mobility of single emigrant women at that time, that of married women was rendered safe by the family structure within which they emigrated. Whereas the mobility of young single women was almost always aligned with the potential for sexual downfall and the upset of the moral order of the colony, that of the married woman was made 'safe' by the fact of her marriage.[73] While they did not deny that they were 'long-suffering wives, loyally supportive of their husbands' undertakings',[74] they were also keen to assert that this supportiveness was not their *only* role in emigration: in the sisters' works, the emigrant mother emerges as integral to the success of settlement – and her children are equally essential for her to developing an attachment to place.[75]

It was also well suited to the sketch, itself a genre that is dedicated to narrating small, anecdotal events. Through their insistence that both the form and the content of the sketch were valid means of narrating the realities of emigration, the sisters reclaimed it as a legitimate form for female writers. They drew parallels between the size of the sketch – the small anecdotes – and the lives they were leading as emigrant mothers busy with their chores and children in the bush. And, by drawing on a late eighteenth-century poetic tradition which asserted that to be able to 'see small' was to be able to see reality, they invested their work with the quality of the 'truth'.

Katie Trumpener argues in *Bardic Nationalism* that, while England is the mother country that has inexplicably expelled Moodie, 'Canada is apostrophized as an allegorical nurse, who nourishes its foundling immigrants and serves as Moodie's muse'.[76] Metaphors of the colonies as 'children' of the 'motherland' of England were commonplace both in the nineteenth century and now, although there seems to be little consensus on the exact nature of the relationships. Bina Freiwald, for example, argues that the language of Moodie and Parr Traill constructs Canada as 'the great fostering mother',[77] while Moodie herself refers to England as the 'illustrious parent from whom [Canada] sprang' (25). The play on the 'mother-land' is only too clear in *Backwoods*, where the emigrant 'child' writes back not only to her mother, but also her native 'motherland'. Thus, while Trumpener notices that Moodie is 'a female writer preoccupied with her own maternity',[78] she does not interrogate the relationship between the metaphor of England as the mother country and the fact that Moodie is both an author and a mother.

In both Moodie's and Parr Traill's work, mothers have an important role to play in the process of emigration. Not only do they carry their children across the Atlantic to the new world,[79] they are also responsible for cultivating a correct colonial attitude in their children. Developing pride in the Canadian environment, and passing it on to their children was extremely important to both sisters. Moodie urges 'British mothers of Canadian sons!' to 'Make your children proud of the land of their birth, the land which has given them bread [. . .] do this, and you will soon cease to lament your separation from the mother country' (26). Parr Traill's short sketch 'Society in the Bush' echoes a similar sentiment. The sketch, which appeared in *Sharpe's London Journal* in 1849, depicts a small gathering of established emigrants discussing the changes in how new emigrants were received into the community since they themselves had arrived. When a young Canadian-born girl petulantly teases her elderly friend that he 'always praises the British ladies', the gentleman replies, 'Yes, my dear, I love Britain, her institutions, her people, and all that belongs to her [. . .] I rejoice in your love for your native soil; but while you are proud of being a Canadian, do not forget that you are a *British* Canadian.'[80] In 'A Bundle of Emigrants' Letters', Caroline Chisholm writes of settlements:

> from little communities thus established, other and larger communities will rise in time, bound together in a love of the old country still fondly spoken of as Home, in the remembrance of many old struggles shared together, of many new ties formed since.[81]

Parr Traill seems to be drawing upon this idea of the colony as a natural and organic community, at once bound together to Britain through patriotic pride and nostalgia, and at the same time, developing and establishing itself as it grows. While the sisters evidently depict the older generation as having a responsibility in cultivating a correct colonial outlook in the younger generation, they also view the relationship as a reciprocal one. Children play an important part in helping mothers remember Britain and feel at home in the colonies. Of her first child, Katie, Moodie writes in *Roughing It*:

> She was a sweet, lovely flower herself, and her charming infant graces reconciled me, more than aught else, to a weary lot. Was she not purely British? Did not her soft blue eyes, and sunny curls, and bright rosy cheeks for ever remind me of her Saxon origin, and bring before me dear forms and faces I could never hope to behold again? (111)

At the end of *Roughing It*, when her children are awaiting the return of John from the wars, Moodie says '[n]ever did eager British children look for the first violets and primroses of spring with more impatience than my baby boys and girls watched, day after day, for the first snow-flakes that were to form the road to convey them to their absent father' (323). The fact that Moodie distinguishes between British children who look for 'violets and primroses' and Canadian children who look for 'the first snow-flakes' shows that instead of being *reminded* of Britain when she looks at her children, Moodie draws a comparison between the two and feels a closer affinity with the Canadian landscape. Again, Parr Traill echoes the sentiment that a mother feels an affective attachment to where her children are born in her poem, 'The Canadian Emigrant's Farewell', which appeared in *Home Circle*. The poetic voice, an emigrant mother who has had her children in Canada, and is now leaving it bids it adieu:

> I love thy dark and lonely woods,
>   Thy waters gushing free
> Through forest glen, or rocky bed, –
>   Oh, they are dear to me!

The final crux of the poem:

> And dear the loved and lowly cot
>   Where a mother's joy I felt.
>
> Farewell – farewell my children's home,
>   The birth-place of the free![82]
> With saddened heart and tearful eyes
>   I turn my steps from thee.

In the works of the two sisters, then, the emigrant mother plays an important part in the success of the colonies; both in producing the young, healthy children needed to populate it further, and in teaching them the correct colonial attitude and the correct way of remembering Britain. But this relationship is reciprocal. As the mothers give birth and have children, in turn, they develop an attachment to their new lands. *Roughing It* and *Backwoods* grapple with the issue of how to cultivate an attachment to Canada, without entirely forgetting Britain. While the sisters sometimes depict the relationship between Britain and Canada through the metaphor of mother and the child, they also *literalise* this relationship and show instead the active part that mothers play in ensuring the sustainability of this colonial relationship.

Emigration literature did not participate in a one-way transfer from Britain to the colonies, or vice versa. This is also the case with Moodie and Parr Traill: while their works were published in Britain for most of the nineteenth century, they were circulated in various forms and editions in both Britain and Canada, as well as in North America. Such stories circulating in print delocalised places of settlement: as in the emigrants' letters, places became texts that travelled to different areas, and generated and accrued new meanings as they did so. Whether they circulated in Britain or in Canada, the nationalistic impetus of the stories would have been keenly felt, demonstrating the importance of text to cultivating a relationship across geographical boundaries. One reviewer in *Blackwood's Edinburgh Magazine* urged its female readers to recognise the differences between their material situation and that of their 'sisters' in the bush:

> Ladies of Britain, deftly embroidering in carpeted saloon, gracefully bending over easel or harp, pressing, with nimble finger, your piano's ivory, or joyously tripping in Cellarian circles, suspend, for a moment, your silken pursuits, and look forth into the desert at a sister's sufferings![83]

Here, the reviewer refers to Moodie as the British female reader's 'sister', thus drawing on a metaphorical relationship of sisterhood to emphasise an affinity between female readers in Britain and Moodie in the colonies. However, as with the metaphorical mother–child relationship, which renders the colonial work of emigrant mothers invisible, this metaphorical relationship also renders invisible the actual bonds of sisterhood which produce *Roughing It* and *Backwoods*. Moodie and Parr Traill secured their London publishers for *Roughing It* and *Backwoods* through their eldest sister, Agnes Strickland, who had become famous through her *Lives of the Queens of England* (1850). As well as being a prolific contributor to major literary periodicals, she was also briefly the editor of the *Lady's Magazine*. She helped secure Richard Bentley as a publisher for *Roughing It* and for each of Moodie's subsequent publications. *Backwoods* was initially rejected by three publishers before Agnes secured Charles Knight, the publisher for the Society of Diffusing Knowledge. Furthermore, tellingly, when Parr Traill's short stories and sketches appeared in London periodicals, such as *Chambers's Edinburgh Journal*, *Bentley's Miscellany*, *Sharpe's London Journal* and *Home Circle*, for example, Agnes invariably had an item placed in the same issue. Editors were keen to point out the relationship between the two authors. The transatlantic exchange worked both ways: through Moodie's links to Lovell, both their sisters, Agnes and Jane Strickland, placed their work in the *Literary Garland*.[84]

The reviewer for *Blackwood's Edinburgh Magazine* constructs the British female reader as being from an upper-middle-class background in order to highlight the stark differences between life in Britain and in the bush. However, most reviews stressed that *Roughing It* was an invaluable aid to emigration. While the reviewer for the *Rambler* said that the book provided 'light and entertaining literature for the general reader', he also mentioned that it gave 'useful hints to any of the upper classes of society who may be contemplating emigration to Canada',[85] continuing:

> her [Moodie's] privations and sufferings were both frequent and [. . .] so severe [. . .] that all educated persons accustomed to the refinements and luxuries of European society, and contemplating emigration to a foreign land, would do well to study this narrative before putting themselves in the way of encountering them.[86]

Another reviewer in the *Athenaeum* writes enthusiastically that the book should occupy 'a natural, and almost a necessary, place on the table of every one who cares for the Literature of Emigration'.[87] Perhaps ironically, Moodie's reviewers place *Roughing It* in the same category of texts that she so decried in the opening pages of the book – propaganda written for personal interest and purportedly aiding emigration. Moodie may have detested this propaganda, but despite her stark portrayal of bush life, she did not aim to dissuade people from emigrating. Cattermole's leaflets, pamphlets and lectures and many others like them spurred Moodie on to cultivate her fragmentary aesthetic in *Roughing It* – and so to write a text that, by being 'truthful', had a greater chance in producing successful emigrants. Like Cattermole, Moodie holds out the promise of success, but in her book, the promise is an attenuated one. Success is not an immediate consequence of emigration, but comes with time. Importantly, neither sister sought to dissuade the women from emigrating. Instead, both seek to *better equip* them for emigration by raising awareness of the initial period of difficulty. As Parr Traill succinctly puts it in her introduction, 'Forewarned, forearmed' (9). Moodie begins the book with her claim to truth, and she ends it in a similar fashion, reminding the reader that she wishes to provide a 'faithful picture of life in the backwoods of Canada' (330). In her closing remarks, she writes:

> To the poor, industrious working man it [Canada] presents many advantages; [because] he works hard; puts up with coarse scanty fare, and

submits, with good grace, to hardships that would kill a domesticated animal at home. Thus he becomes independent, inasmuch as the land that he has cleared finds him in the common necessaries of life; but it seldom, if ever, accomplishes more than this. (330)

By disclosing what she calls 'the secrets of the prison house' and debunking the myth that Canada is the land of plenty and ease, Moodie hopes to avoid setting up unrealistic and false expectations that made it extremely difficult for her as a newly arrived emigrant (330). Alongside this economic promise is an affective one: that, like her, they too can make Canada their own.

In their own ways, then, Moodie and Parr Traill shared many of the concerns of booster literature explored in the first chapter of this volume. Though they do not share the culture of suspicion that marks the genre of printed emigrants' letters, nonetheless, they participate in the circulation of positive stories of emigration. Their work is characterised by the drive to produce authentic narratives, but this desire for authenticity is not grounded in a fear of the loss of the personal connections that print entails in the context of printed emigrants' letters. As the few preceding pages have shown, for Moodie and Parr Traill, the material production of their works is rooted in filial relations and bonds of sisterhood: print *maintains*, rather than breaks off, personal connections. Instead, their drive to produce authentic narratives is embedded in an effort to sway the bias of much emigration literature: producing a narrative of emigration written from a female viewpoint highlights the gendered difficulties of settlement and thus better prepares emigrant women for life in the bush. This highlights the complex power dynamics often at work in emigration literature: as middle-class emigrants forced to emigrate as a result of their genteel poverty, the sisters, especially Moodie, feel their loss of status keenly in the colony which has little regard for it. They have to find their literary feet and establish a voice for themselves to counter the male-driven emigration propaganda, and yet at the same time, there is no denying that they are complicit in the act of colonisation and settlement. The sisters appropriated the sketch to narrate their experiences, but they did so in ways that bolstered their claims to authenticity. While they drew on the sketch's established association of stable communities to invest their own work with these qualities, at the same time, they also used the fragmentary aesthetics of the sketch to narrate the confusing, complex disaggregation of experiences that emigration entailed.

Notes

1. Susanna Moodie, *Roughing It in the Bush*, ed. Michael A. Peterman (London: Norton, 2007 [1852]), p. 130. All further quotations from this book are taken from this edition and referenced in-text, unless otherwise stated.
2. Catharine Parr Traill, *The Backwoods of Canada*, ed. D. M. R. Bentley (Toronto: McClelland & Stewart, 1989 [1836]), p. 90. All further quotations from this book are taken from this edition and referenced in-text, unless otherwise stated.
3. Carl Ballstadt, Elizabeth Hopkins and Michael A. Peterman (eds), *I Bless You in My Heart: Selected Correspondence of Catharine Parr Traill* (Toronto: Toronto University Press, 1996), p. 39 (13 May 1832).
4. Quoted in Charlotte Gray, *Sisters in the Wilderness: The Lives of Susanna Moodie and Catharine Parr Traill* (London: Duckworth, 2001), p. 9.
5. Moodie published her poems, sketches and stories in leading journals such as the *Athenaeum* and *Chambers's Edinburgh Journal*, but also in ladies' magazines such as *La Belle Assemblée*, prior to her marriage. She also published a volume of poetry, *Enthusiasm; and Other Poems* in 1831 through Smith & Elder and in the same year, through her associations with Thomas Pringle, became the amanuensis for the slave narrative *The History of Mary Prince*. See Carl Ballstadt, 'Editor's Introduction', in Susanna Moodie, *Roughing It in the Bush, or Life in Canada* (Ottawa: Carleton University Press, 1988 [1852]), pp. xvii–lx (p. xxii) and Gray, *Sisters in the Wilderness*, p. 26.
6. Michael A. Peterman, 'Editor's Introduction', in Catharine Parr Traill, *The Backwoods of Canada*, ed. Michael A. Peterman (Ottawa: Carleton University Press, 1997 [1836]), pp. xix–lxix (p. xx).
7. Ballstadt, 'Editor's Introduction', p. xx.
8. Ibid. p. xvii. John Moodie's *Ten Years in South Africa: Including a Particular Description of the Wild Sports of that Country* (London: Bentley, 1835) is very much written from a male viewpoint and thus falls foul of the criticism that Moodie and Parr Traill level at accounts of emigration in print.
9. Carl Ballstadt, Elizabeth Hopkins and Michael A. Peterman (eds), *Susanna Moodie: Letters of a Lifetime* (Toronto: University of Toronto Press, 1985), p. 55 (late January 1831). Volume subsequently referred to as Ballstadt et al., *Lifetime*.
10. John had served in the Napoleonic Wars as a subaltern in the 21st Royal North British Fusiliers. Ballstadt, 'Editor's Introduction', p. xviii.
11. Galt was another who turned to writing about his experiences as an emigrant in order to alleviate financial difficulty. Amongst other emigrant-inspired works, he wrote a semi-fictional account of emigration, *Bogle Corbet; Or the Emigrants* (London: H. Colburn and R. Bentley, 1831) and *The Autobiography of John Galt* (London: Cochrane and M'Crone, 1833).

12. Gray, *Sisters in the Wilderness*, pp. 39–40.
13. Peterman, 'Editor's Introduction', pp. xx–xxi.
14. Gray, *Sisters in the Wilderness*, p. xi.
15. Ballstadt et al., *Lifetime*, p. 61.
16. Probably the only imaginative engagement with Parr Traill's work is *The Bush-Ladies in Their Own Words: Susanna Moodie, Catharine Parr Traill, Anne Langton, Anna Jameson* (Victoria: Scirocco Drama, 2000), a contemporary play by Molly Thom, where the two sisters and two other emigrant settlers meet and share their experiences of bush life. The most famous reworking of Moodie's *Roughing It* is Margaret Atwood's *The Journals of Susanna Moodie* (Toronto: Oxford University Press, 1970), a collection of poems that explores Moodie's rage at and frustration with her new life.
17. For an account of George Putnam's pirated edition, see Ballstadt, 'Editor's Introduction', pp. xxxii–xxxiv. For an account of the 1871 Canadian edition, see Ibid. pp. xxxvi–xxxvii. The revised 1871 text was bought 'up-to-date' with a preface by Susanna Moodie aptly called 'Canada: A Contrast'.
18. Richard Sha, *The Visual and Verbal Sketch in British Romanticism* (Philadelphia: University of Pennsylvania Press, 1998), pp. 22–7.
19. Alison Byerly, 'Effortless Art: The Sketch in Nineteenth-Century Painting and Literature', *Criticism* 41 (1999), pp. 349–64 (p. 351).
20. Amanpal Garcha, *From Sketch to Novel: The Development of Victorian Fiction* (Cambridge: Cambridge University Press, 2009), p. 13.
21. Sandra A. Zagarell, 'Narrative of Community: The Identification of a Genre', *Signs* 13 (1988), pp. 498–527 (p. 499).
22. See Garcha, *From Sketch to Novel*, pp. 9–11; Zagarell, 'Narrative of Community', pp. 500–1; and Josephine McDonagh, 'Rethinking Provincialism in Mid-Nineteenth-Century Fiction: *Our Village* to *Villette*', *Victorian Studies* 55 (2013), pp. 399–424 (p. 404). For an alternative reading of the sketch in the context of the city and urban culture, see Tanya Agathocleous, *Urban Realism and the Cosmopolitan Imagination in the Nineteenth Century: Visible City, Invisible World* (Cambridge: Cambridge University Press, 2011), especially 'The Cosmopolitanism of the Victorian Urban Sketch', pp. 73–87.
23. Ballstadt et al., *Lifetime*, p. 12. See Letters 15, 19, 21 and 24 in this volume for Moodie's letters to Mitford.
24. Carl Ballstadt, 'Susanna Moodie and the English Sketch', *Canadian Literature* 51 (1972), pp. 32–8, repr. in Susanna Moodie, *Roughing It in the Bush*, ed. Michael Peterman (London: Norton, 2007), pp. 419–25.
25. Yoxford is a village about ten miles from Reydon in Suffolk, where the Moodies lived.
26. Cameron and Maude, *Assisting Emigration to Upper Canada*, p. 48; p. 132.
27. Gray, *Sisters in the Wilderness*, p. 40.

28. Cameron and Maude, *Assisting Emigration to Upper Canada*, p. 306, n. 18.
29. William Cattermole, *Emigration: The Advantages of Emigration to Canada* (London: Simpkin and Marshall, 1831), p. iii.
30. Ibid. p. 10; p. 11; p. 18.
31. Ibid. p. 3.
32. Catharine Parr Traill, *The Female Emigrant's Guide and Hints on Canadian Housekeeping* (Toronto: Maclear, 1854).
33. Catherine Helen Spence, *Tender and True: A Colonial Tale*, 2 vols (London: Smith and Elder, 1856), i, pp. 200–1.
34. Garcha, *From Sketch to Novel*, p. 16.
35. Ibid. p. 26.
36. Ballstadt et al., *Lifetime*, p. 90 (14 February 1833).
37. Ibid. p. 93 (23 January 1835).
38. Byerly, 'Effortless Art', p. 356.
39. Northrop Frye, 'Conclusion to a Literary History of Canada', in *The Bush Garden: Essays on the Canadian Imagination* (Ontario: Anansi, 1971), pp. 213–51 (p. 220). Gerson argues that this question is 'a central paradox of Canadian sensibility': Carole Gerson, *A Purer Taste: The Writing and Reading of Fiction in English in Nineteenth-Century Canada* (Toronto: University of Toronto Press, 1989), p. 50.
40. Frye, 'Conclusion to a Literary History', p. 220.
41. See Carl Berger, *Science, God and Nature in Victorian Canada* (Toronto: University of Toronto Press, 1983). Despite the scientific discovery of Canada's age, Parr Traill still writes that the limestone in her area has 'fossil remains, evidently of very recent formation', pp. 37–40.
42. Michael A. Peterman, 'Introduction', in Susanna Moodie, *Roughing It in the Bush* (London: Norton, 2007 [1852]), pp. vii–xvii (pp. xii–xiii); Carole Gerson, *A Purer Taste*, pp. 1–35; pp. 41–3; Faye Hammill, *Literary Culture and Female Authorship in Canada, 1760–2000* (Amsterdam: Rodopi, 2003), pp. 36–45.
43. Diane Bessai, 'Counterfeiting Hindsight', *World Literature Written in English* 23 (1984), pp. 353–66 (p. 363).
44. Sandra Djwa, 'Canadian Poets and the Great Tradition', *Canadian Literature* 65 (1975), pp. 42–52 (p. 45).
45. Susan Glickman, *The Picturesque and the Sublime: A Poetics of the Canadian Landscape* (Montreal: McGill-Queen's University Press, 1998), p. 21.
46. Norman Page, 'Introduction', in Norman Page and Peter Preston (eds), *The Literature of Place* (Basingstoke: Macmillan, 1993), pp. xi–xii (p. xii).
47. Michael A. Peterman, '"Splendid Anachronism": The Record of Catharine Parr Traill's Struggles as an Amateur Botanist in Nineteenth-Century Canada', in Lorraine McNullen (ed.), *Re(dis)covering Our Foremothers: Nineteenth-Century Canadian Women Writers* (Ottawa: University of Ottawa Press, 1990), pp. 173–85 (p. 177). Peterman borrows

the phrase 'splendid anachronism' from Berger, *Science, God and Nature*, p. 35.
48. Catharine Parr Traill, *Studies of Plant Life in Canada, or, Gleanings from Forest, Lake and Plain* (Ottawa: A. S. Woodburn, 1885), p. 60.
49. John Barrell, *The Idea of Landscape and the Sense of Place 1730–1840: An Approach to the Poetry of John Clare* (Cambridge: Cambridge University Press, 1972), pp. 120–1.
50. Ibid. pp. 121–2.
51. Wallace Stegner, *Where the Bluebird Sings to the Lemonade Springs: Living and Writing in the West* (New York: Random House, 1992), p. 205.
52. McDonagh, 'Rethinking Provincialism', p. 409.
53. D. M. R. Bentley, 'Afterword', in Catharine Parr Traill, *The Backwoods of Canada*, ed. D. M. R. Bentley (Toronto: McClelland & Stewart, 1989 [1836]), pp. 291–301 (p. 291).
54. Raymond Williams, *The Country and the City* (London: Vintage, 2016), p. 241.
55. Frye, 'Conclusion to a Literary History', p. 239.
56. For an interpretive use of Frye's phrase, 'one-woman garrison', see Shelley Boyd, '"Transplanted into Our Gardens": Susanna Moodie and Catharine Parr Traill', *Essays on Canadian Writing* 84 (2009), pp. 35–57 and Marian Fowler, '*Roughing It in the Bush*: A Sentimental Novel', in John Moss (ed.), *Beginnings*. Series: *The Canadian Novel*, rev. edn, 4 vols (Toronto: Ontario Arts Council and Canada Council), ii, pp. 80–96 (p. 93). Helen M. Buss, however, argues that an unquestioning acceptance of Frye's phrase has led to a blind spot in our understanding of pioneer women's relationship to their new environments. See Helen M. Buss, 'Women and the Garrison Mentality: Pioneer Women Autobiographers and their Relation to the Land', in Lorraine McMullen, *Re(Dis)covering Our Foremothers*, pp. 123–36.
57. William Herbert New, *Land Sliding: Imagining Space, Presence, and Power in Canadian Writing* (Toronto: University of Toronto Press, 1997), p. 83.
58. This seems to be a common complaint amongst middle-class emigrant gentlewomen. Parr Traill also wrote of this in her 'Female Servants in the Bush', *Sharpe's London Journal* (January 1852), pp. 22–6.
59. See also Gillian Whitlock, 'Exiles from Tradition: Women's Life Writing', in Gillian Whitlock and Helen Tiffin (eds), *Re-Siting Queen's English: Text and Tradition in Post-Colonial Literatures* (Amsterdam: Rodopi, 1992), pp. 11–24 for an interesting discussion comparing the construction of the self in *The History of Mary Prince* (1829) and *Roughing It*.
60. Catharine Parr Strickland, *Prejudice Reproved; Or, The History of the Negro Toy-Seller* (London: Harvey & Darton, 1826), p. iii.
61. Carole Gerson, 'Nobler Savages: Representations of Native Women in the Writings of Susanna Moodie and Catharine Parr Traill', *Journal of Canadian Studies* 32 (1997), pp. 5–21 (p. 7).

62. Ibid. p. 9.
63. Ibid. p. 8.
64. Ibid. p. 8, p. 5.
65. Jean M. O'Brien, *Firsting and Lasting: Writing Indians out of Existence in New England* (London: University of Minnesota Press, 2010), p. 105; p. 107. See also Johannes Fabian, 'Time and Writing About the Other', in *Time and the Other: How Anthropology Makes Its Object* (New York: Columbia University Press, 1983), pp. 71–104. Saree Makdisi also explores the complex dynamics between race, temporality and modernity in defining 'the Other' in *Romantic Imperialism: Universal Empire and the Culture of Modernity* (Cambridge: Cambridge University Press, 1998).
66. Gerson, 'Nobler Savages', p. 13.
67. Shirley Foster, *Across New Worlds: Nineteenth-Century Women Travellers and their Writings* (London: Harvester Wheatsheaf, 1990), p. 22.
68. See Byerly, 'Effortless Art', p. 350. See also Sha, *Visual and Verbal Sketch*, especially the third chapter, 'Perverting Female Propriety: Women's Verbal Sketches as Proper Displays of Perversion', pp. 104–44.
69. Foster, *Across New Worlds*, p. 22.
70. Sha, *Visual and Verbal Sketch*, p. 82.
71. Fiona Stafford, *Local Attachments: The Province of Poetry* (Oxford: Oxford University Press, 2010), p. 25.
72. Ibid. pp. 25–6. The apologetic tones of Parr Traill and Moodie suggest that they are aware that they are entering arenas – both in writing and in the experience of emigration – that were predominantly male.
73. See Rita S. Kranidis, *The Victorian Spinster and Colonial Emigration: Contested Subjects* (Basingstoke: Macmillan, 1999), pp. 20–1; pp. 66–7.
74. Foster, *Across New Worlds*, p. 8.
75. Though clearly gendered, this notion of community is different from those that have previously been suggested by feminist critics, such as Nina Auerbach, who focuses on the power of all-female communities, Josephine Donovan, who discusses women writers in New England, and Sandra Zagarell who argues that the writing of communities was primarily gendered. See Nina Auerbach, *Communities of Women: An Idea in Fiction* (Cambridge, MA: Harvard University Press, 1978); Josephine Donovan, 'Sarah Orne Jewett and the World of Mothers', in *New England Local Color Literature: A Women's Tradition* (New York: Frederick Ungar, 1983), pp. 99–118; and Zagarell, 'Narrative of Community'.
76. Katie Trumpener, *Bardic Nationalism: The Romantic Novel and the British Empire* (Princeton: Princeton University Press, 1997), p. 233.
77. Bina Freiwald, '"The Tongue of Woman": The Language of the Self in Moodie's *Roughing It in the Bush*', in *Re(Dis)covering Our Foremothers: Nineteenth-Century Canadian Women Writers*, ed. Lorraine McMullen (Ottawa: University of Ottawa Press, 1990), pp. 155–72 (p. 166).

78. Trumpener, *Bardic Nationalism*, p. 235.
79. Moodie emigrated with her first child, Catharine Mary Josephine, who was under five months old at the time. Catharine was born on 14 February 1832. Moodie sailed on 1 July 1832.
80. Catharine Parr Traill, 'Society in the Bush', *Sharpe's London Journal* (July 1850), pp. 129–34 (p. 129), original emphasis.
81. Caroline Chisholm, 'A Bundle of Emigrants' Letters', p. 20.
82. Catharine Parr Traill, 'The Canadian Emigrant's Farewell', *Home Circle* (7 July 1849), p. 19.
83. Frederick Hardman, 'Forest Life in Canada West', *Blackwood's Edinburgh Magazine* (March 1852), pp. 355–65 (p. 355).
84. The title of Agnes's poem, 'The Last Look', *Literary Garland* (June 1849), p. 263, suggests that it may be concerned with emigration. In fact, the poem is an exploration into the various different types of 'last looks', from those cast by pilgrims onto their homes, to those given by dying ones to those they love. Jane Strickland's contributions were similarly unrelated to emigration. One was a serialised story, 'The Buccaneers of Tortuga' from January to March 1850, and the other was a short story 'The Rustic Coquette', *Literary Garland* (May 1850), pp. 203–6.
85. Anon., 'A Blue-Stocking in the Bush', *Rambler* (October 1852), pp. 322–6 (p. 322).
86. Ibid. p. 333, original emphasis.
87. 'Roughing it in the Bush; or, Life in Canada', *Athenaeum* (28 February 1852), pp. 247–8 (p. 248).

Chapter 4

Emigration Paintings: Visual Texts and Mobility

This chapter extends the focus of this book, which has so far been on the textual output of emigration culture, into the realm of visual art. It takes as its focus five paintings, produced during the mid-century: Ford Madox Brown's *The Last of England* (1855), Richard Redgrave's *The Emigrant's Last Sight of Home* (1858), Thomas Webster's *A Letter from the Colonies* (1852), James Collinson's *Answering the Emigrant's Letter* (1850) and Abraham Solomon's *Second Class – The Parting* (1854). With the exception of Brown's painting, which was first exhibited at Liverpool City Art Gallery, all the paintings here were first shown at the Royal Academy in London. All the paintings discussed here were first shown at the Royal Academy in London, when emigration peaked as a result of the discovery of gold in Australia. It is no surprise, then, that three out of the five paintings discussed here depict emigration to that country. Brown's *The Last of England* was famously inspired by the emigration of his friend and sculptor Thomas Woolner, to Australia in 1852. It is possible that Collinson may have known Brown through the Pre-Raphaelite Brotherhood, but regardless of whether or not he did, emigration was a hugely important subject to him. This chapter looks at two of Collinson's paintings of emigration.[1] While Brown is the only artist in this study to be directly inspired by an actual instance of emigration, Webster and Redgrave were both working in, and familiar with, agricultural areas from which large numbers of people were emigrating.

Positioning these paintings alongside the textual cultures of emigration has a twofold purpose. Firstly, it demonstrates just how pervasive the cultural effects of settler emigration in Britain were. By mid-century, emigration had become a legitimate subject for artists: one art critic wrote that, as a 'serious subject of interest', 'recourse' to emigration 'is always to be applauded'.[2] This enthusiasm for emigration as subject matter by both artists and audience alike is attested to by the prolific range and number of paintings that were produced throughout the course of the nineteenth century, and the sheer quantity of their reviews in art periodicals. One critic has identified over 300 images of emigration which were produced between 1830 and 1870.[3] Emigration was a popular choice for many British artists: not only did it allow them to reflect on a contemporary phenomenon, it also naturally threw up themes of sorrow, parting, loss and despair and thus provided them with a rich source of emotion that they could tap into and portray.[4] Furthermore, by depicting emigration, British artists could simultaneously participate in the national push for increasing the status of 'genre' paintings, while at the same time critiquing and questioning how to depict the effect of emigration on family life.[5]

Secondly, positioning the textual alongside the visual aligns itself with a nineteenth-century mode of seeing that understood the visual and the textual as two sides of the same coin. Martin Meisel, in his monumental *Realizations*, is one of the first critics to bring our attention to this. He argues that 'in the nineteenth century all three forms [novels, painting and drama] are narrative *and* pictorial; pictures are given to storytelling and novels unfold through and with pictures. Each form and each work becomes a site of a complex interplay of narrative and picture', and suggests that there may be 'ways of organising and perceiving representational art that cut across medium and genre and constitute *a common style*'.[6] In other words, Meisel argues for a shift towards recognising the commonalities between novels and art, rather than stressing their generic differences.

Meisel's reading opens up opportunities for interdisciplinary research, but it also raises a number of questions. Evidently, not all genres are the same: the search for a common style needs to take into account class and gender differences in a work's reception. Are all genres accessible to the same groups of people? Narrative paintings of emigration and emigration literature had very different agendas: the purpose of one was to instruct and cultivate taste, the other was to encourage people to emigrate and provide practical support. A collection of printed emigrants' letters is aimed at a significantly different audience from that of a painting of emigration exhibited at the Royal Academy, one of London's oldest and most renowned art institutions. The contexts in which they were read and viewed, for example, were often at variance: a collection of letters is easily transportable and can be read on the move and in most places. Royal Academy exhibitions were often busy and crowded. One critic in the *Art Union*, for example, complains on the first day of the exhibition, 'the crowd and the dust effectually kept us from the sight of all works on or under "the line", [and] we were, as we have intimated, compelled to look only round the walls above'.[7] George Bernard O'Neill's painting of a viewing at the Royal Academy, *Public Opinion* (1863), shows that two decades later, little had changed. Would those of limited means – those who were the most likely to emigrate – have been able to afford the time and expense of attending these exhibitions, especially if viewing was so difficult? These questions are complicated by the fact that the nineteenth-century art world of 'high' culture was becoming available to the working-class public. As Hilary Beck has shown, engravings of paintings opened up the world of high art to other classes.[8] As engraved prints, emigration paintings received a wider exposure than they otherwise would have done. Edward Hopley's *A Primrose from England* (1855) which depicts a primrose arriving from Britain to Australia, initially exhibited at the Royal Academy, was engraved three years later in 1858, in the *Illustrated London News*. It has not been possible to track whether the individual paintings discussed in this chapter were reproduced and where they circulated as such a task was beyond the scope of this project, but it is reasonable to suggest that the paintings may have been known to potential emigrants.

In spite of the complex questions that it raises, Meisel's argument has been influential in bringing to critics' attention the ways in which words and images 'blended' into each other.[9] Of particular relevance here is the work of Rachel Teukolsky in *The Literate Eye* and Gerard Curtis in *Visual Words*. In her study of the rise of the art press in the periodical culture of the time, Teukolsky argues that the 'Victorian experience of art was shaped by a flurry of accompanying captions, poems, guidebooks, and other linguistic signs, producing a wholesale entwining of writing and seeing'. Looking at art was a 'scripted, linguistic, culturally conditioned experience'.[10] Gerard Curtis further argues that we need to take into the account the increasing 'literariness' of Victorian images: 'Longer descriptive titles for paintings, the development of catalogue descriptions, and the explosive growth in a whole genre of narrative and illustrative paintings from novels and poetry mean that artists used text as part of the painting's "reading process" in a form of inverted ekphrasis.'[11] The paintings discussed in this chapter each engage with text in different ways. The catalogue entries for Ford Madox Brown's *The Emigrant's Last Sight of Home* and Richard Redgrave's *The Last of England* are both accompanied by lines of poetry, which shapes our reading of the painting in fundamentally important ways. Emigrants' letters and maps in Thomas Webster's *A Letter from the Colonies* and James Collinson's *Answering the Emigrant's Letter* bring disparate places into contact with each other. Emigration advertisements in the background of the picture frame the narrative in Abraham Solomon's *Second Class – The Parting*. In their varying uses of text, these paintings position the viewer as reader and thus emphasise that reading is an integral part of the experience of emigration.

Attending closely to the relationships between word and image set up in these paintings, this chapter uncovers the mutual ways in which representations of emigration shaped the aesthetics of British genre painting and the ways nineteenth-century paintings of emigration provided a counter-narrative to the pro-emigration stories circulating in booster literature and, as the next chapter will show, the novel. Contrary to the popular stories of emigration as a successful move, genre paintings of emigration stressed a different aesthetic: they centred on the pain of departure, the temporality of never seeing one's home again and the uncertainties of remaking one's home in a foreign place. Even in paintings that depict settler life, such as R. J. Hammerton's *Emigrants Receiving News from England* exhibited at the Royal Society of British Artists in 1843 and Harden S. Melville's *The Squatter's Hut, News from Home*, exhibited at the Royal Society of British Artists in 1851,[12] there is little reference to the wealth and success that booster literature claimed was to be found in the colonies. Crucially, however, these responses are *not* divergent from those circulating in print, but rather ones that constitute themselves *with and against* those in print.[13] Like the texts of emigration culture, such as the letters, diaries and handbooks, for example, these paintings did not simply act as a historical record of human experience. 'Pictures,' as Lynda Nead points out, 'are more than passive conveyors of visual evidence: they do not reflect other forms of historical experience, but actively work on and may alter those structures.'[14] The dynamic between text and image across these paintings becomes a site of enquiry into the connections between the far-flung places of the colonies, the 'heart' of England in the countryside and the possibilities of recreating 'home' abroad. It argues that on the one hand, these pictures draw on the familiar markers of genre painting – of comfortable, if not lavish, family life and, in the case of Webster and Collinson, rural cottage scenes. Yet, despite the pictorial emphasis on home, these are not scenes of stability or settlement. Rather than reproducing the mythic image of an unchanging 'Merrie England', these genre paintings question and trouble the meaning of home in a time of increasing demographic mobility. Through the representations of emigrants' letters, maps and advertising bills, these paintings reinforce the idea that emigration is underpinned by textual mobility and build up a particular visual vocabulary that reflects on the conditions of being mobile. In all five paintings, the texts are mobile: as well as being texts that move, they are also texts that initiate movement.

Forced Departures

Leave-taking was a popular subject matter for artists: scenes of families leaving, such as Ford Madox Brown's *The Last of England* (1855; Figure 6) and Richard Redgrave's *The Emigrant's Last Sight of Home* (1858; Figure 7), allowed artists to explore the nature of the relationship between Britain and the colonies. The subject matter of leave-taking necessarily threw up a rich depth of emotion that artists could tap into and portray in their work, be they images of bustling

Figure 6 Ford Madox Brown, *The Last of England*, 1855, oil on panel, 82.5 x 75 cm © Birmingham Museums Trust

Figure 7 *The Emigrant's Last Sight of Home*, 1858, Richard Redgrave. Purchased with assistance from an anonymous donor 1977. Oil on canvas, 69.9 x 98.4 cm ©Tate, London 2017

port scenes, as in Henry O'Neil's *The Parting Cheer* (1861) or of more intimate goodbyes, such as Paul Falconer Poole's *The Emigrant* (1858). In the nineteenth century, to make the audience 'feel' – and feel correctly – was a measure of the quality of one's work. Much of the poignancy of these scenes of leavetaking is generated by the sense of finality that emigration brings. In the titles of their works, Brown and Redgrave were keen to impress upon the viewer that this would be the 'last' time that the emigrants would be in their familiar environments. For these emigrants, emigration constitutes a clean break from Britain. Yet, rather than stressing solely pathos at this sense of finality, Brown and Redgrave use the accompanying poetry in their respective catalogue exhibitions to incorporate the emotional tumult of the emigrants into a critique of emigration. Rather than portraying it as an act of volition, with success ensured at the end of the voyage, both artists portray emigration as a departure forced by circumstance, rather than choice.

The Last of England took three years to complete. As mentioned previously, it was inspired by the emigration of Brown's friend, the sculptor Thomas Woolner, who emigrated out to Australia as part of the gold rush in 1852.[15] He worked on the painting, 'for the most part in the open air on dull days [. . .] on cold days', as he wanted to capture the flushed hues of the cold skin. 'I have thought it necessary to imitate' 'the minuteness of detail', in order to bring 'the pathos of the subject more home to the beholder'.[16] Brown worked outside consistently, even in the winter months for three to four hours at a stretch, sometimes with '[b]lanket round feet, two coats shawl & gloves on, very cold in spite'.[17] His wife, Emma, and first child, Catherine, sat for the painting, and endured the 'the most in human weather' with him.[18] The effect of the outdoor light can clearly be seen in the final painting. The faces of the couple looking out are tinged with red from the cold and the effect of the wind is emphasised by the circular design of the painting: the curve of the umbrella, sails and rope at the front of the picture follow the edges of the painting and mimic the stray hair as it whips across the woman's face and her bonnet ribbons as it is lifted by the wind. In one hand, she holds that of her husband in a comforting grip, and in the other, she holds the hand of her young baby, who lies on her lap, guarded from the wind by her grey shawl. The figure of the mother in the family all together is a common trope in emigration paintings. In the centre of Paul Falconer Poole's *The Emigrant's Departure* (1838), for example, the emigrant mother holds her child's hand in one and her sister's hand (who is not emigrating) in the other, symbolically connecting the old world and the new. Nestled between the mother and father in Brown's painting is a pile of books. Their presence points to the interrelationship between text and the emigration. Whereas she looks softly askance out to her left, her husband appears far more tense and withdrawn; a deep, fierce frown furrows his forehead, scarcely hidden by his hat. Behind them is a crowd of people. Few figures can be made out in full, but one of them is a labourer, shaking his fist at the receding white cliffs of Dover. The overall atmosphere of *The Last of England* is not one of joy, anticipation and excitement, but of anxiety and frustration.

Visually, *The Last of England* could not be more different from Redgrave's *The Emigrant's Last Sight of Home*. The painting presents us with an English village set in rolling hills. The emigrants are placed in the foreground of the picture. The father stands facing the hills. His arms are outstretched, and with his hat in hand, he salutes his village goodbye. One of his sons stands looking at the rural scene, the attention of two daughters has been caught by something in the distance. His wife sits on a little tuft with another child near her and a baby in her lap, looking to where her daughter is excitedly pointing.[19] One nineteenth-century critic wrote enthusiastically that '[n]othing can be more excellent than the drawing of "The Emigrant's Last Sight of Home"'.[20] The *Art Journal* commented that in painting the landscape, Redgrave had 'thrown himself into a fervency of devotion rarely witnessed'.[21] Another art critic wrote that it is 'a genuine bit of English scenery'.[22] Redgrave's composition, however, is more than an exercise in faithfully depicting a rural scene. Rather than posing a dichotomy between the emigrants and the land, it questions the relationship between them.

Accompanying the entry for Redgrave's painting in the Royal Academy exhibition catalogue are two couplets from Oliver Goldsmith's poem, *The Traveller* (1764):

> Have we not seen, round Britain's peopled shore,
> Her useful sons exchanged for useless ore?
> Forced from their homes, a melancholy train,
> To traverse climes beyond the western main.[23]

Goldsmith's poem, like his later poem *The Deserted Village* (1770), is a reflection on the effect of the Enclosure Acts of the eighteenth century, where common land was enclosed and villagers were consequently evicted from their homes. By choosing these lines to frame the narrative of his painting, Redgrave draws similarities between eighteenth-century eviction and nineteenth-century emigration. While 'useless ore' in Goldsmith's poem refers to the money that landowners made from enclosure, the words take on a new meaning as they become framed by – and frame – Redgrave's painting. Given the context of the gold rush of the 1850s, it's likely that the husband in the painting is a potential gold-digger, moving with his family to search for 'useless ore' in Australia. If this is the case, emigration is portrayed not as a move that strengthens the nation, but instead as one that weakens it: it is an unequal exchange between 'useful sons' who could profit England by continuing to labour there and the 'useless ore' that cannot match their worth. The *Illustrated London News* severely criticised Redgrave's choice of lines, writing that:

> the time is gone by for such maudlin stuff as this, and artists, if they would minister to the requirements of the age in 'Britain's peopled shore', and in new homes 'beyond the Western main' would do wisely to adopt a more ennobling view of a great social and political movement.[24]

However 'genuine' Redgrave's depiction of the English countryside may have been, to the reviewer of the *Illustrated London News*, Redgrave had not embraced the spirit of the age by casting emigration as a forced expulsion rather than a positive choice.

Similarly to Redgrave's *The Emigrant's Last Sight of Home*, Brown's *The Last of England* posits the idea that emigration was a failure on the part of Britain to keep her men. The painting was first exhibited in Liverpool City Gallery in 1856, but it is the 1865 exhibition in London that continues to be the most important in the eyes of contemporary scholars, on account of the exhibition catalogue that Brown wrote himself. In this catalogue, Brown not only includes a lengthy description of the painting and how he painted it, but also a sonnet that provides a context for the painting:

> "The last of England! o'er the sea, my dear,
>   Our home's to seek amid Australian fields.
>   Us, not the million-acred island yields
> The space to dwell in. Thrust out! Forced to hear
> Low ribaldry from sots, and share rough cheer
>   With rudely nurtured men. The hope youth builds
>   Of fair renown, bartered for that which shields
> Only of the back, and half-formed lands that rear
> The dust-storms blistering up the grasses wild.
>   There learning skills not, nor the poet's dream,
>   Nor aught we loved as children shall we see."
> She grips his listless hand and clasps her child,
>   Through rainbow-tears she sees a sunnier gleam,
>   She cannot see a void, where *he* will be.[25]

In the dynamic between word and image in Brown's sonnet and painting, we see the same preoccupation as in the case of Redgrave. Despite being 'million-acred', England 'Thrust[s]' out her able-bodied men who are 'forced' to make their homes 'amid Australian fields'. The discontent of the emigrants in Brown's painting, however, arises from the fear that emigration upsets established class structures. In the catalogue, Brown writes that, 'in order to present the parting scene in its fullest tragic development', he has 'singled out a couple from the middle classes, high enough through education and refinement, to appreciate all they are now giving up, and yet depressed enough in means to have to put up with the discomforts and humiliations to a vessel "all one class"'.[26] The painting picks up on the complex interrelations between emigration and class. Behind the middle-class couple, a working-class man shakes his fist at the receding cliffs of Dover. The middle-class man shares this anger and frustration: not only is his forehead furrowed in a frown, his back is symbolically turned on England.

At the time that Redgrave and Brown produced their paintings, they were both going through a period of emotional lows. In his diary, Redgrave writes, 'Alas! I feel I take less pleasure than I formerly did in life and its works.'[27] However, whereas with Redgrave this appears to have been little more than a general tiredness, Brown seemed to be suffering from a more deep-seated malaise. Anxious over his financial situation, and scared that he was not held in high regard by the public, he writes in his diary:

> What chance is there for me out of all the Bodies, Institutions, Art unions & accademies & Commissions of this country, Classes sects or cotteries, Nobles dealers patrons rich men or friends. Which one takes an interest in me or my works. Is it encouraging to go on? Is it not rather a clear affirmation of my not being required by the British Public [sic].[28]

Some days later, he wrote, 'Very absent & dejected no prospect but going to India',[29] but he seems to have been discouraged by his friends: 'I breakfasted with Lowes Dickinson to day & he says that there is a fortune to be made in India, but he does not think me the man to do it. I shall not go at present at any rate.'[30] Throughout the time that Brown painted *The Last of England* he was plagued with money problems: he pawned his belongings regularly, borrowed money from family members, and waited for two of his paintings destined for the Paris Universal Exhibition to be sold.[31]

The negative portrayal of emigration in their paintings may have stemmed from the artists' personal anxieties at the time, but it also shapes the larger discourse surrounding emigration. The paintings critique Britain for being unable to keep her able-bodied men on her shores: emigration is a choice that these emigrants have been forced to make. Nonetheless, the possibility of success remains open-ended. The crowd of hands behind the couple in *The Last of England* can be read as a metonym of the hard work and labour that is needed in the colonies, while the name of the ship, *Eldorado*, could be either an indication of the success that is to come or a reminder that the search for gold overseas is a mythic ideal.

The Emigrant's Letter

Both Ford Madox Brown and Richard Redgrave depict the family, as an entire unit, moving over to the colonies. Letter scenes, which depict either emigrants' families in England or emigrants in the colonies receiving letters from their loved ones, probe into how the relationship between parted friends and family is sustained after emigration.

Webster's *A Letter from the Colonies* (Figure 8) shows a postman having just delivered a letter at a rural cottage to an elderly couple and a young lady, perhaps their daughter. The younger woman has left her needlework at the table, and come round to look at the letter the elderly man holds up to the light in his left hand. Opposite them, the older woman looks anxiously at them both. Meanwhile, the postman leans in through the open window, smiling at the elderly woman, with his hand outstretched, waiting for his payment. A light breeze lifts the gingham curtains, and through the window a clear blue sky can be seen; sunlight plays through the green boughs of a tree in the garden. Despite the seeming ordinariness of the scene, the mood is one of tense apprehension.[32]

Webster gained great acclaim during his life for his depictions of simple village and school life; like most of artists discussed here, this is his only painting to depict emigration.[33] As with most of his work, *A Letter from the Colonies* was well-received by the press. Webster plays to the audience's expectations in this painting by following several of the markers of genre painting:[34] a rural setting, the depiction of a family at home, everyday items lying around the house. The topicality of emigration, and its constant presence in print culture of the time, as well as in the lived experience of people, meant that

Figure 8 *A Letter from the Colonies*, 1852, Thomas Webster. Presented by J. G. Milner 1986. Oil on wood, 41.3 x 52.1 cm, ©Tate, London 2017

viewers would have recognised and identified with the subject matter of the delivery of an emigrant's letter. The critic for the *Athenaeum* wrote that the painting 'is another of Mr Webster's telling pictures, which come home at once to every spectator, learned or unlearned'.[35] The reviewer's assertion that the painting is a 'telling' one suggests that the painting lets slip an occluded truth beyond the mundane subject matter of the delivery of the letter. That this hidden meaning should 'come home at once' to all who view the painting suggests that the ambiguity and emotional complexity of this painting would have been recognised by the nineteenth-century audience.

In her chapter, 'Ramsgate Sands', Caroline Arscott argues that '[i]n narrative painting we are given that crucial second phase of narrative, upon which the resolution depends'. Narrative painting depicts a situation that 'is assumed to stand between the past and a future'; 'although a resolution will follow as a consequence of the second phase', it is 'not always [an] inevitable' one.[36] Webster's painting shows a pause as the elderly man holds up the unopened letter to the young daughter and they gaze upon the handwriting in which the address is written. Given that the letter has been delivered, it is hardly likely that the writing has been blurred during its long voyage to the cottage. There is no reason that the elderly man and young lady should pause to linger over the address on the front, other than to enjoy the sight of familiar handwriting. In *The Postal Age*, David Henkin writes that 'Letter-writers frequently focused on the impact and significance of handwriting, pulling a metonymic string that linked chirography to hand to bodily presence [. . .] Handwritten letters bore the trace of physical contact and not simply the recognizable imprimatur of individual identity.'[37] In Webster's painting, the address is the first sight of the emigrant's handwriting that the elderly man and young lady have: the slight smile at the corner of the woman's mouth shows the pleasure that the sight of a familiar hand brings her. Even before the letter is opened and its contents read, the letter's materiality marks the absence of the emigrant, and as a physical object that has been touched by them, signifies their physical presence.

A Letter from the Colonies depicts two moments of delay. Running alongside the affective moment as the elderly man and young woman pause over the sight of the handwriting is another, quite different narrative as the postman waits to receive his payment from the elderly woman. One nineteenth-century critic wrote that she was in 'an agony of anxiety to hear it [the letter] read',[38] which suggests that the elderly lady is anxious because of the uncertainty of the situation: until the letter has been opened and read, there is no way of knowing whether it contains good or bad news. However, given that she clutches at her money bag, and given the humble interior of the cottage, it could also be that she is worried about paying for the expenses of international postage. This second 'sub-plot' of the painting frames the emigrant's letter, not as an object through which family members extend their kinship ties, but as a commodity in the moment of exchange. I have already looked at the ways in which emigrants' letters enter the commodity market as they are published, in the first chapter of this book, but importantly, this is a scene where the manuscript letter itself is marked by the commodity moment. Epistolary exchange and commodity exchange become one and the same thing here. The emigrant's letter also forms the counter narrative of the painting that stresses not moments of pleasure and anxiety, but of transaction, money and exchange.

Although the elderly woman is tense and withdrawn, the way in which the letter reflects the light into the faces of the elderly man and the young lady suggests that it contains good, rather than bad, news. Julia Thomas suggests that '[b]y picturing these different reactions the painting refuses to commend or criticise emigration and offers instead the possibility of both readings'.[39] I suggest, however, that Webster is not so interested in passing judgement on emigration as a national endeavour as he is in keeping the audience guessing. The complexity of emotion registered in the scene means that until the letter is opened, the audience has no idea which way this narrative will swing.

Emigrants' letters were often marked by delay and an empty expanse of waiting, for both emigrants and their families in Britain. Given that emigrants frequently wrote their letters over days and sometimes weeks, and given the length of time it took for letters to reach Britain, letters often contained news of events that had happened months before. If they were diverted en route, they would be delayed even further. As well as being frustrated by delay, emigrants were also acutely conscious of the costs involved in sending letters. Frederick Hasted, an emigrant to Upper Canada in 1832, explains to his family that

> I have wrote 3 letters before [. . .] Because the postage comes heavy to me, 2s. 2d. every letter I send from here home, therefore I did not intend writing any more yet; but as I had forgot something of material consequence to you, I thought I would spend 2s. 2d. more for your sake [*sic*].

He ends his letter with 'I intended to say more, but have neither time nor room. If you want to know more send a large sheet of paper and money to pay the postage, and I will fill it for you.'[40] Even before the letter entered the print market, emigrants were aware of the fact that their letters were commodities. In his painting, Webster draws upon the themes of delay and the expense of the letter to frame the narrative: the concerns of emigration culture shape the aesthetics of his genre painting. Part of the pleasure of viewing *A Letter from the Colonies* is understanding its refusal to offer only a single reading of the events it depicts. Like the unopened letter, the painting keeps the audience guessing as to what the real events are and how they will turn: the viewer becomes caught up in the moment of suspense, waiting for revelation as the old man holds the unopened letter up to the light.

Troubled Gazes

In *A Letter from the Colonies*, even though the emigrant is not present in the picture itself, the motif of the letter tracks many of the concerns that are central to the emigrant experience: anticipation, pleasure and loss, as well as the emphasis on everyday commodities. In James Collinson's *Answering the Emigrant's Letter*, the letter is opened, its contents are revealed and they are the subject of a family discussion (Figure 9).

As in *A Letter from the Colonies*, *Answering the Emigrant's Letter* is a family scene, although the family depicted is younger. The father sits at the table with his back to the window. He holds in his left hand the opened emigrant's letter: one can see the seal and postage marks and just make out the cross-written lines. He holds a quill loosely in his right hand, and rests it on a map of Australia on the table in front of him. His eldest son sits opposite him at the other end of the table, seeming to act as an amanuensis for the letter as he writes down what the family members around him say. The two middle children, a daughter and a son, crowd enthusiastically round him; the former looks at her elder brother, while the latter looks at the letter being written. Sitting slightly apart from the rest of the family, the mother holds the youngest child – a toddler of about two years – in her lap, putting a sock on its left foot. In an effort to mimic its mother, the toddler also holds a sock in its hands and tries to put it on its right foot. A dog, a symbol of constancy and affection, lies at the feet of the mother, looking up at the family around the table. The fire glows in the grate, and sunlight streams in through the window. Across the heads of her eager children, the mother gives her husband an anxious glance.

Collinson was a member of the Pre-Raphaelite Brotherhood at the time that he painted *Answering the Emigrant's Letter*. He describes it in a letter to William Rossetti as 'a smoky picturesque little interior' and 'a capital Wilkie subject, sure to sell'.[41] Aligning himself with David Wilkie, the 'father' of British genre painting, Collinson was proud of the work, and at the same time, indicates that he is positioning himself firmly within a national school of painting. Rossetti seems to have initially admired the level of detail in *Answering the Emigrant's Letter*, noting in his diary that Collinson is 'finishing up the trees outside to a pitch of the extremest minuteness', although this may have changed later on, as Collinson's earnestness on the painting meant that 'he is unable to go out to do anything in the way

Figure 9 *Answering the Emigrant's Letter*, 1850, James Collinson, oil on panel, 70.1 x 91.2 cm, Manchester Art Gallery, UK / Bridgeman Images

of distributing *Germs*'.[42] Unfortunately, however, when the painting was exhibited at the Academy, it was hung high above the line, 'at a height where all its merits are lost',[43] and this accounts for contemporary critics' complaints that not all the details could be clearly seen. One critic, for example, mentioned that although the 'question of correspondence is sufficiently evident', 'it is impossible to determine that the family council is held on the subject of a letter to an emigrant'.[44] A reviewer for the *Critic* wrote that the painting shows 'nothing short of what an opera glass will reveal'. Although a 'contemporary observes that there are no means of determining that the letter is being written to an emigrant', a 'microscopic investigation would have satisfied him that the principal figure holds a map of the district: and from this the inference is obvious'.[45]

Collinson's painting incorporates three texts: the emigrant's letter, the letter being written in reply and the map that lies open in front of the father. Whereas Webster's painting shows the letter in the moment of one kind of exchange, Collinson's painting shows it in the moment of epistolary exchange. Three of the children form their own little triad of gazes as the eldest child writes the letter. His sister helps him to steady the ink pot; she looks at him with what appears to be concern on her face, while he looks down in concentration at the letter. Meanwhile, their younger brother tries to squeeze in between them to take a look at the letter. While the concentration of gazes around the letter suggests that this is the main narrative of the painting, I argue instead that the climactic point in the narrative lies in the anxious look that the wife gives her husband. Caught up in their own enthusiasm for the letter, the three children are oblivious to this, but, as in Webster's painting, Collinson's *Answering the Emigrant's Letter* depicts a moment of uncertain delay as the father stops his dictation of the letter to glance at his wife.

A number of different readings are encoded into this brief pause: perhaps the wife is warning her husband against putting in a piece of news, perhaps the letter contains bad news, and the couple are wondering what the appropriate mode of consolation could be. However, through its composition, the painting encourages us towards another reading of this moment of delay. It is not merely coincidence that the nineteenth-century reviewer for the *Critic* understood that the letter was from an emigrant to Australia through the map: placed in close proximity to each other, the painting encourages us to read the emigrant's letter and the map of Australia in alignment with each other. Emigrant handbooks and manuals were often sold with maps: these gave prospective readers an idea of the lay of the land before they arrived, but emigrants also found new uses for them, as suited their circumstances. One emigrant to Canada in 1832, for example, wrote to his father:

> by a reference to the map attached to that book, you may trace my route from Quebec to Easthope, by Montreal, Prescot, York, &c. also in the map of the Huron Tract, which is at the foot of the other, you can see how beautifully intersected that part of the block where I live is, with rivers and streams, all of which abound with fish.[46]

Maps were thus useful tools of communication between emigrants and their families: they made the unfamiliar familiar not only in terms of navigation, but also in terms of an affective 'knowing' that was discussed in the third chapter. With his quill poised over the map, perhaps the father is tracking or marking out the route mentioned in the emigrant's letter.

The map, however, is not only a means of visual communication. As is by now well known, it is an important tool of colonial conquest. As G. Clarke argues, 'the map exists as a [. . .] reconstruction of a culture's way with the world'.[47] They are 'not so much objective and scaled equivalents of the land as [. . .] cultural text and ideological image – a political frame of space in which the map is offered as a scaled version of control and, by implication, of possession'.[48] The idea of possession and control is particularly significant here. The emigrant's letter is a text from someone who has already succeeded in possessing some land (or is working towards this), and the map also signifies possession on a national scale. Both these texts are, in effect, texts of colonial acquisition and they are both held by the father, an able-bodied man, with a young, thriving family – in short, the ideal coloniser. As we have seen in the first chapter, emigrants' letters frequently contained encouragements to family members in Britain to follow: the painting may also depict a scene where the father is deciding whether or not to emigrate. The fact that the settler experience is so heavily determined by text, and the fact that the father's quill is poised over the map ready to make its mark strongly suggests a textual inscription that he will then follow up with the act of migrating out.

This reading is supported by the glance that the wife gives her husband. Half fearful and uncertain, with her mouth an anxious line of worry, it is the most striking element in the picture. If her husband follows, like Susanna Moodie and Catharine Parr Traill, she will have little choice but to acquiesce. It is a look that Collinson repeated in his *The Emigration Scheme*, painted two years later as a pendant to *Answering the Emigrant's Letter*. Around the room in this painting are what appear to be two families. A young boy stands facing them, reading out news of an emigration scheme from the *Australian News*. While both the men are flushed with excitement at the prospect of moving abroad (one has the opened emigrant's letter on his lap), the woman near the centre of the painting stares on with a hard, questioning look of fear: will the men have their heads turned by the news of the gold rush? The troubled glances in each of these paintings tinge the comfortable setting of the home with irony: this is a home that may soon be home no more.

The Country and the Colony

In *Epistolarity*, Janet Altman writes that the letter can 'function as a connector between two distant points, as a bridge between sender and receiver': 'the epistolary author can choose to emphasise either the distance or the bridge'.[49] As we have seen in Webster's and Collinson's paintings, the emigrant's letter brings the far-flung places of the colonies into domestic spaces. In doing so, it disrupts the ostensible rootedness and located nature of home. As a mobile object and carrying the written inscriptions of its migrant author, the letter is shown to induce new formations of mobility into settled family scenes. More is at stake in these paintings, however, than a simple contrast between the distant colonies and the home. As I will show below, the relationship between text and image in the paintings also has colonial ramifications.

The cottage interiors, the rustic dress of the figures, and the greenery that can be seen through the windows of Webster's and Collinson's paintings all indicate that the paintings are set in the countryside. As can be seen from Redgrave's *The Emigrant's Last Sight of Home* (and other paintings),[50] the countryside was a popular setting for artists depicting emigration. The prevalence of the countryside setting for emigration pictures could be partly a result of historical fact: many agricultural labourers were forced to migrate as a result of industrialisation and the agricultural depression, and Redgrave and Webster were both well aware of this. Susan Casteras points out that 'Redgrave used his place of summertime residence as the location for this farewell scene' and that the hills depicted 'seem to be Leith Hill, one of the several steep slopes in the area and the highest summit in the southeast of England'.[51] However, as various critics have noted, the peaceful representation of the countryside is more of an aesthetic veneer than it is a historical fact. Leith Hill is in Abinger, which is between the parishes of Dorking and Petworth: in short, in an area that saw the emigration of agricultural labourers. Abinger was among those agricultural parishes in the South that had been desperately poor in the 1830s and '40s, subject to the anguish of the Swing Riots, machine-breaking, rick-burning, unemployment, near starvation, and emigration. Although Webster was living in London when he was painting *A Letter from the Colonies*, he was at this time travelling down to Cranbrook regularly to visit his distant cousin and artist, F. D. Hardy. Webster was familiar with the area and evidently attracted to it: in 1856, he decided to settle in Cranbrook, in order to be nearer to the subject matter of his paintings of village scenes and rural life.[52] Similarly, the introduction of a railway line in Cranbrook in 1842 meant that the population 'substantially declined', as people moved 'to the larger centres of Maidstone and Tunbridge Wells'. In addition, 'foreign food imports and the emigration of labourers to Canada and Australia was causing an agricultural depression'.[53] Yet both Collinson's and Webster's paintings register little, if any, of this agricultural distress.

Such aesthetic cleanliness is driven by an understanding that genre painting should reproduce the same atmosphere of calm and peace that it depicted in the spaces where it was hung. David Wilkie was of the opinion that a 'fine picture is one of our household gods, and kept for private worship: it is an every-day companion'.[54] Richard Redgrave similarly argued that the 'subjects' of British genre paintings, 'are undoubtedly of a less elevated, and of a lower and more familiar character in England, but they are works which a man can live with, and love to look on, obtruding no terrors on his sleeping or waking fancies'.[55] Almost two decades later, the reviewer for *The Times* echoed this sentiment when he asserted that 'if pictures are things to be lived with', the subject must be 'happily chosen'. In a review of Luke Fildes's *The Widower* (1876), for example, the reviewer complains that the painter

> is under a mistake who brings his dirty boots, squalling and scrambling children, parental and sisterly love, and the pathos of an innocent's death-struggle, into such close contact [. . .] It is a great pity that painters do not bear more in mind the fact that their pictures are meant to adorn English living-rooms, and that intense painfulness, overstrained expression, and great vehemence of momentary action or short-lived attitude are all qualities that make pictures unpleasant to live with.[56]

'Abstinence' from such depressing scenes does not necessarily 'condemn the painter to insipidity', for there is an 'abundance of interest, including pathos, to be found in subjects of the present and the past'.[57] Thus, the fact that so many emigration paintings do not depict the distress which motivated emigration is due to an understanding in the art world that saw genre paintings as fulfilling a particular purpose: they both depict a comfortable idyllic home, and, through such depictions, work to produce this interior within the space in which they are situated.

Critics have read the drive for this aesthetic cleanliness of genre paintings as a reaction against the changes of modernity. Lionel Lambourne, for example, argues that they were a result of 'nostalgia' in the face of dramatic change.[58] In *The Dark Side of the Landscape*, John Barrell argues that categorising the aesthetic and stylised representations in nineteenth-century paintings as sentimental idealism does little to enhance our understanding. In his view, the reluctance to depict agricultural distress is a 'myth' to be explored, rather than dismissed: we cannot 'strip away the nostalgia and mythologizing about Merry England or the organic community', because these myths 'really happened as well'. The real question is not what the 'harmonious surface of the painting' hides, but what it tells us.[59]

So what, if anything, does the narrative painting's refusal to depict the social ills at home as a primary force for motivating emigration tell us? In *Rural Scenes and National Representations*, Elizabeth Helsinger argues, 'rural place[s]' acquire symbolic force in paintings as they are also

> made to stand for the whole nation, against the competing claims of other contemporary images, such as the city or the machine [. . .] The rural as national metaphor carries over to the new national context [. . .] This transfer of meaning often brings with it a certain stylization: images and narratives are simplified and codified as they are staged, performed, and quoted for a national audience.[60]

But if the countryside could be read metaphorically as the space of the nation, then so too could the family unit. As Nead argues, 'the family was seen as a "natural" and stable unit which should ideally be located in a natural, rural setting' and the 'specific focus for this construct was around the notion of a village community' because the village was 'rooted in nature and tradition', it was smaller than the industrial cities and towns, and people were familiar and readily identified.[61] With their emphases on the family and the countryside, the paintings of Redgrave, Collinson and Webster evidently play into the idea of painting embodying national values.

Letter scenes mesh texts of emigration culture into the family and village homes and thus encourage us to see the national characteristics of emigration itself. Traditionally, the country is pulled into a binary with the city. In his seminal *The Country and the City*, Raymond Williams argues that whereas the country 'has gathered the idea of a natural way of life: of peace, of innocence, and simple virtue', the city on the other hand, 'has gathered the idea of an achieved centre', but with plenty of '[p]owerful hostile associations', such as 'noise, worldliness and ambition'.[62] This same dynamic was reproduced in emigration literature, where manuals urged emigrants not to stop for long in the ports where their ships docked, for fear of being drawn into a drunken and debauched lifestyle, but to press on into the bush where they could expect to find work and settle quickly. However, letter scenes such as Webster's and Collinson's circumvent depictions of the city entirely, and instead stress a periphery–periphery connection between the country and the colony. Rather than an opposition, however, we are encouraged to see a similarity, and maybe even a continuity between the two. As the families make the decision to migrate, or set sail on the ship, the message seems to be that they will carry the values of the country and all that it stands for with them, to reproduce them in the colonies. Webster and Collinson thus use the conventions of domestic genre painting to explore the impact of emigration on family life back home. In their paintings, the arrival of the emigrant's letter complicates the settled nature of the cottage interiors. The artists thus probe how the textual cultures of emigration connect different spaces – and through encouraging the viewer to see a connection between colony and country, point to the ability of home to be made elsewhere.

Advertising Emigration

In both *A Letter from the Colonies* and *Answering the Emigrant's Letter*, the letters themselves cannot be read. Instead, they become part of the visual vocabulary of the paintings, a motif of mobility. By contrast, in Abraham Solomon's painting, *Second Class – The Parting* (Figure 10) words become part of the fabric of the painting: one can clearly see the wording of the bills advertising emigration at the back of the scene.

Figure 10 *Second Class – The Parting*, 1854, Abraham Solomon, oil on canvas, 76.3 x 54.5 cm, Southampton City Art Gallery, Hampshire, UK / Bridgeman Images

Emigration Paintings 153

In the words of Gerard Curtis, the advertisements in the background are truly 'visual words', that is, words that are painted into the picture's fabric. We see the inside of a train carriage, where a widow has an arm around her young son. Opposite them sits her daughter. She regards her son with concern, but her son looks at his older sister, who looks back anxiously, a handkerchief in hand to wipe away her tears. His belongings are in a carpet bag with a tag on it and tied up in a bundle next to him. Next to it is his bedding. The three are caught in a triangle of gazes, oblivious to the man and woman, presumably a couple, who sit in the carriage behind them. The husband rests his arm on the back of his seat as he turns around to cast a sympathetic glance at the boy. One critic suggested that 'behind, in the next compartment, a sailor, seeing the thing with a practised glance, regards him with sympathy and kindness'.[63] Meanwhile, his wife blushes slightly, perhaps at the embarrassment with what she feels is her husband's intrusion into a private, emotional family scene, and gracefully averts her eyes to look out of the carriage window. Outside, one can make out the ships in the harbour, a portent of what is to come.

It is, however, the advertising bills covering the back of the carriage that provide the painting with its context and give the spectator indications of where the boy is headed. Over the top of the carriage is the sign 'Australian Emigrants Should Be Provided With All. Goulding and Comp[any]. Implements For The Gold Diggings'. Below this is an advertisement of the same size for clothing: 'Try The Monarch Cheap Clothing Mart For All Kinds Of Outfits For Emigrants At Messers Cuttwells and Comp[any]'. On the left of this advertisement is a smaller one advertising 'Cutwells & Co Paletots &c Best In The World',[64] and on the right, another advertising 'Mens And Youths Garments Of Every Description [sic]'. One advertises 'Hill Brothers Co's Line Of Packets Established In 1845 For Sydney The Finest First Class Ship *Cleopatra* of 522 Tons Register' which has a certain 'William Shaw' as the 'Commander' that is setting sail from 'London Docks'. Another calls the attention of those who wish 'To Sail Early In May For Port Philip Direct' on 'The Splendid East Sailor *Mediana*'. The rest of the details on the ship and the captain are obscured by the woman's head.

In *Advertising, Subjectivity and the Nineteenth-Century Novel*, Sara Thornton argues that advertising dramatically changed the cityscape and, by extension, the experience of walking on the streets. The amount of 'printed matter that an average citizen might see on the streets of London and Paris grew vertiginously in the mid-nineteenth century, helped by improved printing technologies, cheaper paper and the thrust given to the advertising of commodities by the Great Exhibition of 1851'.[65] It was not just walls that became covered in advertising: text was, 'literally, on the move',[66] pasted on hoardings, on sandwich boards, on the sides of horse carriages and the inside of buses and along the tracks of railway platforms.[67] As John Orlando Parry's *A London Street Scene* shows, the streets became crowded with bills and advertisements. When the space on any given surface filled up, new bills were posted over old ones, which generated new readings and meanings. Solomon's *Second Class* demonstrates little of this over-pasting, but it picks up on the cacophony of messages that advertising necessarily set into play. Juxtaposed in between and next to the emigration advertisements, ordinary, everyday life goes on. The very first advertisement on the left of the spectator is for a product that advertises 'No More Grey Hair'. Below the slogan, one can just about make out the figure of a woman admiring her black locks.[68] Another advertises 'New Year's Gifts' and 'Presents for Children', which indicate to the spectator the time of year that this scene takes place. The rest of the advertisement is obscured by the mother's head. Through these advertisements, the discourse of emigration is shown to be not distinct and apart from everyday life, but very much enmeshed in it. As Thornton argues, through the palimpsest that these advertisements created, a 'story was being written on the walls which no one had begun and no one could end and which delivered up its message intermittently to those who wished to see it and were able to decipher it'.[69] The juxtaposition of these advertisements creates another layer of meaning: 'No More Grey Hair' promises youth, while the timing of 'New Year' speaks of new beginnings. Placed right above the boy's head, these advertisements seem to reassure the spectator of the former's success in the gold diggings. This promise of success, secreted away in the details of the painting, mimics that of the emigrant's letter in *A Letter from the Colonies*, which seems to emit light, and the idea of control and power through the map in *Answering the Emigrant's Letter*. Furthermore, the advertisement for 'Cowell's Manufactory Watches & Clocks. Chronometer Maker To Her Majesty' picks up on temporality; a theme that we have already seen is of particular concern in emigration painting. Most interesting, however, is the 'Wanted' advertisement for 'A Few Fine Young Men To Enter The Honourable East India Service' placed right above the young boy's head[70] – the idea of men fulfilling the vision of colonial Britain. Thornton suggests that the streets, filled with advertising bills, become 'a new space in which to dream, a space of fantasy'.[71] The advertising bills in Solomon's painting bring visions of the colonies into the enclosed space of the railway carriage and transform it by projecting a fantasy of colonial success.

None of the artists studied in this chapter emigrated, but their interest in emigration as a legitimate subject matter for art demonstrates the extent to which they were aware of its impact on individual families and society at large. Crucially, the artists were not interested in promoting emigration as a solution to social problems at home: rather they display an anxiety that Britain cannot keep its men on its shores and are interested in exploring the other side of the pro-emigration stance of much of emigration literature. It is because the nineteenth-century experience of emigration was mediated by and through text, that text becomes a central part of emigration painting's iconography. Collectively, these paintings absorb how texts negotiated, crossed and collapsed distance, bringing distant places into contact with the known and familiar places at home. Simultaneously, however, they seem to display an unease with the ability of text to generate mobility: rather than emphatically stressing the inevitability of success in the colonies, the possibility of home at a distance is always hidden in the details under the apparent meaning of the arrival of an emigrant's letter, or a scene of departure. In the next chapter, I examine the ways in which the textual culture of emigration shaped the aesthetics of Elizabeth Gaskell's, Charles Dickens's and Catherine Spence's novels. Whereas nineteenth-century paintings problematised the pro-emigration narrative in booster literature, Gaskell's and Dickens's novels picked up on the stock images of successful emigration to the colonies that circulated in emigration literature.

Notes

1. In total, Collinson produced three paintings of emigration – more than any of the artists discussed in this chapter. His third painting, *The Reply*, is now lost. In 1851, the *Art Journal* reviewed the painting, which depicted 'a letter to Australia, written by a boy, the son of a cottager or a small farmer in answer to one received. The work exhibits everywhere the most minute manipulation, but as this does not appear without a microscopic examination, we submit that a better end had been answered by a more generous touch': 'The National Institution', *Art Journal* (1 May 1851), pp. 138–40 (p. 139).

2. 'Fine Arts', *Spectator* (1 May 1852), pp. 422–3 (p. 422). I have not included the painting in my discussion here because Highland Clearances have their own modes of representation, as Patricia Hardy notes in the second chapter of her thesis. See 'The Backward Gaze to the Highlands', pp. 93–140, in Patricia Hardy, 'Victorian Images of Emigration' (unpublished doctoral thesis, Courtauld Institute of Art, 2008).
3. Hardy, 'Victorian Images', pp. 254–78.
4. Susan P. Casteras, '"*Oh! Emigration! Thou'rt the Curse* . . .": Victorian Images of Emigration', *Journal of Pre-Raphaelite Studies* 6 (1985), pp. 1–23 (pp. 5–6). The 'sentimental' quality of Victorian genre painting has been a contested topic of academic debate. See Pamela Fletcher, '"To wipe a manly tear": The Aesthetics of Emotion in Victorian Narrative Painting', *Victorian Studies* 51 (2009), pp. 457–69 for a discussion on how the 'question of feeling' 'defined and complicated the limits between sincerity and vulgarity, interiority and performativity, morality and moralizing, representation and real life, and popular appeal and aesthetic success' (479). Miriam Bailin takes a similar view when she asserts that a discourse of 'sentimentality' in nineteenth-century painting allowed Victorians to explore issues surrounding 'the experience of social mobility', in '"Dismal Pleasure": Victorian Sentimentality and the Pathos of the Parvenu', *ELH* 66 (1999), pp. 1015–32 (p. 1016). See also Fred Kaplan, *Sacred Tears: Sentimentality in Victorian Literature* (Princeton: Princeton University Press, 1987) for a more general discussion on sentimentality and Victorian culture.
5. See Lionel Lambourne, *An Introduction to 'Victorian' Genre Painting: From Wilkie to Frith* (London: HMSO, 1982), p. 5 and Lynda Nead, *Myths of Sexuality: Representations of Women in Victorian Britain* (Oxford: Basil Blackwell, 1988), pp. 18–19. For a brief and concise introduction to the politics of subject matter in British art at this time, see the first two pages of 'The Cranbrook Colony' in Andrew Greg, *The Cranbrook Colony: F. D. Hardy, G. Hardy, J. C. Horsley, A. E. Mulready, G. B. O'Neil, T. Webster* (Wolverhampton: Central Art Gallery, 1977), from which the quotations above are taken. As this book has no page numbers all subsequent references from this book refer to the section from which the quotations are taken.
6. Martin Meisel, *Realizations: Narrative, Pictorial, and Theatrical Arts in Nineteenth-Century England* (Princeton: Princeton University Press, 1983), p. 3. Emphasis added.
7. 'The Royal Academy', *Art Union* (1 June 1845), pp. 179–96 (p. 180).
8. Hilary Beck, *Victorian Engravings* (London: Victoria and Albert Museum, 1973) and Celina Fox, 'Wood Engravers and the City', in Ira Bruce Nadel and F. S. Schwarzbach (eds), *Victorian Artists and the City: A Collection of Critical Essays* (New York: Pergamon, 1980), pp. 1–13 both provide an important background to the production and consumption of engravings.

9. See Rhoda L. Flaxman, *Victorian Word-Painting and Narrative: Toward the Blending of Genres* (Saginaw, MI: UMI Research, 1987), p. 1. I have focused on the literary nature of the art world here, but the commonalities between genre painting and the novel have been interrogated by critics elsewhere. Ruth Bernard Yeazell in *Art of the Everyday: Dutch Painting and the Realist Novel* (Princeton: Princeton University Press, 2008), for example, argues convincingly that the novel's sense of realism is derived from the Dutch genre painting.
10. Rachel Teukolsky, *The Literate Eye: Victorian Art Writing and Modernist Aesthetics* (Oxford: Oxford University Press, 2009), p. 16.
11. Gerard Curtis, *Visual Words: Art and the Material Book in Victorian England* (Aldershot: Ashgate, 1999), p. 57.
12. Hardy, 'Victorian Images', p. 238.
13. See Julie F. Codell, 'Introduction: Imperial Co-Histories and the British and Colonial Press', in Julie F. Codell (ed.), *Imperial Co-Histories: National Identities and the British and Colonial Press* (Madison: Fairleigh Dickinson University Press, 2003), pp. 15–26 (p. 18).
14. Lynda Nead, 'The History in Pictures', *Cultural and Social History* 7 (2010), pp. 485–92 (p. 486).
15. See Virginia Surtees, *The Diary of Ford Madox Brown* (London: Yale University Press, 1981), p. 80 n. 25. Woolner in fact returned from Australia before the painting was completed. In December 1854, Brown records having dinner with Woolner the previous night and records his satisfaction that 'Woolner who ought to know likes [*The Last of England*] well', Surtees, *The Diary*, p. 106 (2 December 1854).
16. Ford Madox Brown, *The Exhibition of Work, and Other Paintings by Ford Madox Brown at The Gallery, 191 Piccadilly* (London: M'Corquodale, 1865), p. 9. Brown's diary provides an insight into the meticulous care he took over accurately capturing the details for this painting. See especially the entries for March 1854 in Surtees, *The Diary*, pp. 124–30.
17. Surtees, *The Diary*, p. 80 ([?] August 1854).
18. Ibid.
19. Susan P. Casteras, '"Social Wrongs": The Painted Sermons of Richard Redgrave', in Susan P. Casteras and Ronald Parkinson (eds), *Richard Redgrave 1804–1888* (New Haven, CT: Yale University Press, 1988), pp. 2–28 (p. 21).
20. 'Royal Academy', *Saturday Review* (28 May 1859), pp. 651–3 (p. 652).
21. 'The Royal Academy Exhibition', *Art Journal* (1 June 1859), pp. 161–72 (p. 161).
22. Council of Four, *A Guide to the Exhibition of the Royal Academy of Arts, 1859: Containing Original, Critical, and Descriptive Notices of 250 Works of Art* (London: Kent, 1859), p. 24; p. 25.
23. *Exhibition Catalogue of the Royal Academy of Arts, the Ninety-First* (London: William Clowes, 1859), p. 12. In the catalogue, the two couplets are given as though one follows from the other, but in the original poem, they are separated by a few lines. For a critical reception of

Goldsmith's poem, see A. Lytton Sells, *Oliver Goldsmith: His Life and Works* (London: George Allen & Unwin, 1974), pp. 105–8 and pp. 288–95.
24. Quoted in Lionel Lambourne, *Victorian Painting* (London: Phaidon, 1999), p. 359.
25. Brown, *The Exhibition of Work*, p. 8, original emphasis.
26. Ibid.
27. F. M. Redgrave, *Richard Redgrave, C.B., R.A.: A Memoir, Compiled from his Diary with Portrait and Three Illustrations* (London: Cassell, 1891), p. 219.
28. Surtees, *The Diary*, p. 96 (3 October 1854).
29. Ibid. p. 132 (11 April 1855).
30. Ibid. p. 153 (9 September 1855).
31. Teresa Newman and Raymond Watkinson, *Ford Madox Brown and the Pre-Raphaelite Circle* (London: Chatto & Windus, 1991), p. 88.
32. Susan P. Casteras, 'Painted Fictions: Commemorating the Everyday in Victorian Art', in *Pre-Raphaelite and Other Masters: The Andrew Lloyd Webber Collection* (London: The Royal Academy of Arts, 2003), pp. 204–27 (p. 205).
33. Kathryn Moore Heleniak, 'Thomas Webster', *Oxford Dictionary of National Biography* < http://www.oxforddnb.com/view/article/28947?docPos=3> [accessed 21 September 2017] (para. 1).
34. See Nead, 'History in Pictures'.
35. 'Royal Academy', *Athenaeum* (15 May 1852), pp. 549–51 (p. 551).
36. Caroline Arscott, 'Ramsgate Sands, Modern Life, and the Shoring-Up of Narrative', in Brian Allen (ed.), *Towards a Modern Art World* (London: Yale University Press, 1995), pp. 157–68 (p. 158).
37. David M. Henkin, *The Postal Age: The Emergence of Modern Communications in Nineteenth-Century America* (Chicago: University of Chicago Press, 2006), pp. 55–6.
38. 'The Exhibition of the Royal Academy', *Art Journal* (1 June 1852), pp. 165–76 (p. 168).
39. Julia Thomas, *Victorian Narrative Painting* (London: Tate Publishing, 2000), p. 80.
40. *Letters from Settlers in Upper Canada*, p. 2; p. 6.
41. William E. Fredeman (ed.), *The P. R. B. Journal: William Michael Rossetti's Diary of the Pre-Raphaelite Brotherhood 1849–1853, Together with Other Pre-Raphaelite Documents* (Oxford: Clarendon, 1975), p. 8 (Wednesday 30 May 1849). Collinson's painting, in fact, remained unsold at the exhibition, along with William Holman Hunt's *A Converted British Family Sheltering a Christian Missionary from the Persecution of the Druids* (1850).
42. Fredeman, *P. R. B. Journal*, p. 8 (Wednesday 30 May 1849); p. 50 (Saturday 2 February 1850). Soon after the exhibition, Collinson resigned from the Academy due to religious differences. In his letter to Gabriel Rossetti, he wrote that 'as a sincere Catholic, I can no longer allow myself to be called a P. R. B. in the brotherhood sense of the

term, or to be connected in any way with the magazine [. . .] Whatever may be my thoughts with regards to their works, I am sure that all the P. R. B.s have both written and painted conscientiously; it was for me to have judged beforehand whether I could conscientiously, as a Catholic, assist in spreading the artistic opinions of those who are not': Ibid. p. 71 (Sunday 21 July 1850). Collinson's conversion also led him to break off his engagement to Christina Rossetti. Neither of the Rossetti brothers, nor Christina Rossetti, comments on this in their diaries and letters. See Lindsay Errington, *Social and Religious Themes in English Art 1840–1860* (London: Garland, 1984), pp. 352–5 for more information on Collinson and his resignation from the Brotherhood; Jan Marsh, *The Pre-Raphaelites: Their Lives in Letters and Diaries* (London: Collins & Brown, 1996), p. 33; and Ronald Parkinson, 'James Collinson', in Leslie Parris (ed.), *Pre-Raphaelite Papers* (London: Tate Gallery/Allen Lane, 1984), pp. 61–75. William Holman Hunt's *Pre-Raphaelitism and the Pre-Raphaelite Brotherhood*, 2 vols (London: Macmillan & Co, 1905), i, pp. 161–5 also provides insight into Collinson's time with the Pre-Raphaelite Brotherhood.

43. Fredeman, *P. R. B. Journal*, p. 70 (Sunday 21 July 1850). Paintings that were exhibited at eye level were described as having been exhibited 'on the line'. 'Above' or 'below' 'the line' thus means above or below eye level. As pictures and reviews of the Royal Academy exhibitions show, space was extremely limited: being exhibited on the line was one of the very few places where a painting could hope to get a good viewing. For more information, see Helene E. Roberts, 'Art Reviewing in the Early Nineteenth-Century Art Periodicals', *Victorian Periodicals Newsletter* 19 (March 1973), pp. 9–20, and Helene E. Roberts, 'Exhibition and Review: The Periodical Press and the Victorian Art Exhibition System', in Joanne Shattock and Michael Wolff (ed.), *The Victorian Periodical Press: Samplings and Soundings* (Leicester: Leicester University Press, 1982), pp. 79–107.

44. 'The Royal Academy', *Art Journal* (1 June 1850), pp. 165–78 (p. 173).

45. 'The Royal Academy Exhibition', *Critic* (1 August 1850), pp. 381–3 (p. 381).

46. *Letters from Settlers in Upper Canada*, p. 4.

47. G. N. G. Clarke, 'Taking Possession: The Cartouche as Cultural Text in Eighteenth-Century American Maps', *Word & Image* 4 (1988), pp. 455–74.

48. Ibid. pp. 455–6.

49. Janet Gurkin Altman, *Epistolarity: Approaches to a Form* (Columbus: Ohio State University Press, 1982), p. 13.

50. In Paul Falconer Poole's *The Emigrant's Departure* (1838), for example, we can see fields through the open door and window.

51. Susan P. Casteras, '"Green Lanes and Chequered Shade": The Landscapes of Richard Redgrave', in Susan P. Casteras and Ronald Parkinson (eds), *Richard Redgrave, 1804–1888* (London: Yale University Press, 1988), pp. 71–85 (p. 80).

52. Greg, *The Cranbrook Colony*.
53. Ibid.
54. David Wilkie, 'Critical Remarks on Works of Art', in Allan Cunningham (ed.), *The Life of Sir David Wilkie*, 3 vols (London: John Murray, 1843), iii, pp. 128–215 (p. 139).
55. Redgrave, *Richard Redgrave*, p. 131.
56. 'Royal Academy', *The Times* (8 May 1876), p. 9.
57. Ibid. I do not have the space to compare and contrast the idyllic representations of emigration with more realistic ones, but for an interesting example of this contrast, see John Absolon's *We Are Out on the Ocean Sailing to our Home Beyond the Deep* (1850) to Hubert von Herkomer's *Passage to the West* (1884).
58. Lambourne, *Introduction to 'Victorian' Genre Painting*, p. 9.
59. John Barrell, *The Dark Side of the Landscape: The Rural Poor in English Painting 1730–1840* (Cambridge: Cambridge University Press, 1980), p. 164.
60. Elizabeth K. Helsinger, *Rural Scenes and National Representation, Britain: 1815–1850* (Princeton: Princeton University Press, 1997), p. 13.
61. Nead, *Myths of Sexuality*, p. 40.
62. Raymond Williams, *The Country and the City*, p. 1.
63. 'Royal Academy', *Athenaeum* (13 May 1854), pp. 593–5 (p. 593).
64. Paletots were a type of coat common in the nineteenth century.
65. Sara Thornton, *Advertising, Subjectivity and the Nineteenth-Century Novel: Dickens, Balzac and the Language of the Walls* (Basingstoke: Palgrave Macmillan, 2009), p. 4, p. 8.
66. Ibid. p. 8.
67. For visual examples of advertising in the city, see Diana Hindley and Geoffrey Hindley, *Advertising in Victorian England, 1837–1901* (London: Wayland, 1972), Plates 1.1, 1.2, 1.5–1.8 and 1.10, n.p.
68. There is another person facing her in the painting, but it is not clear whether this is a gentleman who has also used the product, or the salesperson showing the lady in question how to use it.
69. Thornton, *Advertising*, p. 27.
70. The placement of the East India advert could suggest that the boy is in fact going to join that company, but the fact that there are more emigration advertisements that take central place in the painting, combined with the fact that the painting is dated 1854, so close after the gold discovery of 1851, supports my reading of the young boy as gold-digger.
71. Thornton, *Advertising*, p. 7. See also Lynda Nead, *Victorian Babylon: People, Streets and Images in Nineteenth-Century London* (New Haven, CT: Yale University Press, 2000), p. 58 for a reading of advertising as a visual consumption of place.

Chapter 5

Emigration Aesthetics: Elizabeth Gaskell, Charles Dickens and Catherine Helen Spence

'Have you been in England?' asked Martin.
'In print I have, sir,' said the General, 'not otherwise. We air a reading people here, sir. You will meet with much information among us that will surprise you'.[1]

This brief exchange in *Martin Chuzzlewit* (1844) between Martin and General Choke encapsulates many of the central concerns of emigration literature. The General's answer to Martin that he has been to England 'in print' highlights the ways in which places travel through texts as they become caught up in intersecting and overlapping networks of circulation. The General knows all too well that as places circulate through print, they open up a contested space as things shift and change. It does not occur to the unsuspecting Martin, however, that the information he comes across in emigration literature might 'surprise' him because it is in fact dubious *mis*information.

As this book has demonstrated so far, the circulation of emigration literature produced certain affective regimes. It enabled readers who had yet to experience colonial life first-hand to familiarise themselves with places through text and at a distance. At the same time, this means of knowing was troubled and ambiguous, as the editors and emigrants alike sought to prove to a suspicious public that the text's geographical mobility had not compromised its authenticity. Different kinds of authenticity are at stake here: fears that the text might be compromised in terms of its accurate portrayal of colonial life sat alongside fears that the mobile text no longer authentically mediated kinship ties between emigrants and their families in Britain. Negotiating the distance between Britain and her colonies is thus a key preoccupation of emigration literature. In this chapter, I argue that this preoccupation with how to narrate distance shaped the aesthetics of certain significant mid-century novels. I focus on Charles Dickens's *Martin Chuzzlewit* (1844) and *David Copperfield* (1850), Elizabeth Gaskell's *Mary Barton* (1848) and Catherine Helen Spence's *Clara Morison* (1854). In these novels, emigration literature acquires a particular representational force: the places of settlement are more than a mere passing reference to somewhere that exists in the shadows of the novel, and instead are shown to impact upon the lives of the central characters in formative ways. In *Martin Chuzzlewit*, Martin Chuzzlewit and Mark Tapley emigrate to the fictitious Eden in the United States; in *David Copperfield*, the Micawbers and Peggottys emigrate to Australia; and in *Mary Barton*, Mary and Jem Wilson emigrate to Canada. In *Clara Morison*, the eponymous heroine is sent to make a life for herself in Adelaide following her father's death. As an Australian author writing for a predominantly British audience, Spence's novels offer a way of interrogating the global network of print culture from an Australian vantage point. Like Dickens and Gaskell, she was read both in Britain and in the colonies, and like Dickens, she travelled between England, Europe and America. Emigration literature offered the three authors under study here a profound way of imagining the circulation of people and print between Britain and the colonies. In their novels discussed in this chapter, characters circulate: they move to settlements elsewhere, sometimes temporarily, sometimes permanently, and sometimes they come back to England to visit. This demographic mobility is always accompanied by the textual culture of emigration, whether it be maps, letters or periodicals. That the novel should represent emigration through its textual culture points to the deeply intertwined relationship between emigration and the written word. In their interrogation of the distance that separates emigrant characters from their friends in Britain, these novels draw on the motifs of emigration literature, such as the successful labourer, the lying text, and homesickness. But, in a curious act of doubling, as the novels examine how emigration literature mediates a sense of place, the texts of emigration literature themselves become a motif in the novel. The colonial periodical, the emigrant's letter and the map, for example, are used again and again to probe how emigration literature projects a sense of place and maintains relationships across time and space. Thus, the novels both draw on the motifs of emigration literature *and* use emigration literature as a motif to shape enquiry into how people become connected into a global network of migrations. Emigration in Gaskell's, Dickens's and Spence's novels is a means of engaging with a broader set of questions about the cultural work of emigration literature.

Mary Barton: Recreating the Knowable Community

At the end of *Mary Barton*, the narrator projects her gaze from England to the colonies, to observe a scene of perfect domesticity in a small settlement in Canada:

> I see a long low wooden house, with room enough and to spare. The old primeval trees are felled and gone for many a mile around; one alone remains to overshadow the gable-end of the cottage. There is a garden around the dwelling, and far beyond that stretches an orchard. The glory of an Indian summer is over all, making the heart leap at the sight of its gorgeous beauty.[2]

The narration shifts in both tone and style here to narrate Jem and Mary's Canadian life. After the industrial strife and the melodrama of the novel, the ending in Canada offers the reader a scene of untroubled contentment. 'At the door of the house, looking towards the town, stands Mary, watching the return of her husband from his daily work; and while she watches, she listens, smiling' at her son Johnnie singing a ditty around her (392). Gaskell had never been to Canada, and Canada had never held sway over her imagination in the way that the States had.[3] Her image of settler life is drawn from contemporary accounts of the Canadian bush circulating either as oral narratives, or through print. Through the scene of Jem and Mary in Canada, Gaskell echoes an image that was frequently used in contemporary debates surrounding emigration. Her picture of man having tamed a rural wilderness has close parallels, for example, with that of Thomas Carlyle, in *Chartism*. Carlyle writes:

> in a world where Canadian Forests stand unfelled, boundless Plains and Prairies [are] unbroken with the plough; on the west and on the east, green desert spaces never yet made white with corn; and to the overcrowded little western nook of Europe, our Terrestrial Planet, nine-tenths of it yet vacant or tenanted by nomads, is still crying, Come and till me, come and reap me![4]

For Carlyle, the untamed Canadian forests are a means for England to rectify its problem of excess labour. Gaskell's depiction of life in Canada seems to offer Mary and Jem a solid stability in comparison to the turbulence of Manchester. Through the image of the 'felled' 'primeval' trees, Gaskell evokes the colony as a place that has been worked on by humans, not as a place of pristine untouched nature.

Clearing the bush is one of the first tasks of settlement, and in doing so, Jem has turned the unruly, wild landscape into a suitable place to live. For Carlyle, the supposedly empty space of Canada provides the 'briefless Barristers, chargeless Clergy, taskless Scholars [in England] languishing in all courthouses, hiding in obscure garrets, besieging all antechambers, in passionate want of simply one thing, Work' with the opportunity that they need.[5] The question of work – or, rather, the lack of it – defines *Mary Barton*. After the fire at their mill, the Carsons decide to modernise and lay off hands. John Barton's misery is occasioned by the lack of available opportunities following his redundancy. By contrast, Jem's job as an engineer allows him to move easily to Canada. He becomes an 'instrument-maker to the Agricultural College' that is being newly established 'at Toronto, in Canada': 'It is a comfortable appointment, – house, – land, – and a good percentage on the instruments made' (375). For a novel that concerns itself with the effects of industrialisation on labourer's lives, Jem's job in Canada is particularly apt. It suggests that Canada presents the opportunity for a new community to develop, but in ways that do not repeat the detrimental effects that industrialisation has had on Manchester.

Of all the characters in the novel, Jem is one of the few to have consistent, regular employment. It is not want of work that pushes him to emigrate, but the desire for anonymity that both he and Mary need in order to rebuild their lives following the trial and the death of John Barton. He correctly fears that he 'might find, in spite of a jury's verdict, that too strong a taint was on his character for him ever to labour in Manchester again' (349). He remembers how 'some one suspected of having been a convict was shunned by masters and men' and 'how he himself had thought it did not become an honest upright man to associate with one who had been a prisoner' (349). Even though Jem has done no wrong, his arrest is enough to sully his reputation. Sally Leadbitter, Mary's friend, cannot bring herself to even say what he is: 'Decent men were not going to work with a – no!' (359). For all her gossiping nature, she is right in this: 'As he [Jem] stood in the entrance to the foundry [. . .] many of those employed in the works passed him on their return from breakfast; and, with one or two exceptions, without any acknowledgement of former acquaintance beyond a distant nod at the utmost' (375). His fears are cemented after John Barton's death: 'I could live it down if I stayed in England; but then what would not Mary have to bear? Sooner or later the truth would out; and then she would be a show to folk for many a day as John Barton's daughter' (375). The distance between Canada and Britain offers Jem and Mary the opportunity they need to escape the shame they would have faced, had they stayed in England. The absence of a community who knows them, as well as the chance of employment, ensure the success of their settlement.

Given the narration of the projected gaze in the last scene of the novel, and the narrator's shift in tone, it is in many ways unsurprising that this end scene has been read as detached from the rest of the text. For critics such as Raymond Williams, the book's use of emigration as a solution to the problems it raises constitutes an act of imaginative failure. In *The Country and the City*, he argues that 'in the industrial novels of the mid-nineteenth century [. . .] the idea of emigration to the colonies was seized as a solution to the poverty and overcrowding of the cities'. He points to *Wuthering Heights*, *Great Expectations*, *Alton Locke* and 'many other novels of the period', where emigration is

> a way out from the struggle within English society to [. . .] distant lands; a way out that is not only the escape to a new land but, as in some of the real history, an acquisition of fortune to return and re-enter the struggle at a higher point [. . .] The lands of the Empire were an idyllic retreat, an escape from debt or shame, or an opportunity for making a fortune.

In his view, *Mary Barton* is one of these novels: it 'ends in Canada, in a mood of rural idyll and escape as powerful as any of the earlier English images'. The reading of emigration in novels as an 'escape' has gained currency since Williams initially proposed it. Lynette Felber, for example, echoes Williams's language when she argues that the ending of *Mary Barton*, where the narrator looks out to Jem and Mary's settlement in Canada, is 'underdeveloped and lacks continuity with the primary narrative', and is an 'equivocal' 'solution to the industrial problem' of the novel. Grace Moore similarly argues that Gaskell 'neatly evaded the problem' of 'how to end *Mary Barton*' by 'despatching [Jem] and his new wife to the colonies'. In other words, in the novel, emigration is no more than 'a device to facilitate narrative closure'. The common thread in the body of such criticism seems to be that the 'escape' of the novels lies not so much in the character's escape to new lands, but in the author's escape in not providing a more local solution to the problems that their novels raise.[6]

Suvendrini Perera is one of the few critics to argue otherwise, when she writes that the ending has not been 'read within the same interpretive framework as the rest of the narrative': rather than reading the ending 'as part of the novel's processing and configuration of the specific social situation seen as its main concern', the 'migrations and overseas voyages in novels such as *Mary Barton, Alton Locke, David Copperfield,* and *Great Expectations* are often read within a different frame of reference – one of "magic" or "escape"'.[7] In her view, the 'resolution by migration in *Mary Barton* can be read as the ultimate expression of [a] spatial relationship' between the 'internal and the domestic' that is 'neither sudden nor unprepared for but based on [the novel's] existing network of connections, influences, and transactions'.[8] Perera's comments that the Canadian scene is part of the novel's existing spatial network deserves further consideration. Critics working on the commodity culture of *Mary Barton* have highlighted the ways in which the novel registers the global politics of the cotton trade, a theme that Gaskell picks up again in *North and South*.[9] Canada is also connected to England through more personal networks. Jem returns from his day's work in the forest carrying letters from England. The letters contain news that Will and Margaret 'are to be married on the twenty-fifth of this month, and he's bringing her out here next voyage; and Job Legh talks of coming out [. . .] to try and pick up a few specimens of Canadian insects' (393). The novel recognises the importance of chain migration in consolidating family structures and friendship ties. It is telling that Jem and Mary's long cottage has 'room for more' (392), a symbolic gesture to the vast expanses of Canada which can supposedly support an incoming population.

In its anticipation of the colony's growing population, the novel once again picks up on Carlyle's notion in *Chartism* that emigration would make the British nation stronger:

> Is it not as if this swelling, simmering, never-resting Europe of ours stood, once more, on the verge of an expansion without parallel; struggling, struggling like a mighty tree again about to burst in the embrace of summer, and shoot broad frondent boughs which would fill the whole earth? A disease; but the noblest of all, – as of her who is in pain and sore travail, but travails that she may be a mother and say, Behold, there is a new Man born![10]

Although an abstract space – or precisely because it is an abstract space – Canada is conceived of in *Mary Barton* as a community which is far enough removed from Britain to provide Jem and Mary with the distance that they need, and yet at the same time connected to it through epistolary exchange. The depiction of chain migration through letters at the end of the novel constructs Canada as a safe haven for a microcosmic version of the community in England. The colony is thus shown in the process of becoming a smaller version of the rural Manchester that we saw at the opening scenes of the novel, where the Barton and Wilson families take a walk on Green Heys Fields at the end of the working day. In the end, the colony ends up as a mini-rural Manchester – but with the potential for new beginnings.

Martin Chuzzlewit: A Culture of Suspicion

In 1842, Dickens returned from his first trip to America, a tour that had lasted about five months. As Claire Tomalin argues, he had thought that a trip to America would relieve him from 'the pressure of constant writing', 'give himself a mental shake' and provide him with the opportunity to 'gather enough material from his travels to make a book'.[11] While the trip provided him with material enough for two books, his travelogue *American Notes* (1842) which he published four months after his return to England, and *Martin Chuzzlewit*, the trip had nonetheless fallen far short of Dickens's expectations. The pressure of being a celebrity, coupled with the refusal of the Americans to take the issue of international copyright law seriously, quickly led to soured relations between Dickens and the American public. By the end of the five-month tour, Dickens was looking forward to coming home. The voyage back opened his eyes to what the working classes endured when they emigrated across the Atlantic. In *American Notes*, he notices the steerage passengers, about a hundred people, living in 'a little world of poverty':

> as we came to know individuals among them by sight [. . .] we became curious to know their histories, and with what expectations they had gone out to America, and on what errands they were going home, and what their circumstances were.[12]

Upon enquiring, he finds that

> Some of them had been in America but three days, some but three months, and some had gone out in the last voyage of that very ship in which they were now returning home. Others had sold their clothes to raise the passage-money, and had hardly rags to cover them; others had no food, and lived upon the charity of the rest [. . .] After hoarding up, and borrowing, and begging, and selling everything to pay the passage, they had gone out to New York, expecting to find its streets paved with

gold; and had found them paved with very hard and real stones. Enterprise was dull; labourers were not wanted; jobs of work were to be got, but the payment was not. They were coming back, even poorer than they went. (245)

This passage strongly resonates with scenes in *Martin Chuzzlewit*, where Martin is obliged to pawn his clothes and 'reduce his wardrobe to the narrowest limits consistent with decent respectability' (193) in order to pay for his passage out, and returns with less than when he went away. Given the tenor of the rest of *American Notes*, it is interesting that Dickens's comments on the voyage out in it are not embedded in a critique of America or the myth of the American dream, but on the 'whole system of shipping and conveying these unfortunate persons', which 'stands in need of thorough revision' (244–5). In short, he lays the blame for the mismanagement of steerage passengers at the door of the British government:

> If any class deserve to be protected and assisted by the Government, it is that class who are banished from their native land in search of the bare means of subsistence [. . .] The law is bound, at least among the English side, to see that too many of them are not put on board any ship: and that their accommodations are decent: not demoralising and profligate. It is bound, too, in common humanity, to declare that no man shall be taken on board without his stock of provisions being previously inspected by some proper officer, and pronounced moderately sufficient for his support upon the voyage. (244–5)

This last concern is, no doubt, driven by the story of a man who 'was discovered nearly at the end of the voyage, not before' who 'had had no sustenance whatever but the bones and scraps of fat he took from the plates used in the after-cabin dinner, when they were put out to be washed' (244). Dickens had no hand to play in the various reforms of the Passenger Acts through the 1840s that saw steerage conditions gradually improve.[13] However, the humanitarian concern in the passages above indicates not only that by the early 1840s he was forming an interest in the fates of those who emigrated, but that he also recognised the need for appropriate legal measures to be in place in order to provide those less well off with a safe and healthy passage out.

Written and published in 1844 after his return from America, *Martin Chuzzlewit* is one of the few novels in which Dickens follows his protagonist overseas. Upon learning that he has fallen out of favour with Mr Pecksniff, the younger Martin Chuzzlewit decides to emigrate to America, in the hope of returning with enough money and marrying his grandfather's ward, Mary. As he makes his preparations for the voyage, Mark Tapley arrives at his lodgings, offering to accompany him on his adventures. Their stay in America is miserable: falling foul of the country's newspapers, which Dickens paints as corrupt, they travel up the country to Eden, a place sold to them as a thriving town, but which is in fact, a malaria-ridden swamp. First Martin falls ill, then Mark. Eventually both recover sufficiently to come back to England.

The American chapters of the novel have generated much interest, but perhaps the most unusual reading of them comes from Nancy Metz, who suggests that through the emigration scenes, Dickens 'hoped to draw public attention to the most common "preventable" mistakes made by emigrants'.[14] In other words, the novel acts as a pseudo-emigration guide for its readers:

> it is clear that Dickens composed the Eden subplot, at least in part, as an elaborate study in the 'How Not to Do It' of trans-Atlantic emigration. Martin and Mark systematically illustrate through their decisions, or observe in the choices made by others the consequences of all that the handbooks typically warn against. In the process and by implication, the American chapters give dramatic structure to a wide range of useful information and advice: how much the passage cost and how long it took, which provisions were needed, what dangers and contingencies were involved in the journey, where to seek employment on arrival, when to travel and where to settle, which skills were necessary for clearing the land and subduing an unclaimed frontier.[15]

In Metz's reading, the novel itself participates in the truth economy of emigration literature by acting as a kind of guide, providing instruction and information for readers intending to emigrate. While this is a compelling reading, it in no way takes into account the context of *Martin Chuzzlewit*'s publication and Dickens's overall dislike of the States. Safely on board the ship with all his luggage in order, and before the ship set sail, he is filled with excitement, 'in the best of spirits, and full of hope'.[16] However, the pressure of being famous, of being followed, autographed, painted and sculpted soon took its toll. In his letters, he writes of having 'almost paralyzed his right arm, by constantly shaking hands'.[17] In addition to gathering new material for a book and taking a break from writing during his trip to America, Dickens was 'intending to raise the question of international copyright and the pirating of his books in America, which deprived him of the income on which he as a writer depended'.[18] His letters at this time are filled with his frustration at not having his concerns over what he called, 'the unjust and iniquitous state of the law in that country, in reference to the wholesale piracy of British works' taken seriously.[19] Unfavourable reviews in the American press of *American Notes* did little to abate his anger and frustration.[20] As Tomalin argues, in the American chapters of *Martin Chuzzlewit* (1844) Dickens found another opportunity to further emphasise all that he liked least about America, 'pointing out, with savage humour' the 'corrupt newspapers, violence, slavery, spitting, boastfulness and self-righteousness, obsession with business and money, greedy, graceless eating, hypocrisy about supposed equality, the crude lionizing of visitors'.[21] Even before Martin and Mark's ship 'touched the shore', she is 'boarded and over-run' by 'a legion' of 'news-boys', shouting out the news they had on sale. The names of the papers – the *Sewer*, *Stabber*, *Family Spy*, *Private Listener*, *Peeper* and *Keyhole Reporter* – say it all about Dickens's intense dislike of the American newspaper publishing industry (220). A few pages later, when Martin meets Mr Jefferson Brick, War Correspondent of the *Rowdy Journal*, he asks him 'whether this paper of ours [. . .] deals in forgery? In forged letters [. . .] solemnly purporting to have been written at recent periods by living men' (227). No doubt, this is a reference to 'a crudely forged letter attributed to him in a New York Newspaper'.[22]

It is hardly likely, then, that *Martin Chuzzlewit* is an instruction to readers on how to settle properly in America. If anything, in order for Dickens to adequately show his disillusionment with the country, Martin's plan of settlement must come to nothing: his failed emigration is imbricated in a critique of America and her institutions. Metz argues that Martin and Mark's failure is 'the predictable outcome of a long chain of judgement errors made by a pair of novice travellers'.[23] On the contrary, Martin and Mark are not entirely unsuspecting travellers. When Mark cheerfully tells Martin that he has heard a 'military officer' say that the 'Walley of Eden' is filled with 'fleas', 'wampires' and venomous 'snakes', he hastens to reassure him that the officer was most likely 'one of another Company I dare say, and only made up the story that we might go to his Eden, and not the opposition one' (295). Martin tells General Choke that he is willing to settle in Eden 'subject to your opinion and the agent's advice' (299). It is 'serious news' to him to hear that the General is in fact 'a member of the Eden Land Corporation [him]self' as he had previously hoped that he might obtain some 'disinterested advice' (299). Despite his 'secret misgivings on the subject', Martin agrees to 'see the agent, see the maps, and plans' and then 'conclude to go or stay' (300). Sure enough, when they reach the office, a map of Eden, 'a great plan which occupied one whole side of the office', catches his eye (304). Eden comes across as a 'flourishing city', an 'architectural city!' where there are 'banks, churches, cathedrals, market-places, factories, hotels, stores, mansions, wharves; an exchange, a theatre; public buildings of all kinds, down to the office of the *Eden Stinger*, a daily journal; all faithfully depicted in the view before them' (307). The original illustration by Phiz, 'The Thriving City of Eden as it Appeared on Paper', shows Martin and Mark standing enthralled in front of the map, while the emigration agent, Scadder – a gaunt man with a knowing smirk around his mouth – lurks in the background, smoking his pipe. The map of Eden is not unusual in any way – like many of the maps of new settlements, it has a planned infrastructure and well developed roads.[24] There are signs for a botanical garden, school, cemetery, hospital, theatre, chapel, wharf, baths and river. Predictably, at the centre of the town is a church and water pump. Yet when they reach Eden, the 'monotonous desolation of the scene' strikes them:

> A flat morass, bestrewn with fallen timber; a marsh on which the good growth of the earth seemed to have been wrecked and cast away, that from its decomposing ashes vile and ugly things might rise; where the very trees took the aspect of huge weeds, begotten of the slime from which they were sprung, by the hot sun that burnt them up; where fatal maladies, seeking whom they might infect, came forth at night, in misty shapes, and creeping out upon the water, hunted them like spectres until day; where even the blessed sun, shining down on festering elements of corruption and disease, became a horror; this was the realm of Hope through which they moved. (325)

The accompanying illustration by Phiz, 'The Thriving City of Eden as it Appeared in Fact', shows a dejected Martin, sitting next to a log stump with a few sketches on it, with his head in his hands looking out over the swamp. In true settler mode, Mark grips onto the branch of a tree, with an axe in his left hand, as if he is about to start felling the tree. Two notices on the two log huts behind them show that one is the office of 'Chuzzlewit & Co. Architects and Surveyors' and the other is the 'Bank and National Credit Office'. Amidst the gloom of the swamp, these two log huts are the only references to the organised, 'thriving' city that Martin and Mark saw on the map of Eden in Scadder's office. The irony of the situation is clear – apart from a couple of trees in the background, there is nothing to fell and no land to clear, because most of it is swampy marshland, unfit for settlement.

In Scadder's office, Mark realises that the map is a poor semblance of the truth when Scadder admits that the market-place – and indeed, many of the public buildings – 'ain't built' yet (307). 'The soil being very fruitful, public buildings grow spontaneous, perhaps' (307), Mark comments sarcastically, hoping to draw Martin's attention to the contradictions in Scadder's account of Eden. Scadder, in fact, is not an outright cheat. He tells Martin the truth when Martin asks if there are 'several architects there', answering that there 'ain't a single one' (307). He is reluctant to sell them the land, 'at one time requesting them to think of it, and call again in a week or a fortnight; at another, predicting that they wouldn't like it; at another, offering to retract and let them off, and muttering strong imprecations upon the folly of the General' (308-9). Martin's own preliminary caution, and Mark's subsequent distrust, show that the two participate in the culture of suspicion that emigration literature produced and was embedded in. Yet this does not prevent Martin from being misled: he buys into the version of Eden that the map projects notwithstanding all the markers around him.

The map of Eden fits into a wider concern of the novel on the nature of texts and their ability to seduce the reader into believing that they are true. Merry, Pecksniff's younger daughter, tries to pacify her drunken husband Jonas that she has been reading 'all night long' while sitting up for him: 'The strangest story, Jonas! And true, the book says'. Jonas replies:

> 'Was there anything in it about a man's being determined to conquer his wife, break her spirit, bend her temper, crush all her humours like so many nutshells? [. . .] That'll be a true story though, before long; for all the book says nothing about it. It's a lying book, I see. A fit book for a lying reader.' (395)

By their very nature, books can seduce people into buying and believing them. On his visit to Salisbury, Tom Pinch takes a walk among the markets and shops, only to come across bookshops, 'whence a pleasant smell of paper freshly pressed came issuing forth':

> And in the window were the spick-and-span new works from London, with the title-pages, and sometimes even the first page of the first chapter, laid wide open: tempting unwary men to begin to read the book, and then, in the impossibility of turning over, to rush blindly in, and buy it! (64)

The notion of men being seduced by the materiality of the book and 'rushing blindly in' to buy it shows how the commodity status of the book is secured through the book's appeal to the senses. The first part of this book established that the authenticity effect played an integral part in the commodification of emigrants' letters. The first and third chapters have shown that the fear of misinformation is a constant theme of emigration literature: *Martin Chuzzlewit* continues the idea of the misrepresentations and anxieties in print and relates them to the context of emigration.

If the map of Eden sets into circulation one set of images of the place, Martin sets another going upon his return, talking about it 'in pretty strong terms' (459). In doing so, Martin participates in the oral round of narratives that led him to emigrate in the first place. The map is the only piece of 'information' that Martin reads in his decision to emigrate. He reads little else by way of handbooks, letters or guides. Interestingly, however, much of the information and ideas that he gleans is through word of mouth and through stories of *oral* communication. It is significant, for example, that a few pages before he decides to up and leave for America, he hears John Westlock say that 'I feel sorry that I didn't yield to an impulse I often had, as a boy, of running away from him [Pecksniff] and going abroad.' When Martin questions, 'Why abroad?', Westlock replies, 'In search [. . .] of the livelihood that I couldn't have earned at home. There would have been something spirited in that' (174). Martin's sudden decision to emigrate is driven no doubt by his own desire to carry out something as 'spirited'. A few pages later, after he takes his decision to travel to America, he comes across a coach guard who tells him of a certain 'Lummy Ned of the Light Salisbury' who 'had set up in the public line here, and couldn't meet his engagements, so he cut off to Liverpool one day, without saying anything about it, and went and shipped himself for the U-nited States' (189). Martin takes a 'sudden interest' (188), and asks the coach guard 'several questions', all of which are of practical importance, such as

> how long had the fortunate guard of the Light Salisbury been in crossing the Atlantic; at what time of year he had sailed; what was the name of the ship in which he had made the voyage; how much had he paid for the passage-money; did he suffer greatly from sea-sickness? (189)

The coach guard provides ready answers, but unbeknown to Martin, 'his friend possessed little or no information' on 'these points of detail'; thus 'either answering obviously at random, or acknowledging that he had never heard, or had forgotten' (189). The circulation of oral narratives of emigration is also evidently important, but the novel registers the ways in which these can be just as false as textual ones. Achieving total objectivity when it comes to representing distant places, and producing an objective account of how to emigrate are almost impossible. There is not a single source in the novel that Martin goes to that provides him with the correct information.

Martin's emigration to America fails in material terms, and '[i]n health and fortune, prospect and resource, they came back poorer men than they had gone away' (471). Nonetheless, the trip has a lasting influence on his character and outlook on life. Firstly, he learns how not to be selfish in America. The 'knowledge of himself' and his selfishness finally dawns upon him. '[I]n the hideous solitude of that most hideous place', 'he felt and knew the failing of his life, and saw distinctly what an ugly spot it was'. 'Eden was a hard school to learn so hard a lesson in; but there were teachers in the swamp and thicket, and the pestilential air, who had a searching method of their own' (452). Secondly, moving away from England teaches Martin the value of being at home and what home actually means:

> Often at night when Mark and Martin were alone, and lying down to sleep, they spoke of home, familiar places, houses, roads, and people whom they knew; sometimes in the lively hope of seeing them again, and sometimes with a sorrowful tranquillity, as if that hope were dead. (454)

He realises that 'though home is a name, a word, it is a strong one; stronger than magician ever spoke, or spirit answered to, in strongest conjuration' (471). Here, Dickens is clearly drawing on the homesickness he experienced on his trip to America. In May, a couple of months before he arrived back home, he wrote to John Forster,

> As the time draws nearer, we get FEVERED with anxiety for home . . . Kiss our darlings for us. We shall soon meet, please God, and be happier and merrier than ever we were, in all our lives . . . Oh home-home-home-home-home-home-HOME!!!!!!!!!!!![25]

While Martin's settlement may have failed in material terms, nonetheless it has taught him important lessons which have a greater staying power.

Thus, in his depiction of Eden in the America chapters of *Martin Chuzzlewit*, Dickens draws upon stock characters and tropes in the literary culture of settler emigration. We need only to cast half a glance backwards over this book to discover that Dickens's character and tropes in *Martin Chuzzlewit*, such as the scheming Land Company, the lying agents, the false representations of settlements are all motifs that occur again and again in emigration literature. Think, for example, of James and Harriot Parks in the first chapter of this book who warn against further family members relying on 'Mr Becks' if they want any edible food on the voyage out, or of the third chapter, where Moodie expresses her intense dislike of Cattermole for circulating propaganda in her home town. Thus, while the emigration scenes of *Martin Chuzzlewit* are a critique of America and its institutions, they simultaneously register a wider preoccupation at the time surrounding the veracity of emigration literature and its ability to project visions of places that readers had no practical experience of.

David Copperfield: Textual Connections

By the time Dickens finished *David Copperfield* in November 1850, Urania Cottage, his home for fallen women, had been running for about three years. Dickens's vision of emigration as a successful means of rehabilitating fallen women into society clearly shapes the novel's plot: at the end of the novel, Little Em'ly and Martha both emigrate along with Mr Peggotty, leaving behind their old lives to start new ones in Australia. After moving from job to job, and successfully exposing Uriah Heep for fraud, Mr Micawber is once more left unemployed. He emigrates out with his family on the same ship as the Peggottys on the suggestion of David's aunt, Betsy Trotwood, and with her financial support.

As in *Mary Barton*, where Canada affords Jem and Mary the anonymity they need to begin their lives again, so too in *David Copperfield*, Australia provides Little Em'ly and Martha with an opportunity for fresh starts. 'Our future life,' Mr Peggotty informs David, 'lays over the sea': 'No one can't reproach my darling in Australia. We will begin a new life over theer!'[26] Sure enough, Little Em'ly finds her calling on board the ship. She takes care of 'some poor folks aboard [the ship] as had illness among 'em' and of the 'children in our company' (846). In the colony, this transforms into a way of life: she is 'fond of going any distance fur to teach a child, or fur to tend a sick person [and] liked by young and old; sowt out by all that has any trouble' (847). Moving to Australia may be a means of removing herself from the dangers of falling back into her old way of life, but even in the colonies, she remains apart from the other settlers. She lives with Mr Peggotty 'in a solitary place, but among the beautifullest trees, and with the roses a-covering our Beein to the roof' (847). As Mr Peggotty points out, 'the solitoode done her good', for 'No one knows how 'tis' that Em'ly is so young and unmarried (847). Like her literary sister Ruth in Gaskell's *Ruth*, Little Em'ly is exiled from married life and instead carves herself out a different trajectory in order to redeem herself. Her removal from society to the backwoods symbolises her new-found purity, as a nurse and teacher. She is fundamental to the development and continuity of her community. Martha marries a 'young man, a farm-laborer' (847) in her second year and settles down to become a hard-working farmer's wife in the bush, but she too, lives far removed from society 'fower hundred mile away from any voices but their own and the singing birds' (848). The solitude that marks the lives of these fallen women in the colonies is a stark contrast to the busy, public life of Mr Micawber. He begins life as a labourer 'in the Bush', 'turning to' the land 'with a will', 'that theer bald head of his, a perspiring in the sun' (849). He works his way up the social ladder to become 'a Magistrate' in 'Port Middlebay Harbor [. . .] a town' (849) and a 'diligent and esteemed correspondent' for the colonial periodical *Port Middlebay Times* (849).

Unlike *Martin Chuzzlewit* and *Mary Barton*, *David Copperfield* is written in first-person narrative. As David does not emigrate himself, he cannot describe Australia for the reader, nor can he narrate the settler's experience through a projected gaze. As David notices, the issue of the *Port Middlebay Times* contains two of Micawber's letters, 'an advertisement of a collection of similar letters by him, to be shortly republished, in a neat volume, "with considerable additions;" and [. . .] the Leading Article was his also' (851). The newspaper reports a social dinner which Micawber's family have attended. They appear to have settled well: his eldest child, Wilkins, and his daughter are both married and hold good positions in society.

In the face of his earlier incompetence, Micawber's success in Australia has been understood by some critics as a fantastical and unrealistic solution. Moore, for example, argues that 'Dickens seems to equate success in the colonies with some kind of colossal bluff':

> For the impecunious Micawbers it [Australia] is a place where they can effortlessly prosper, and where Mr Micawber's empty rhetoric can achieve a success that it would never have found in his English existence. Thus, the prosperity of the Micawbers, the Peggottys and even Mr Mell on the one hand confirms the popular belief that emigration would lead to prosperity, while on the other, the sheer absurdity of the resolution is ironic.[27]

For Moore, Micawber's success in the colonies is neither real nor reproducible: it is a farce of a resolution. In *Postal Plots*, Laura Rotunno argues that Micawber 'fails' to rise to the 'position of respected writer – the position reserved for the eponymous hero of the novel'.[28] Although Rotunno states that his letters are 'culturally significant' because they conform to a long tradition of letter-writing that stretches back to the eighteenth century, she does not make a connection between Micawber's letter-writing and his successful settlement in Australia.

Micawber is a prolific letter-writer, who dominates many of the scenes in the novels through his epistolary, rather than bodily, presence. 'Letters!' marvels David's aunt, 'I believe he dreams in letters!' (775). As this book has demonstrated, letters and periodical culture are integral parts of the emigrant experience. Circulating in both personal and public networks, letters were important for the maintenance of family relationships and for encouraging potentially curious readers to emigrate. Emigrants during the voyage to Australia performed their settlement on board the ship through an imagined print periodical culture. Emigrant authors, such as Susanna Moodie, turned to colonial periodicals as initial outlets for their literary endeavours.[29] As we saw earlier, even Eden in *Martin Chuzzlewit* has its own periodical, the *Eden Stinger*. When Micawber tells Betsey Trotwood that emigration 'was the dream of my youth, and the fallacious aspiration of my riper years' (743), David thinks with wry amusement that Micawber 'had never thought of it [emigration] in his life' (743). While Micawber may not have done so, nonetheless, his letters pre-empt the idea of home and settlement in a number of different ways.

In one of his letters to David, he writes that he is 'bidding adieu to the modern Babylon' and is 'about to establish myself in one of the provincial towns of our favoured island, (where the society may be described as a happy admixture of the agricultural and the clerical)' (514). The description that he gives of a town which is part agricultural, part clerical and in a provincial area could well be taken to refer to a settlement in Sydney or Melbourne, but in actual fact, he is going to move to Canterbury: 'It may be expected that on the eve of a migration which will consign us to a perfectly new existence [. . .] I should offer a few valedictory remarks to two such friends as I see before me' (520). In a later letter, Mrs Micawber takes up the language of emigration and settlement in another context, when she writes to David that 'The pecuniary means of meeting our expenses, kept down to the utmost farthing, are obtained from him with great difficulty, and even under fearful threats that he will Settle himself (the exact expression)' (609). Dickens plays on the word 'settle': while Mrs Micawber's use of it refers to Micawber's potential suicide, the verb also speaks of the future when Micawber will indeed be settled in Australia and will turn his literary skills into fame and fortune. Thus, even before his move to Australia, Micawber considers himself as an emigrant, an itinerant figure needing to establish himself.

Given all of this, it is entirely appropriate that, as an emigrant, Micawber should become a letter-writer of some acclaim in a flourishing Australian periodical. His success and appearance in print at the end of the novel is a culmination of what has been the novel's subtext all along. In his own way, Mr Peggotty is also as successful as Micawber. 'We've allus thrived,' he explains to David.

> We've worked as we ought to't, and maybe we lived a leetle hard at first or so, but we have allus thrived. What with sheep-farming, and what with stock-farming, and what with one thing and what with t'other, we are as well to do, as well could be. (846)

Both *Mary Barton* and *David Copperfield* reproduce the familiar narrative trajectory that equates emigration with success. There is, however, something curiously banal about how Gaskell and Dickens construct emigration in their novels. Rather than probing the central features of emigration literature, the two authors reproduce in their novels stock images such as the successful emigrant and the hardworking sheep farmer that emigration literature set into circulation. The novel thus draws on the tropes of emigration literature in order to shape its own aesthetics and discourse on emigration. While it may not be a form of booster literature, nonetheless, this re-circulation of emigration motifs in the novel reaffirms particular ways of thinking about emigration.

Catherine Helen Spence: Shifting the Network

Catherine Helen Spence's literary career embodies the network of the textual and literary connections across the colonial world depicted at the end of *David Copperfield*. Following her father's failed speculation in 'foreign wheat',[30] her family emigrated to South Australia in 1839, when she was only fourteen. From a young age, Spence knew that she 'wanted to be a teacher first, and a great writer afterwards', in this order because the 'qualifications of a teacher would help me to rise to literary fame'.[31] Spence carried these aspirations to South Australia. Within five years of her arriving, she found the 'occasional opportunity'[32] to write in the *South Australian*, her brother-in-law, Andrew Murray's, newspaper. Through Murray's subscription to a 'Reading Club', she also had access to English and Australian newspapers and magazines. Spence's autobiography demonstrates the tension of having a strong British literary heritage but writing in Australia about Australia for a predominantly British audience. She compares her decision to write an autobiography with Margaret Oliphant's, who had been inspired to write her own autobiography after reading the *Life of George Eliot* by John Morley. She aligns herself with Charlotte Brontë, who also had her first novel rejected, but the second one accepted, by Smith, Elder & Co. A great admirer of George Eliot, Spence sought out a meeting with Eliot on her trip to London in 1865, and, despite the meeting not going very well, continued to 'read everything, poetry and prose that came from George Eliot's pen' and lectured on her works at the Mutual Improvement Society at her Unitarian Church. This strong literary interest was coupled with a great concern regarding the welfare of settler women and children. In her autobiography, she writes that 'more important' than accessing literature from Britain 'was the fact that we took hold of the growth and development of South Australia, and identified ourselves with it'.[33] Spence campaigned in Australia, America and Britain for electoral reform and for women's suffrage in Australia; the latter was won in 1895 in South Australia, the same year in which women were allowed to stand for Parliament.[34] Along with Caroline Emily Clarke, she spearheaded plans for rehousing children in the Destitute Asylum with families; she was the first woman on the advisory board for the Education Department, and the first president of the Women's Non-Party Political Association. She was involved in the work of the Women's Land Reform League, Women's National Council, Women's Liberal League, the National Council of Women, and the International Council of Women, amongst other organisations. Her novels reflected her interests in women's rights in the colonies. *Mr Hogarth's Will* (1865), for example, was written so that 'all the world would see how badly capable and industrious women were paid'.[35] This section considers how Spence's first novel, *Clara Morison* (1854), frames Clara's emigration both within the particularities of a gendered, South Australian context and within a global network of print culture.

In *Clara Morison*, the Australian colonies are depicted as hybrid places, with distinctive identities independent of Britain, and part of a globally interconnected world. Clara's uncle writes her letters of introduction from Edinburgh, but upon arrival in South Australia, she finds that they are 'quite valueless'.[36] One is addressed to an acquaintance in Sydney, another in Hobarton, while the third is addressed to a man of 'bad character' who Mr Campbell warns 'you must not know' (28). Writing against this lack of 'knowledge of Australian geography' (28), Spence fills the seemingly homogeneous space of 'Australia' with depictions of inter- and intra-colonial migrations. Following the rush of the 'entire male population' to the diggings in Melbourne, there are '[n]one but women and children to be seen everywhere' in South Australia (iv). A Jewish man, Mr Samuels, replaces the German lodger, Mr Haussen, at Mrs Handy's house. Withering compares South Australia to India, announcing that she should 'prefer' India of the two (98). The Victorian gold rush is pulled into comparison with the Californian one through Mr Handy, who 'had gone to California on a gold-hunting expedition' (29). By situating the relationship between metropole and colony within a wider network of colonial and global relationships, Spence writes against the notion of the Australian colonies as a geographical nowhere and instead depicts them as being embedded within their very own geographical nexus. Tellingly, in Spence's second novel, *Tender and True* (1856), Australia retains its identity as a specific location and it is Natal that becomes the country to which characters disappear: 'disgusted with Adelaide', Marshall decides to emigrate there, even though he doesn't 'know much about it'.[37]

Spence's assertion of the distinct geographical identities of South Australia exists alongside her efforts to articulate the colony's modernity by claiming its synchronicity with the print rhythms of Britain. Clara is an avid reader: she 'knew what book such a thing was in, what part of the book, and almost at what page' (2). Having expected the colonies to be barren of a reading culture, she brightens at the thought of being able to 'get a sight of Dickens' works here' (34). Clara and Reginald bond over a shared love of literature, talking about Scott, Carlyle and Macaulay for example. Reginald's boast of being able to read 'the newest works of Dickens, Bulwer and Thackeray' in the colony (34) shows that despite the distance and time it takes for things to be shipped out, the colonies are on the same temporal rhythm as Britain. Spence reiterates this in her autobiography:

> I recollect a newcomer being astonished at my sister Mary having read Macaulay's *History*. 'Why, it was only just out when I left England,' said he. 'Well, it did not take longer to come out than you did,' was her reply.[38]

In *Time and the Other*, Johanne Fabian argues that communities that have different temporal rhythms from those of the metropolitan centre are often labelled 'primitive'. As we have seen in the first chapter, emigrants writing back home to their families were at pains to portray the colonies as vibrant places, where they could purchase the newest things.[39] In a similar vein, as though she were trying to allay criticisms of the colonies as 'backward' or primitive places, Spence asserts that South Australia is connected to Britain through its synchronicity with global print rhythms.

Yet despite wanting to mediate the sense of South Australia as a distinctive locality, with its own spatial and temporal co-ordinates, to her predominantly British audience through her novels, *in* her novels Spence questions the extent to which places can be effectively mediated through text. As with *Martin Chuzzlewit*, *Clara Morison* picks up on the contradictory and often confusing nature of emigration literature. On her voyage out, the Captain and Mrs Whitby 'talked of the colony of South Australia with raptures', but when Clara hears that their trip out with her is their first one, she feels that 'their praises were no recommendation' (7). Eager for extra information, she 'read every book that she could procure about the colony she was bound for, but the accounts were so contradictory, that she came to no conclusion' (7–8). Reginald's reference to 'Mrs Todgers', the lady of the boarding house in *Martin Chuzzlewit* where the Pecksniffs stay while in London, suggests Spence's awareness that she is taking part in a larger conversation about the cultural place of emigration literature and its mediation of both place and lived experience. That the Captain and his wife can talk about Australia as though they have been there, from their reading alone, gestures towards the vitality of emigration literature but also the slippages that occur between oral and textual narratives, and between read and lived experience. Eager for information on how her son is faring, 'Mrs Reginald reads every description of colonial news, from the Adelaide newspapers which her son sent her, to the shorter notices of the colonies given by the London journals'. Her conclusion is that 'Charles was quite lost at a sheep station in South Australia' (187). The first time that Minnie visits Reginald in the bush, she marvels at his 'palace of a sheep-station', which is replete with 'books, pictures, fireirons' and wanting only 'picture-hangings and a carpet'.[40] Yet none of this homeliness – sense of place – comes across to Mrs Reginald. Despite reading all that she is able to about Australian sheep stations, and receiving Reginald's sketches of neighbourhood and the 'full weight of foreign post well filled' from him (45), she is none the wiser about the specificities of his sheep station. Reginald remains 'lost' to her in a geographical abstraction.

Rather than positing a binary relationship where the 'home' and the 'world' have fixed, stable markers, the novel instead builds a more complex relationship between the two through its depiction of the Great Exhibition. Clara maintains that the Great Exhibition is a place where her sister Susan can go to 'see the world', she herself is 'seeing life' in Australia: the 'world' is both far away from London, but, in an expression of colonial might, it also *is* London (93). In *Globalization and the Great Exhibition*, Paul Young argues that the Exhibition's 'national form of segregation', 'made perfect capitalist sense' and 'allowed for the study and comparison of individual nations', not just individual exhibits.[41] Australia certainly became a huge market for Britain in terms of wool, but Spence's emphasis is not so much on international trade as it is on the settlers' awareness that they, and by extension, the colony of South Australia, are part of 'so wonderful a display' (57) for the rest of the world to see. Dent cannot contain his pride when he announces that the 'Burra malachite is not to be despised even in the world's fair' (188). Harris laments that it is 'a thousand pities' that the 'monster' nugget of gold could not have been sent in time for the Exhibition, for it would have been 'the greatest wonder in the Exhibition', overshadowing the other 'articles near it' (137). Although South Australia is both the 'world' as experienced by Clara and represented in the Great Exhibition, it is also the 'locality' in which Dent finds Mrs Reginald: 'I have no doubt, from the locality in which I find you, that you are the mother of my friend, Charles Reginald, of Taringa, in the north' (189). 'Locality' here means more than the specific region of South Australia: it refers to the kind of affective 'knowing' that is based upon personal experiences and connections that were explored in the third chapter of this book. Upon seeing Escott's wool, Langton claims that he should 'know it among a thousand' (188) and notices that Escott 'still has Humberstone with him'. Overhearing this, Mrs Reginald is struck by the fancy that some of the wool may have been sent by Charles: 'Can there be any of Charles's wool in the Exhibition?' she asks Julia (188). In much the same way as with the emigrants' tokens discussed in the first chapter of this book, the material objects in the Exhibition are a means of providing a connection between Mrs Reginald and her son. We have already seen how the geographical mobility of texts opens up contested spaces of representation, and as Peter Hoffenberg notes, the sheer fact of '[d]istance made some Australian exhibits seem exotic' at the Great Exhibition.[42] Yet the South Australian exhibits in Spence's novel are not made foreign through the distance they travel: their distinctive sense of locality travels *with* them, so that they are immediately recognisable to Dent and so that it is possible for Mrs Reginald to imagine an affinitive connection through them to her son. Spence thus rewrites the Great Exhibition as a site of local connections so that the event is less about exhibiting Britain's colonial possessions than it is about the colonies articulating their sense of being at home in the metropolitan centre. In *Clara Morison*, then, Spence interrogates the complex networks of print and material culture in the context of settler emigration, even as she straddles the divide in writing out of an Australian context for a predominantly British audience.

'Merely Crossing': Emigration Literature and the Novel

Thus far, this chapter has explored the way in which Gaskell, Dickens and Spence drew upon emigration literature to shape their own novels. In their different ways, they examine the different ways in which the circulation of emigration literature produces moments of emigration. In this section, I want to consider how the depiction of the global circulation of emigration literature produces a distinct spatial imaginary in the novels discussed so far. Before Mr Peggotty in *David Copperfield* leaves David for Australia, the two of them 'spoke, with some approach to cheerfulness, of Mr Peggotty's growing rich in a new country, and of the wonders he would describe in his letters' (717). However, David comes to know of how his former friends are faring, not through personal correspondence, but because Mr Peggotty travels all the way back to England to see him and his family with an issue of the *Port Middlebay Times*. Through its depiction of the print and textual networks produced out of emigration, the novel examines the relationships between Britain and the colonies. It depicts a world in which geographically distant places are only partially interconnected through the global mechanisms of print circulation (i.e. the shipping of newspapers from one country to another, or the establishment of printing presses abroad). Local instances of coincidence and chance meetings are also just as important in sustaining relationships over time and space in the context of resettlement.

David's literary fame is such that news of it has reached Australia. Mr Peggotty 'points' to where Micawber has published a public letter of appreciation directly addressed to David:

> My dear Sir,
> [. . .] though estranged (by the force of circumstances over which I have had no control) from the personal society of the friend and companion of my youth, I have not been unmindful of his soaring flight [. . .] Go on, my dear sir! You are not unknown here, you are not unappreciated [. . .] Go on, my dear sir, in your Eagle course! The Inhabitants of Port Middlebay may at least aspire to watch it, with delight, with entertainment, with instruction! (851)

This is Micawber's first letter to David since he has emigrated, and in a curious inversion, he writes him a personal note via public means. The notion that David is not 'unknown' or 'unappreciated' and that the 'inhabitants' of Port Middlebay will continue to follow his 'soaring flight' demonstrates David's global reach, and the power of the print market to keep different parts of the globe connected by providing a common reading base.

David comes to hear of other characters aside from Micawber through the issue of the *Port Middlebay Times* that Mr Peggotty brings back to him. David is 'pleased' to see 'the name of Doctor Mell' in the paper, the 'formerly poor pinched usher to my Middlesex magistrate' (850). But the novel imagines the circulation of print in broader terms as well. Just as colonial newspapers find their way back to England and the figures are instantly recognisable to those who read it, so too in the colony do people carry English newspapers that are instantly recognisable to settlers. Mr Peggotty explains how he and Little Em'ly come to hear of the death of Steerforth, the man who seduces Little Em'ly.

> Theer come along one day, when I was out a-working on the land, a traveller from our own Norfolk or Suffolk in England (I don't rightly mind which), and of course we took him in, and giv him to eat and drink, and made him welcome. We all do that, the colony over. (847)

The traveller who comes to their home in Australia has 'an old newspaper with him, and some other account in print of the storm' in which Steerforth dies: this is how Little Em'ly comes to hear of it

(847). The novel thus imagines print to connect characters into a wider network than their face-to-face contacts, but it almost never portrays print flowing smoothly through its routes of global circulation. More often than not characters become caught up in this wider network because other characters travel between places and bring printed texts with them. In other words, the novel imagines print as being portable in the proper sense of the word: characters move with text, and as the mobile text begins to circulate, it forges new connections.

David Copperfield thus imagines how the colonies and Britain are enmeshed in a network of portable print. This emphasis on circulation produces a very distinct spatial imaginary. In the same way that emigration literature, the letters, and the handbooks and manuals, for example, all try to produce a certain aesthetics of place, where the colonies are like home, or are very far away from home, the novel posits a more confused and confusing relationship between the colonies and Britain. Moore argues that:

> the fact that Dickens never saw this country [Australia] – to which he exiled two of his own sons – gave it a strangely illusory quality that made it both real, and yet not real. As a result there is something not quite real about the lives of the characters he ships off to the settlement, and the wealth that they accumulate. In *David Copperfield*, for instance, Dickens seems to equate success in the colony with some kind of colossal bluff [. . .] and suggests an authorial warning that the Australia Dickens depicts is, quite literally, a utopia – a no-such-place.[43]

As I have argued above, the novel reads as more of an endorsement of the familiar images of emigration, rather than a critique of it. If Australia is a utopia in the novel, it is no more a utopia than it is in emigration literature. In the same way, the spatial interconnections between the colonies and home in the novels are troubled and curiously morphed. The idea of the colony as an abstract, fictional place is pressed upon the reader through Micawber's actions after he makes the decision to emigrate. David notices that Micawber 'practises' for Australia before he goes:

> Shall I ever recall that street of Canterbury on a market-day, without recalling him, as he walked back with us; expressing, in the hardy roving manner he assumed, the unsettled habits of a temporary sojourner in the land; and looking at the bullocks, as they came by, with the eye of an Australian farmer! (745)

A few pages later, David makes a similar observation:

> Mr Micawber [. . .] in his adaptation of himself to a new state of society, had acquired a bold buccaneering air, not absolutely lawless, but defensive and prompt. One might have supposed him a child of the wilderness, long accustomed to live out of the confines of civilisation, and about to return to his native wilds. (782)

Both these quotations show that Micawber *acts* emigration out. In the same way that the emigrants on board the *Alfred* and *True Briton* perform settlement on board the ship in order to prepare themselves for the actual task of settlement in Australia, so too for Mr Micawber emigration is something that can be performed and practised prior to the actual event. Emigration can be lived as a fiction before it becomes a fact. The fictionalising of emigration, however, results in a curious morphing of geographical distance.

In the novel, distance is recognised for what it is only when Mr Peggotty admits that 'It's a mort of water [. . .] fur to come across, and on'y stay a matter of fower weeks' (846). Before they emigrate, the Micawbers are convinced that they will not only return, but that their emigration will not cause the cutting of relations with England. Mrs Micawber reminds her husband that he is 'going out [. . .] to this distant clime, to strengthen, not to weaken, the connexion between yourself and Albion' (787). When David tries to dissuade Micawber from emigrating to Australia, on account of the fact that it is a very long way away, he muses that 'It is merely crossing [. . .] merely crossing. The distance is quite imaginary'. David recalls,

> how odd it was, but how wonderfully like Mr Micawber, that, when he went from London to Canterbury, he should have talked as if he were going to the farthest limits of the earth; and, when he went from England to Australia, as if he were going for a little trip across the channel. (787)

This distortion of distance occurs in *Mary Barton* as well: when Mary leaves Manchester for the first time in her life, as she starts her search for Jem, she feels an overwhelming sense of loss as the train pulls out of the station: 'She was losing sight of the familiar objects of her childhood for the first time; and unpleasant as those objects are to most, she yearned after them with some of the same sentiment which gives pathos to the thoughts of the emigrant' (282-3). When Jem decides that he wants to leave Manchester, he says that he'd 'as lief' leave England as well and go to Canada (376). Spence draws upon a similar sentiment in *Clara Morison* and *Tender and True*. When both Clara and Susan exclaim that Australia is a long way to go, her uncle pushes aside their concerns, arguing, 'What matter for distance? [. . .] If Clara were to take a situation at all, you must be separated; the greater the distance the better for her' (3). In *Tender and True*, Mary's husband Marshall assures her that Australia is 'just like England, only a little hotter'.[44] In these novels, the colony and England are not separate, distinct places. Instead, in the spatial imagination of the characters they morph into each other, so that places within England are imagined as distant from each other and the colonies are imagined as proximate.

In the novels discussed in this chapter, emigration is far from an escape strategy on the part of the authors, an easy means of resolving difficult plots or characters. Such arguments not only undermine the literary skill of the authors, but they also fail to acknowledge the social context within which they were writing. Emigration was clearly intensely important to both Gaskell and Dickens as a legitimate means of philanthropy, and to all three authors as a legitimate subject of fiction. If emigration literature set into circulation a certain way of conceiving settlement in the colonies, then Gaskell's, Dickens's and Spence's novels took up these representations: the repetition of certain themes in their novels solidifies this way of conceiving emigration. Yet this was not an unthinking absorption of the world around the authors: at the same time as drawing on the motifs of emigration literature, the authors also turn emigration literature into a motif. In their novels, the textual culture of emigration becomes a site for the interrogation of what it means to inhabit a wider world and to be connected to friends and family in distant places through text. Their novels take up emigration literature's preoccupation with settlement in new and distant places. As the first half of this book has demonstrated, emigration literature produced its colonial ideology through its skewed spatial relations. Over and again, emigration literature tried to make the unfamiliar familiar, and to make the far away near. Wherever possible, it concentrated on the similarities between Britain and the colonies in order to collapse the sense of geographical distance. Yet at the same time, given the immense finality of most people's migrations in the nineteenth century, emigration literature could not deny that the distance between emigrants and their families in Britain was also insurmountable. When it comes to representing emigration, the novels discussed in this chapter owe their distortion of distance to emigration literature. The distortion of distance in the novel captures the complex ways in which emigration and its literature reverberated across other cultural modes of expression. As a genre of the nation, it makes sense that the novel imagines the textual and print culture of emigration as integral to this process of establishing a knowable community within the context of the global network of the British Empire.

Notes

1. Charles Dickens, *Martin Chuzzlewit*, ed. Margaret Cardwell (Oxford: Oxford University Press, 1998 [1844]), p. 299. All further quotations from this book are taken from this edition and referenced in-text, unless otherwise stated.
2. Elizabeth Gaskell, *Mary Barton*, ed. Macdonald Daly (London: Penguin, 1996 [1848]), p. 392. All further quotations from this book are taken from this edition and referenced in-text, unless otherwise stated.
3. See, for example, Gaskell's letters to her American friend, Charles Eliot Norton: Elizabeth Gaskell, *The Letters of Mrs Gaskell*, ed. J. A. V. Chapple and Arthur Pollard (Manchester: Mandolin, 1997). pp. 606–11 (5 April 1860).
4. Thomas Carlyle, *Chartism*, 2nd edn (London: James Fraser, 1842), p. 112. For more information on Carlyle's changing views on emigration, see Bossche, *Carlyle and the Search for Authority*, pp. 96–7 and pp. 114–15.
5. Carlyle, *Chartism*, p.112.
6. Williams, *The Country and the City*, p. 404; Lynette Felber, 'Gaskell's Industrial Idylls: Ideology and Formal Incongruence in *Mary Barton* and *North and South*', *Clio* 18 (1988), pp. 55–72 (p. 60); Grace Moore, *Dickens and Empire: Discourses of Class, Race and Colonialism in the Works of Charles Dickens* (Aldershot: Ashgate, 2004), p. 11.
7. Suvendrini Perera, *Reaches of Empire: The English Novel from Edgeworth to Dickens* (New York: Columbia University Press, 1991), p. 52.
8. Ibid. p. 52.
9. See Suzanne Daly, 'Mechanization, Free Trade, and Imperialism: Cotton', in *The Empire Inside*, pp. 36–60; Elaine Freedgood, 'Coziness and Its Vicissitudes: Checked Curtains and Global Cotton Markets in *Mary Barton*', in *The Ideas in Things*, pp. 55–80. For a more general reading of the commodity world in Gaskell's industrial novels, see Christoph Lindner, *Fictions of Commodity Culture: From the Victorian to the Postmodern* (Aldershot: Ashgate, 2003), pp. 17–41.
10. Carlyle, *Chartism*, pp. 112–13.
11. Claire Tomalin, *Charles Dickens: A Life* (London: Penguin, 2011), p. 127. The resulting works were *American Notes* and *Martin Chuzzlewit*. To cover the expenses of the trip to America, Dickens was paid in advance for 'the American book and the Monthly Work'. See Charles

Dickens, *The Letters of Charles Dickens: 1842–1843*, ed. Madeline House, Graham Storey and Kathleen Tillotson, 12 vols (Clarendon: Oxford, 1965–2002), iii (1974), p. 1 (1 January 1842).
12. Charles Dickens, *American Notes for General Circulation*, ed. Patricia Ingham (London: Penguin, 2000 [1842]), p. 244. All further quotations from this book are taken from this edition and referenced in-text, unless otherwise stated.
13. Oliver MacDonagh has three chapters charting the changes made to legislation of the Passenger Acts during the 1840s in *A Pattern of Government Growth, 1800–1860: The Passenger Acts and their Enforcement* (London: MacGibbon & Kee, 1961), pp. 138–221.
14. Nancy Aycock Metz, '"Fevered with Anxiety for Home": Nostalgia and the "New" Emigrant in *Martin Chuzzlewit*', *Dickens Quarterly* 18 (2001), pp. 49–61 (p. 60).
15. Ibid. pp. 51–2.
16. Dickens, *Letters*, iii, p. 10 (3 January 1842).
17. Ibid. p. 151 (22 March 1842).
18. Tomalin, *Charles Dickens*, p. 127.
19. Dickens, *Letters*, iii, p. 257 (7 July 1842).
20. See Robert McParland, *Charles Dickens's American Audience* (Plymouth: Lexington, 2010) for a study of Dickens's critical reception in America, particularly pp. 67–82.
21. Tomalin, *Charles Dickens*, p. 141.
22. Ibid. p. 141.
23. Metz, '"Fevered with Anxiety"', p. 52.
24. Phiz's illustration of Eden is similar to the maps that John Galt drew for his city, Guelph.
25. Dickens, *Letters*, iii, p. 248 (26 May 1842).
26. Charles Dickens, *David Copperfield*, ed. Nina Burgis (Oxford: Oxford University Press, 2008 [1850]), p. 711. All further quotations from this book are taken from this edition and referenced in-text, unless otherwise stated.
27. Grace Moore, *Dickens and Empire: Discourses of Class, Race and Colonialism in the Works of Charles Dickens* (Aldershot: Ashgate, 2004), p. 12.
28. Laura Rotunno, *Postal Plots in British Fiction, 1840–1898: Readdressing Correspondence in Victorian Culture* (New York: Palgrave Macmillan, 2013), p. 46.
29. For a discussion of the early forms of literature in Australia, see Elizabeth Webby, 'Writers, Printers, Readers: The Production of Australian Literature before 1855', in *The Penguin New Literary History of Australia* (London: Penguin, 1988), pp. 113–25 (p. 113).
30. Catherine Helen Spence, *Ever Yours, C. H. Spence: Catherine Helen Spence's An Autobiography (1825–1910), Diary (1894) and Some Correspondence (1894–1910)*, ed. Susan Magarey and Barbara Wall (Kent Town: Wakefield Press, 2005), p. 26.

31. Ibid. p. 29.
32. Ibid. p. 48.
33. Ibid. p. 49.
34. Spence stood as a candidate in 1897, but was unsuccessful.
35. Spence, *Ever Yours*, p. 78. The novel was initially serialised in the Adelaide magazine, *Weekly Mail*, between 1863 and 1864.
36. Catherine Helen Spence, *Clara Morison: A Tale of South Australia during the Gold Fever*, 2 vols (London: John W. Parker, 1854), i, p. 28. All further references to this novel are made in the text.
37. Catherine Helen Spence, *Tender and True: A Colonial Tale*, 2 vols (London: Smith & Elder, 1856), ii, p. 102.
38. Spence, *Ever Yours*, p. 49.
39. See p. *** in this book.
40. Catherine Helen Spence, *Clara Morison: A Tale of South Australia during the Gold Fever*, 2 vols (London: John W. Parker, 1854), ii, p. 249.
41. Paul Young, *Globalization and the Great Exhibition: The Victorian New World Order* (Hampshire: Palgrave, 2009), p. 67; p. 70.
42. Peter H. Hoffenberg, 'Nothing Very New or Very Showy to Exhibit?: Australia at the Great Exhibition and After', in Jeffrey A. Auerbach and Peter H. Hoffenberg (eds), *Britain, the Empire, and the World at the Great Exhibition of 1851* (Hampshire: Ashgate, 2008), pp. 93–120 (p. 98).
43. Moore, *Dickens and Empire*, p. 12.
44. Catherine Helen Spence, *Tender and True*, i, pp. 199–200.

Conclusion: Structures of Mobility

The legacy of nineteenth-century settler emigration persists well into twentieth- and twenty-first century literary thought and practice. We occupy a world in which migration has lost none of its vigour, its aesthetic or rhetorical appeal. Current debates on migration are as much about national identity, the free movement of labour and capital, and differing contexts of home-making, as they are about national borders, refuge and asylum. Not only has the visual urgency and topicality of migration increased in the media, its cultural politics continues to provide authors and artists with a rich and fascinating source of enquiry. What are the resonances of a study on white settler-colonial emigration which emerges at a time of rampant national debates on global migrations? Perhaps most importantly, writing this book against this contemporary moment has bought home the pressing need to draw out the distinctions between different structures of mobility, the literatures they produce, and the critical framework with which to analyse them. The movements of nineteenth-century settler emigrants, post-1950 diasporic migrants, and contemporary refugees and asylum seekers, for example, are all determined by very different structural dynamics. In turn, these broader categories are marked by internal differences and specificities. Susannah Moodie, for example, who writes against a male tradition of emigration literature in *Roughing It in the Bush* but opens her book with pejorative and condescending comments about the Irish emigrants around her, exposes the nuanced, uneven web of colonial settler migration. Necessarily, attending to the structural specificities of nineteenth-century settler emigration and drawing out the distinctions between different forms of mobility requires a different set of critical vocabulary from that which we use to talk about twentieth- and twenty-first-century emigration.

As this book as demonstrated, nineteenth-century settler emigration had a pervasive and deep-rooted hold on the Victorian cultural imagination, and the lived practicalities of private lives both in Britain and the colonies. It had far-reaching consequences into the twentieth and twenty-first centuries. Exploring the intersections between colonial emigration and its literary outputs provides us with new ways in which to understand and interrogate the complex and varied workings of mid-century empire. It has necessarily entailed interrogating the silences and occlusions of these texts: part of the ethical and political difficulties of researching and writing this book has been the question of how to examine the cultural work of emigration literature without privileging the voice of the settler emigration over that of indigenous peoples. The texts under study here are complicit both in the violence through which settler colonies were made, and the act of colonial erasure: their emphasis on founding new homes in the colonies and in transporting that information back to a British audience makes invisible the violence of and resistance to colonisation and settler emigration. John Absolon's painting, *We Are Out on the Ocean Sailing to our Home Beyond the Deep* (1850), for example, frames the emigrant ship as home and touches upon neither the harsher realities of settler emigration nor the often fraught nature of the passage out. Similarly, emigrants' letters, filled with news about the acres of land which have been bought, almost always make no mention of the colonial violence that leads to the acquisition of these lands. Ironically, it is only when Catherine Helen Spence travels to America, and meets the family of the abolitionist William Lloyd Garrison, that her attention is drawn to the 'injustice and rapacity of the white Caucasians', and she 'began to be a little ashamed of being so narrow in my views on the coloured question':[1] this does not prompt her, however, to question the condition of South Australia as a settler colony.

Throughout this book, I have maintained the 'world-making' potential of emigration literature: the texts of emigration literature did not merely reflect the environments through which it and emigrants moved, but co-constituted this world, producing new environments *as* they moved. In *The Victorian Geopolitical Aesthetic*, Lauren Goodlad writes that 'form is a medium through which transnational processes are encountered, figured, and to some extent influenced'.[2] In *Atlas of the European Novel*, Franco Moretti writes, 'each genre possesses its own space [...] *and each space its own genre*'.[3] This intertwined relationship between literary form, genre and spatial aesthetics is particularly pertinent to the mobile world of emigration literature. As we have seen throughout this book, mobility exerts a pressure on the form and materiality of emigration literature. In their different ways, printed emigrants' letters, manuscript shipboard periodicals and settler accounts are all physical objects that are determined by the condition of being geographically mobile. Printed letters are produced from manuscript ones that travel back to England, shipboard periodicals are produced on the move, and Moodie and Parr Traill's accounts of settlement are produced in Canada, but published in England and enjoy circulation in North America. As is by now well established in contemporary scholarship, print in the nineteenth century is fundamentally mobile. The print market, circulating libraries, second-hand markets and printing presses in the colonies – only some of the mechanisms of circulation in the nineteenth century – all participated in keeping texts moving through overlapping and competing networks. In the context of emigration literature, however, the text's mobility opens up a contested space of interrogation. Through their circulation, emigration literature transferred the reality of one place to another, but, as I have shown throughout this book, this transfer is uneven. As texts that move from one place to another, they become open to suspicion regarding their authenticity. With little to no first-hand knowledge of the distant colonies that emigration literature described, it became difficult for the reader to know whether what they were reading was factually correct or not. Recognising this, editors and authors were keen to assert the materiality of the text and material conditions of their making in order to convince a potentially doubtful reading public of the text's authenticity. As circulating objects negotiating the distance between Britain and the colonies, the texts of emigration literature produce a new, combined aesthetic of mobility and materiality.

In moving through space, the texts of emigration literature also move across different formal and generic boundaries – from manuscript to print and back again, from literary to visual realism, and between the letter and the novel, for example. As this book has demonstrated, each stage of the emigrant experience – the decision to move, the voyage itself, and the process of settling – produces, and is produced by, a proliferation of text. Bringing genres that have hitherto received little, if any, critical attention to light and putting them into conversation with more canonical genres breaks down binaries, not only between textual and visual culture, but also between the genres of textual culture as well. Positioning print against manuscript, word against image, fact against fiction opens up new fields of interrogation and demonstrates the pervasive influence of settler emigration's textual culture. This is testified to by its prevalence in genres and media that are not directly produced out of the practices of settler emigration, such as narrative paintings and novels. When nineteenth-century novels and paintings depict emigration, they do so through the texts of emigration culture, be they maps, periodicals, newspapers or letters. They draw on the tropes of emigration literature – on the image of the hard-working agricultural labourer, on the fear that texts are economical with the truth, and on the extension of kinship ties over space and time. Simultaneously, however, emigration literature becomes a motif in texts that are not directly produced out of the practices of emigration. The novels and narrative paintings discussed in this book draw on the textual culture of emigration in order to probe its cultural impact. Through their representation of the texts of emigration culture, novels and paintings consolidate ways of thinking about the distance between Britain and her colonies produced by emigration literature, and at the same time, produce new ways of thinking about the national place of settler emigration through their engagement with it.

In mediating the boundaries of space and form, emigration literature produces its own distinct hybrid spatial imaginary. 'Exposing the geography'[4] of emigration literature sheds new light on mid-Victorian colonial discourse. The utopian ideals of emigration literature circulate images both of nature abundant in resources, and in need of taming through clearings: on the one hand, the colonies are the perfect place for replicating the British home in miniature; yet on the other hand, the easy portability of home, or its 'transplantability', is belied by the sheer volume of literature instructing emigrants on how to move. While the fact of distance between Britain and the colonies was a vast logistical undertaking for the colonial administration, in emigration literature, the space from Britain across the Atlantic to Canada, or across the Indian Ocean to Australia and New Zealand is a network of complicated exchanges of emotion, texts, peoples and things, rather than a numerical, objective fact. Through its circulation, emigration literature mediated the perceived reality of one place to another, but, as I have shown throughout this book, this mediation is ruptured and troubled. The ambiguous spatial politics of emigration literature, where the colonies are both alike and different from Britain, demonstrates the extent to which emigration literature is fraught with difficulties of its own representation. Examining the simultaneous erasure and enlargement of distance in emigration literature thus shows the importance of spatial hybridity to the complex and multifaceted ideology of settler colonialism, and its provocative and troubled legacies.

Notes

1. Catherine Helen Spence, *Ever Yours*, p. 153, p. 152.
2. Lauren Goodlad, *The Victorian Geopolitical Aesthetic: Realism, Sovereignty, and Transnational Experience* (Oxford: Oxford University Press, 2015), p. 28.
3. Franco Moretti, *Atlas of the European Novel*, p. 35, original emphasis.
4. Doreen Massey, *For Space* (London: Sage, 2005), p. 64.

Bibliography

Manuscript Sources

Alfred: Weekly Magazine of the Emigrant Ship, Alfred, No. 1–2, 12 Oct.–28 Dec. 1839. Sydney, Mitchell Library, A1680: microfilm CY 2072, frames 1–70.

Anon., *Letter Addressed to 'My Dear Children' Giving an Account of a Voyage in the* Orient *from Plymouth to Adelaide in 1863*. Sydney, Australian National Maritime Museum, 00006831.

Blacket, Edmund, *Journal of a Voyage from London to Sydney on the Ship* Eden, *13 June–4 November 1842*. Sydney, Mitchell Library, Z B1596: microfilm CY 2072.

Charlwood, Edward, *The 1863 Shipboard Diary of Edward Charlwood: From England to Australia*, facsim. edn (Warrandyte: Burgewood Books, 2003 [1863]).

Clapham, John, *Diary of his Voyage to Sydney, 1860–1861, with Transcription by Margaret Kentley, 1975*. Sydney, Mitchell Library, MLMSS 6944: microfilm CY 4319.

Clarke, William, *Diary of Emigrant on Board the* Invercargill *and during his First Few Days in New Zealand, Jun.–Oct. 1879*. London, National Maritime Museum, TRN/19.

Claughton, Joseph, *Transcript of the Diary kept by Joseph Claughton during his Voyage to Australia on the Ship* Fanny, *1852, and while at the Gold Diggings in Victoria, 1852–1853*. Sydney, Mitchell Library, MLDOC 366: microfilm CY 4827.

Cornell, Edward, *Journal Kept on Board the Royal Mail Clipper* Red Jacket *from Liverpool to Melbourne, May to Aug. 1856*. London, National Maritime Museum, TRN/20.

Curr, Henry, *Diary: Covering the First Six Weeks of his Voyage from England to Australia on the Full-Rigged Ship* Morning Light *in 1856*. Sydney, Vaughan Evans Library, 3 0001 00014741 5.

Darvall, Eliza Charlotte, *Diary, 8 Sept.–29 Dec. 1839, with biographical note 1968*. Sydney, Mitchell Library, MLMSS 1547: microfilm CY 2978.

Darvall, Emily, *Typescript Extract of Diary of Miss Emily Darvall, Kept during the Voyage of the 'Alfred' from England to Australia in 1839*, in *Thomas Lodge Murray-Prior papers, 1843–1889, together with Miscellaneous Family Papers*. Sydney, Mitchell Library, MLMSS 3117/11 Item 2: microfilm CY 4336.

Edwards, Nicholas Solomon, *Diary of a Voyage to Port Adelaide, South Australia aboard the* Arabian, *22 December 1849–14 March 1850*. Sydney, Mitchell Library, MLMSS 4906: microfilm CY 3422.

Gosling, Francis Alexander, *Journal of a Voyage from London to Sydney on Board the* Alexander *in 1836*. Sydney, Australian National Maritime Museum, 00001689.

Grove, Captain James, *Manuscript Diary on a Voyage from Cork, Ireland, to New South Wales on Board the Wooden Sailing Ship* Eliza *in 1832*. Sydney, Australian National Maritime Museum, 000006850.

Hopkins, James, *Journal of Passenger on the* Schomberg *on her Last Voyage from Liverpool bound to Melbourne, 6 Oct.–26 Dec. 1855*. London, National Maritime Museum, XJOD/1.

Kay, Benjamin, *Diary Kept on* Pestonjee Bomanjee *from London to South Australia* (1838). Sydney, Australian National Maritime Museum, 000016993. Typescript diary held at Sydney, Vaughan Evans Library, REF MS PES <147183>.

Knight, Henry, *Diary 21 November 1852 to 24 April 1853 Made on a Voyage from Gravesend, England to Sydney, New South Wales on the Emigrant Sailing Ship,* Java. Sydney, Mitchell Library, MLMSS 2405/Folder 1X: microfilm MAV/FM3/870.

Lines, Charles Henry, *Papers, 1850–91, including Diary, 15 Aug.–5 Nov. 1852, Kept on a Voyage from Gravesend to Melbourne, on the Clipper* Ballarat. Sydney, Mitchell Library, Z MLMSS 3348: Microfilm CY 3943.

Lovell, John, *Journal Kept by a Crewman, in the Barque* Elizabeth, *taking Emigrants from Bristol to Melbourne, between January and May 1853*. London, National Maritime Museum, JOD/79.

Miller, Thomas F., *Diary Kept by Passenger in the* Walmer Castle, *Gravesend to Melbourne, 9 Nov. 1869–29 Jan. 1870; Melbourne to Tasmania, 30 Jan.–28 Mar. 1870; and returning in the* Lady Jocelyn, *29 Mar.–12 Jul. 1870*. London, National Maritime Museum, MS JOD/180.

Murray, James, *Manuscript Diary on a Voyage from London to Adelaide on Board the Wooden Sailing Ship* Hyderabad *in 1853–54*. Sydney, Australian National Maritime Museum, 000003910.

Oldham, N. *Journal of a Voyage from London to Sydney, on Board the* Bengal, *24 Oct. 1839–21 Feb. 1840*. Sydney, Mitchell Library, Z MLMSS 1303: microfilm CY 2477.

Open Sea: Weekly Journal No. 1–11, 7 July–Sept. 1868, on the ship True Briton. Sydney, Mitchell Library, A1645: microfilm CY 2072, frames 177–249.

Richardson, Arthur, *Emigrant Letters from Arthur Richardson in America to his Family in Springfield, Lurgan, Ireland 1838-1843* (Dublin, National Library of Ireland, MS 46.759).
Saddington, Robert, *Journal of a Voyage from Liverpool to Sydney in the Great Britain Steam Ship, Captain B. R. Mathews in the Autumn of 1853*. Sydney, Australian National Maritime Museum, 00002139.
Severn, Thomas, *Diary on Voyage to Australia and a Letter Written to his Father in England, 1852*. London, National Maritime Museum, PST/42.
Smith, Revd John Jennings, *The Journal of a Voyage to Australia in the Bark* Amelia Thompson, *Captain William Dawson in 1839*. Sydney, Australian National Maritime Museum, 000006039.
Sobraon Occasional Published on Board the Sobraon *during her Outward Voyage to Melbourne, 7 October–26 December 1875*. Sydney, Mitchell Library, MLMSS 7715/Item 1.
Swain, James George Hogg, *Manuscript Diary of a Voyage from England to Sydney in 1859 by a Passenger on the Ship* La Hogue. Sydney, Australian National Maritime Museum, 000018189. Typescript diary held at Sydney, Vaughan Evans Library, REF MS LAH (93148).
Taylor, Francis C., *Journal Kept in the* Stag *on her Voyage from Deptford taking Emigrants to Adelaide, South Australia, Feb.–Jun. 1850*. London, National Maritime Museum, JOD/75.
Wellings, Henry, *Journal, May 27–Sept. 30 1858*. Sydney, Mitchell Library, MLMSS 1963: microfilm CY 1684.
Withers, Alfred, *Diary on* James Baines (1857). London, National Maritime Museum, MS JOD/171 plus mfm SMF/258.

Pre-1900 Printed Sources

An Act for the Amendment and Better Administration of the Laws Relating to the Poor in England and Wales (London: Saunders and Benning, 1834).
§Anon., 'A Blue-Stocking in the Bush', *Rambler* (October 1852), pp. 332–6.
— 'British Artists: Their Style and Character. No. X, Thomas Webster', *Art Journal* (1 November 1855), pp. 293–6.
— 'Emigration and Marriage', *London Journal and Weekly Record of Literature, Science and Art* (26 September 1857), pp. 61–2.
— 'Fine Arts', *Spectator* (1 May 1852), pp. 422–3.
— 'Fine Arts', *Examiner* (8 May 1852), p. 294.
— '*Roughing It in the Bush; Or, Life in Canada*', *Athenaeum* (28 February 1852), pp. 247–8.
— 'The Royal Academy', *Art Journal* (1 June 1850), pp. 165–78.
— 'Royal Academy', *Athenaeum* (15 May 1852), pp. 549–51.
— 'Royal Academy', *Athenaeum* (13 May 1854), pp. 593–5.
— 'Royal Academy', *Saturday Review* (28 May 1859), pp. 651–3.
— 'Royal Academy', *The Times* (8 May 1876), p. 9.
— 'The Emigration Cry', *Sharpe's London Magazine* (July 1852), pp. 352–61.

— 'The Exhibition of the Royal Academy', *Art Journal* (1 June 1852), pp. 165–76.
— 'The National Institution', *Art Journal* (1 May 1851), pp. 138–40.
— 'The Royal Academy Exhibition', *Critic* (1 August 1850), pp. 381–3.
— 'The Royal Academy Exhibition', *Art Journal* (1 June 1859), pp. 161–72.
— 'The Royal Academy', *Art Union* (1 June 1845), pp. 179–96 (p. 180).
— 'The Royal Academy', *Art Journal* (1 June 1854), pp. 157–72.
— 'The Royal Academy', *Art Journal* (1 June 1863), pp. 105–16.
Australasian News (S.S. Australasian: n. pub., 1885).
Backwoodsman, A, *Statistical Sketches of Upper Canada* (London: John Murray, 1832).
Barclay, Charles, (ed.), *Letters from the Dorking Emigrants who went to Upper Canada in the Spring of 1832* (Dorking: Robert Best Ede, 1832).
P. M. Braidwood and A. J. Cape (eds), *Parramatta Times: Issued on board the S. S. Parramatta during her voyage from Sydney to London, April 2nd to May 25th 1886* (Liverpool: D. Marples, 1886).
Brown, Ford Madox, *The Exhibition of Work, and Other Paintings by Ford Madox Brown at The Gallery, 191 Piccadilly* (London: M'Corquodale, 1865).
Brydone, James Marr, *Narrative of a Voyage, with a Party of Emigrants, Sent out from Sussex, in 1834, by the Petworth Emigration Committee* (Petworth: John Phillips, 1834).
Buchanan, A. C., *For the Information of Emigrants arriving at New York, and Who Are Desirous of Settling in Canada* (Quebec: Office of His Majesty's Chief Agent for the Superintendance of Emigrants in Upper and Lower Canada, 1834).
Buller, Charles, 'Colonisation – The Only Cure for National Distress – Mr Charles Buller's Speech', *Fraser's Magazine* (July 1843), pp. 735–50.
— *Systematic Colonization: Speech of Charles Buller* (London: John Murray, 1843).
Burton, John Hill, *The Emigrant's Manual: Australia, New Zealand, America, and South Africa* (Edinburgh: William & Robert Chambers, 1851).
Byrne, J. C., *Twelve Years' Wanderings in the British Colonies*, 2 vols (London: Richard Bentley, 1848).
— *Emigrant's Guide to New South Wales Proper, Australia Felix, and South Australia*, 9th edn (London: Effingham Wilson, 1849).
Carlyle, Thomas, *Chartism* (London: James Fraser, 1840).
Cattermole, William, *Emigration: The Advantages of Emigration to Canada* (London: Simpkin and Marshall, 1831).
Chadfield, Philip B., *Out at Sea; Or, the Emigrant Afloat, Being a Hand Book of Practical Information for the Use of Passengers on a Long Sea Voyage* (Derby: Chadfield & Son, 1862).
Chisholm, Caroline, *Comfort for the Poor! Meat Three Times a Day!! Voluntary Information from the People of New South Wales, Collected in that Colony by Mrs Chisholm in 1845–46* (London: John Ollivier, 1847).

— *Emigration and Transportation Relatively Considered in a Letter Dedicated, by Permission, to Earl Grey*, 3rd edn (London: John Ollivier, 1847).
— 'A Bundle of Emigrants' Letters', *Household Words* (30 March 1850), pp. 19–24.
— *The A. B. C. of Colonization in a Series of Letters* (London: John Ollivier, 1850).
— *The Story of the Life of Mrs Caroline Chisholm, the Emigrants' Friend, and her Adventures in Australia* (London: Trelawny Saunders, 1852).
— *What Has Mrs Caroline Chisholm Done for the Colony of New South Wales?* (Sydney: James Cole, 1862).
Cobbe, Frances Power, 'What Shall We Do with Our Old Maids?', *Fraser's Magazine for Town and Country* (November 1862), pp. 594–610.
Cobbett, William, *The Emigrant's Guide: In Ten Letters Addressed to the Tax-Payers of England Containing Information of Every Kind, Necessary to Persons who are About to Emigrate including Several Authentic and Most Interesting Letters from English Emigrants, Now in America to their Relations in England* (London: the author, 1829).
Collins, S. H., *The Emigrant's Guide to and Description of the United States of America: Including Several Authentic and Highly Important Letters from English Emigrants now in America, to their Friends in England* (New York: J. S. Ozer, 1971 [1830]).
Copies and Extracts of Letters from Settlers in Upper Canada (London: Marchant, 1833).
Council of Four, *A Guide to the Exhibition of the Royal Academy of Arts, 1859: Containing Original, Critical, and Descriptive Notices of 250 Works of Art* (London: Kent, 1859).
Counsel for Emigrants, and Interesting Information from Numerous Sources; With Original Letters from Canada and the United States (Aberdeen: John Mathison, 1834).
Dickens, Charles, 'A Preliminary Word', *Household Words* (30 March 1850), pp. 1–2.
— 'Home for Homeless Women', *Household Words* (23 April 1850), pp. 169–75.
— *Martin Chuzzlewit*, ed. Margaret Cardwell (Oxford: Oxford University Press, 1998 [1844]).
— *American Notes for General Circulation*, ed. Patricia Ingham (London: Penguin, 2000 [1842]).
— *David Copperfield*, ed. Nina Burgis (Oxford: Oxford University Press, 2008 [1850]).
— *Great Expectations*, ed. Margaret Cardwell (Oxford: Oxford University Press, 2008 [1861]).
Dilke, Charles, *Greater Britain: A Record of Travel in English-Speaking Countries during 1886 and 1867* (London: Macmillan, 1869).

Doyle, Martin, *Hints on Emigration to Upper Canada, Especially Addressed to the Middle and Lower Classes in Great Britain and Ireland*, 2nd edn (Dublin: William Curry, 1832).
Exhibition Catalogue of the Royal Academy of Arts, the Ninety-First (London: William Clowes, 1859).
Galt, John, *Bogle Corbet; Or the Emigrants* (London: H. Colburn and R. Bentley, 1831).
— *The Autobiography of John Galt* (London: Cochrane and M'Crone, 1833).
Gaskell, Elizabeth, *The Moorland Cottage and Other Stories*, ed. Suzanne Lewis (Oxford: Oxford University Press, 1995).
— *Mary Barton*, ed. Macdonald Daly (London: Penguin, 1996 [1848]).
— *North and South*, ed. Patricia Ingham (London: Penguin, 2003 [1855]).
— *Cranford*, ed. Elizabeth Porges Watson, intro. Dinah Birch (Oxford: Oxford University Press, 2011 [1863]).
George, Frances, 'An Emigrant's Glance Homewards', *Household Words* (10 April 1852), p. 80.
George, Frances and Henry Morley, 'From a Settler's Wife', *Household Words* (13 March 1852), pp. 585–8.
Greg, William Rathbone, 'Why Are Women Redundant?', *National Review* (28 April 1862), pp. 434–60.
Hardman, Frederick, 'Forest Life in Canada West', *Blackwood's Edinburgh Magazine* (March 1852), pp. 355–65.
Heaphy, Charles, *Narrative of a Residence in Various Parts of New Zealand: Together with a Description of the Present State of the Company's Settlements* (London: Smith & Elder, 1842).
Hood, John, *Australia and the East: Being a Journal Narrative of a Voyage to New South Wales in an Emigrant Ship, with a Residence of Some Months in Sydney and the Bush, and the Route Home by Way of India and Egypt in the Years 1841 and 1842* (London: John Murray, 1843).
Illustrations to 'Adventure in New Zealand' by Edward Jerningham Wakefield. Lithographed from Original Drawings Taken on the Spot by Mrs Wicksteed, Miss King, Mrs Fox, Mr John Saxton, Mr Charles Heaphy, Mr S. C. Brees and Captain W. Mein Smith, R.A. (London: Smith & Elder, 1845).
Information Published by His Majesty's Commissioners for Emigration Respecting the British Colonies in North America (London: Charles Knight, 1832).
Instructions to Surgeon Superintendents of Government Emigrant Ships (London: George Eyre and Andrew Spottiswode, 1858).
Kingston, William Henry (ed.), *Colonist* (London: Trelawney W. M. Saunders, 1848).
Kingston, William Henry Giles, *The Emigrant Voyager's Manual* (London: Trelawney Saunders, 1850).

Knox, James and Henry Morley, 'Going Circuit at the Antipodes', *Household Words* (3 January 1852), pp. 344–8.
Letters from Settlers & Labouring Emigrants, in the New Zealand Company's Settlements of Wellington, Nelson, & New Plymouth, from February 1842 to January 1843 (London: Smith & Elder, 1843).
Letters from Settlers in Upper Canada (London: Marchant, 1834).
Mackay, Alexander, 'An Emigrant Afloat', *Household Words* (31 August 1850), pp. 534–9.
Malthus, Thomas R., *An Essay on the Principle of Population*, ed. Geoffrey Gilbert (Oxford: Oxford University Press, 2004 [1798]).
Mangles, Ross D., *How to Colonize: The Interest of the Country and the Duty of the Government* (London: Smith & Elder, 1842).
Meredith, George, 'Familiar Things', *Household Words* (6 December 1851), p. 254.
Mereweather, John Davies, *Life on Board an Emigrant Ship: Being a Diary of a Voyage to Australia* (London: T. Hatchards, 1852).
Mitford, Mary Russell, *Our Village* (London: The Folio Society, 1997).
Mixed Playbill for Gil Blas!; Mr. Eden Clarke; Willy Reilly and his Own Dear Cooleen Bawn; The Vokes Family; Raising the Wind, Pavilion Theatre (n.p.:, n.pub, 26 July 1861).
Moodie, John, *Ten Years in South Africa: Including a Particular Description of the Wild Sports of that Country* (London: Bentley, 1835).
Moodie, Susanna, *Roughing It in the Bush*, ed. Michael A. Peterman (London: Norton, 2006 [1852]).
O'Neil, Henry, *Lectures on Painting Delivered at the Royal Academy* (London: Bradbury & Evans, 1866).
Redgrave, F. M., *Richard Redgrave, C.B., R.A.: A Memoir, Compiled from his Diary with Portrait and Three Illustrations* (London: Cassell, 1891).
Redgrave, Richard and Samuel Redgrave, *A Century of British Painters* (Oxford: Phaidon, 1947 [1881]).
Rodney World (Melbourne: n. pub., 1885).
Salmagundi: A Weekly Hash, Prepared on Board the Light Brigade (London: John Wilson, 1863).
Scrope, G. Poulett Esq. (ed.), *Extracts of Letters, from Poor Persons who Emigrated Last Year to Canada and the United States. Printed for the Information of the Labouring Poor and their Friends in this Country* (London: James Ridgway, 1831).
Seeley, J. R., *The Expansion of England*, ed. John Gross (Chicago: University of Chicago Press, 1971 [1883]).
Sequel to the Counsel for Emigrants, Containing Interesting Information from Numerous Sources; With Original Letters from Canada and the United States (Aberdeen: John Mathison, 1834).
Sidney, Samuel, *Sidney's Emigrant's Journal and Traveller's Magazine* (London: W. S. Orr, 1849).

— 'An Australian Ploughman's Story', *Household Words* (6 April 1850), pp. 39–43.
— 'Two-Handed Dick the Stockman: An Adventure in the Bush', *Household Words* (4 May 1850), pp. 141–4.
— 'Three Colonial Epochs', *Household Words* (31 January 1852), pp. 433–8.
Sidney, Samuel and John Sidney (eds), *Sidney's Emigrant Journal* (London: W. S. Orr, 1848–9).
Smith, Benjamin (ed.), *Twenty-Four Letters from Labourers in America to their Friends in England*, 2nd edn (London: Edward Rainford, 1829).
Sockett, Thomas (ed.), *Emigration: Letters From Sussex Emigrants who Sailed from Portsmouth, in April 1832, on Board the Ships,* Lord Melville *and* Eveline, *for Upper Canada: Extracts from Various Writers on Emigration to Canada, and from Canadian Newspapers, with Reference to the Letters: Capt. Hale's Instructions to Emigrants: and a Gazetteer of the Places Named in the Letters* (London: John Phillips, 1833).
— (ed.), *Canada: Letters from Persons who have Emigrated to Upper Canada under the Management of the Petworth Emigration Committee* (Petworth: John Philips, 1834).
— *Emigration: A Letter to a Member of Parliament, Containing a Statement of the Method Pursued by the Petworth Committee, in sending out Emigrants to Upper Canada, in the Years 1832 and 1833, and a Plan upon which the Sums required for Defraying the Expence of Emigration May Be Raised* (London: John Phillips, 1834).
— (ed.), *Continuation of Letters from Sussex Emigrants in Upper Canada* (Petworth: John Phillips, 1836).
Somersetshire News: A Ship Newspaper, Issued on Board the S.S. Somersetshire, on Her Passage from Plymouth to Melbourne (Melbourne: Sands and McDougall, 1869).
Spence, Catherine Helen, *Clara Morison: A Tale of South Australia during the Gold Fever*, 2 vols (London: John W. Parker, 1854).
— *Tender and True: A Colonial Tale*, 2 vols (London: Smith & Elder, 1856).
— *Mr Hogarth's Will*, 3 vols (London: Richard Bentley, 1865).
Strickland, Agnes, 'The Last Look', *Literary Garland* (June 1849), p. 263.
Strickland, Jane, 'The Buccaneers of Tortuga', *Literary Garland* (January 1850–March 1850).
— 'The Rustic Coquette', *Literary Garland* (May 1850), pp. 203–6.
The Act for the Amendment of the Poor Laws with a Practical Introduction, Notes and Forms by John Frederick Archibald (London: Saunders and Benning, 1834).
Traill, Catharine Parr [Strickland], *Prejudice Reproved; Or, The History of the Negro Toy-Seller* (London: Harvey & Darton, 1826).
— *The Young Emigrants; Or, Pictures of Canada*, facsim. edn (New York: Johnson, 1969 [1826]).
— 'The Canadian Emigrant's Farewell', *Home Circle* (7 July 1849), p. 6.
— 'Society in the Bush', *Sharpe's London Journal* (July 1850), pp. 129–34.

— *The Female Emigrant's Guide and Hints on Canadian Housekeeping* (Toronto: Maclear, 1854).
— *The Canadian Settler's Guide*, 7th edn (Toronto: Printed at the office of Toronto Times, 1857).
— *Studies of Plant Life in Canada, or, Gleanings from Forest, Lake and Plain* (Ottawa: A. S. Woodburn, 1885).
— *The Backwoods of Canada*, ed. D. M. R. Bentley (Ontario: McClelland & Stewart, 1989 [1836]).
— *The Backwoods of Canada*, ed. Michael Peterman (Ottawa: Carleton University Press, 1997 [1836]).
[Vincent, Frank and Henry Morley], 'John Chinaman in Australia', *Household Words* 17 (April 1858), pp. 416–20.
W., J. M., 'A Few Words about Mr Sidney Herbert's Emigration Scheme', *Sharpe's London Journal* (January 1850), pp. 99–103.
Walcott, Stephen, 'Instructions to Surgeons of Emigrant Ships Sailing under Government Superintendence' (London: William Clowes, 1843).
Wilcox, John, *Practical Hints to Intending Emigrants for our Australian Colonies* (Liverpool: Henry Greenwood, 1858).
Wilkie, David, 'Critical Remarks on Works of Art', in Allan Cunningham (ed.), *The Life of Sir David Wilkie*, 3 vols (London: John Murray, 1843), iii, pp. 128–215.

Secondary Criticism

Adams, Percy G., *Travel Literature and the Evolution of the Novel* (Lexington: University Press of Kentucky, 1983).
Agathocleous, Tanya, *Urban Realism and the Cosmopolitan Imagination in the Nineteenth Century: Visible City, Invisible World* (Cambridge: Cambridge University Press, 2011).
Alexander, Lynn Mae, *Women, Work and Representation: Needlewomen in Victorian Art and Literature* (Columbus: Ohio State University Press, 2003).
Allinson, Helen, *Farewell to Kent: Assisted Emigration from Kent in the Nineteenth Century* (Sittingbourne: Synjon, 2008).
Altick, Richard D., *The Presence of the Present: Topics of the Day in the Victorian Novel* (Columbus: Ohio State University Press, 1990).
Altman, Janet Gurkin, *Epistolarity: Approaches to a Form* (Columbus: Ohio State University Press, 1982).
Anderson, Amanda, *Tainted Souls and Painted Faces: The Rhetoric of Fallenness in Victorian Culture* (London: Cornell University Press, 1993).
Anderson, Benedict, *Imagined Communities: Reflections on the Origin and Spread of Nationalism*, rev. edn (London: Verso, 2006).
Appadurai, Arjun, 'Introduction: Commodities and the Politics of Value', in Arjun Appadurai (ed.), *The Social Life of Things: Commodities in*

Cultural Perspective (Cambridge: Cambridge University Press, 1986), pp. 1–63.
— *Modernity at Large: Cultural Dimensions of Globalization* (London: University of Minnesota Press, 1997).
Archibald, Diana C., *Domesticity, Imperialism, and Emigration in the Victorian Novel* (Columbia: University of Missouri Press, 2002).
Armstrong, Frances, 'Gender and Miniaturization: Games of Littleness in Nineteenth-Century Fiction', *English Studies in Canada* 16 (1990), pp. 403–16.
Armstrong, Nancy, *Desire and Domestic Fiction: A Political History of the Novel* (Oxford University Press, 1987).
Arscott, Caroline, 'Ramsgate Sands, Modern Life, and the Shoring-Up of Narrative', in Brian Allen (ed.), *Towards a Modern Art World* (London: Yale University Press, 1995), pp. 157–68.
Arscott, Caroline and Janet Wolff, '"Cultivated Capital": Patronage and Art in Nineteenth-Century Manchester and Leeds', in Gordon Marsden (ed.), *Victorian Values: Personalities and Perspectives in Nineteenth-Century Society* (London: Longman, 1990), pp. 29–41.
Atwood, Margaret, *The Journals of Susanna Moodie* (Toronto: Oxford University Press, 1970).
Auerbach, Nina, *Communities of Women: An Idea in Fiction* (London: Harvard University Press, 1978).
Augé, Marc, *Non-Places: Introductions to an Anthropology of Supermodernity*, trans. John Howe (London: Verso, 1995).
Bailin, Miriam, '"Dismal Pleasure": Victorian Sentimentality and the Pathos of the Parvenu', *ELH* 66 (1999), pp. 1015–32.
Baines, Dudley, *Migration in a Mature Economy: Emigration and Internal Migration in England and Wales, 1861–1900* (Cambridge: Cambridge University Press, 1985).
Bakhtin, M. M., *The Dialogic Imagination: Four Essays*, trans. M. Holquist (Austin: University of Texas Press, 1981).
Ball, Adrian and Diana Wright, *SS Great Britain* (Newton Abbot: David & Charles, 1981).
Ballstadt, Carl, 'Editor's Introduction', in Susanna Moodie, *Roughing It in the Bush, or Life in Canada* (Ottawa: Carleton University Press, 1988 [1852]), pp. xvii–lx.
— 'Susanna Moodie and the English Sketch', *Canadian Literature* 51 (1972), pp. 32–8, repr. in Susanna Moodie, *Roughing It in the Bush*, ed. Michael A. Peterman (London: Norton, 2007 [1852]), pp. 419–25.
Ballstadt, Carl, Elizabeth Hopkins and Michael A. Peterman (eds), *Susanna Moodie: Letters of a Lifetime* (Toronto: University of Toronto Press, 1985).
— *Letters of Love and Duty: The Correspondence of Susanna and John Moodie* (Toronto: University of Toronto Press, 1993).
— *I Bless You in My Heart: Selected Correspondence of Catharine Parr Traill* (Toronto: University of Toronto Press, 1996).

Bannet, Eve Tavor, *Empire of Letters: Letter Manuals and Transatlantic Correspondence, 1680–1820* (Cambridge: Cambridge University Press, 2005).
Barker, Hannah, *Newspapers, Politics and English Society, 1695–1855* (Harlow: Longman, 1999).
Barlow, Paul and Colin Trodd, 'Introduction. Constituting the Public: Art and its Institutions in Nineteenth-Century London', in ed. Paul Barlow and Colin Trodd (eds), *Governing Cultures: Art Institutions in Victorian London* (Aldershot: Ashgate, 2000), pp. 1–25.
Barnes, John, Bill Bell, Rimi Chatterjee, Wallace Kirsop and Michael Winship, 'A Place in the World', in David McKitterick (ed.), *The Cambridge History of the Book in Britain, 1830–1914*, 6 vols (Cambridge: Cambridge University Press, 2009), vi, pp. 595–634.
Barrell, John, *The Idea of Landscape and the Sense of Place, 1730–1840: An Approach to the Poetry of John Clare* (Cambridge: Cambridge University Press, 1972).
— *The Dark Side of the Landscape: The Rural Poor in English Painting 1730–1840* (Cambridge: Cambridge University Press, 1980).
Barst, Julie M., 'Pushing the Envelope: Caroline Chisholm, Colonial Australia, and the Transformative Power of Postal Networks', *Prose Studies: History, Theory, Criticism* 33 (2011), pp. 200–16.
Barthes, Roland, *S/Z*, trans. Richard Miller (London: Cape, 1975).
— *The Pleasure of the Text*, trans. Richard Miller (New York: Hill and Wang, 1975).
— *Image, Music, Text*, trans. Stephen Heath (London: Fontana, 1977).
— 'The Reality Effect', in *The Rustle of Language*, trans. Richard Howard (Oxford: Basil Blackwell, 1986), pp. 141–9.
Barton, David and Nigel Hall (eds), *Letter Writing as a Social Practice* (Philadelphia: John Benjamins, 1999).
Basu, Paul and Simon Coleman, 'Introduction: Migrant Worlds, Material Cultures', *Mobilities* 3 (2008), pp. 313–30.
Baucom, Ian, *Out of Place: Englishness, Empire, and the Locations of Identity* (Princeton: Princeton University Press, 1999).
Baudrillard, Jean, *The System of the Object*, trans. James Benedict (London: Verso, 1996).
Beck, Hilary, *Victorian Engravings* (London: Victoria and Albert Museum, 1973).
Beebee, Thomas O., *Epistolary Fiction in Europe, 1500–1850* (Cambridge: Cambridge University Press, 1999).
Beer, Gillian, 'Carlyle and Mary Barton: Problems of Utterance', in Francis Barker (ed.), *1848: The Sociology of Literature* (Colchester: University of Essex, 1978), pp. 242–55.
Beetham, Margaret, 'Towards a Theory of the Periodical as a Publishing Genre', in Laurel Brake (ed.), *Investigating Victorian Journalism* (London: Macmillan, 1990), pp. 19–32.

Belich, James, *Replenishing the Earth: The Settler Revolution and the Rise of the Anglo-World, 1783–1939* (Oxford: Oxford University Press, 2009).
Bell, Bill, 'Fiction in the Marketplace: Towards a Study of the Victorian Serial', in Michael Harris and Robin Myers (eds), *Serials and Their Readers, 1620–1914* (Winchester: St Paul's Bibliographies, 1993), pp. 125–44.
— *A Half-Century of Publishing: Smith & Elder Imprints 1817–1870* (Bristol: Simon Eliot and Michael Turner, 1996).
— 'Crusoe's Books: The Scottish Emigrant Reader in the Nineteenth Century', in Bill Bell, Philip Bennett and Jonquil Bevan (eds), *Across Boundaries: The Book in Culture and Commerce* (Winchester: St Paul's Bibliographies, 2000), pp. 116–29.
— 'Bound for Australia: Shipboard Reading in the Nineteenth Century', *Journal of Australian Studies* 25 (2001), pp. 5–18.
Bell, Duncan, 'Victorian Visions of Global Order: An Introduction', in Duncan Bell (ed.), *Victorian Visions of Global Order: Empire and International Relations in Nineteenth-Century Political Thought* (Cambridge: Cambridge University Press, 2007), pp. 1–25.
— 'The Victorian Idea of a Global State', in Duncan Bell (ed.), *Victorian Visions of Global Order: Empire and International Relations in Nineteenth-Century Political Thought* (Cambridge: Cambridge University Press, 2007), pp. 159–85.
— *The Idea of Greater Britain: Empire and the Future of World Order, 1860–1900* (Princeton: Princeton University Press, 2007).
Benjamin, Walter, *Illuminations*, ed. and intro. Hannah Arendt, trans. Harry Zorn (London: Pimlico, 1999).
Bentley, D. M. R., 'Afterword', in Catharine Parr Traill, *The Backwoods of Canada*, ed. D. M. R. Bentley (Toronto: McClelland & Stewart, 1989 [1836]), pp. 291–301.
— 'Breaking the "Cake of Custom": The Atlantic Crossing as a Rubicon for Female Emigrants to Canada?', in Lorraine McMullen (ed.), *Re(dis)covering Our Foremothers: Nineteenth-Century Canadian Women Writers* (Ottawa: University of Ottawa Press, 1990), pp. 91–122.
— '*The Last of England*, the Literature of Emigration, and "The Pathos of the Subject"', *The Journal of Pre-Raphaelite Studies* 5 (1996), pp. 35–44.
Bentley, Jerry H., Renate Bridenthal and Kären Wigen (eds), *Seascapes: Maritime Histories, Littoral Cultures, and Transoceanic Exchanges* (Honolulu: University of Hawaii Press, 2007).
Berger, Carl, *Science, God and Nature in Victorian Canada* (Toronto: University of Toronto Press, 1983).
Bermingham, Ann, 'The Simple Life: Cottages and Gainsborough's Cottage Doors', in Peter de Bolla, Nigel Leask and David Simpson (eds), *Land, Nation and Culture, 1740–1840: Thinking the Republic of Taste* (Basingstoke: Palgrave Macmillan, 2005), pp. 37–62.

Bessai, Diane, 'Counterfeiting Hindsight', *World Literature Written in English* 23 (1984), pp. 353–66.

Bhabha, Homi K., 'Introduction: Narrating the Nation', in Homi K. Bhabha (ed.), *Nation and Narration* (London: Routledge, 1990), pp. 1–7.

— 'The World and the Home', in Anne McClintock, Aamir Mufti and Ella Shohat (eds), *Dangerous Liaisons: Gender, Nation and Postcolonial Perspectives* (Minneapolis: University of Minnesota Press, 1997), pp. 445–55.

Billington, Josie, *Faithful Realism: Elizabeth Gaskell and Leo Tolstoy: A Comparative Study* (Lewisburg: Bucknell University Press, 2002).

Birch, Sylvia, 'An Introduction to Elizabeth Gaskell's Short Stories', *Gaskell Society Journal* 15 (1993), pp. 11–16.

Blainey, Geoffrey, *The Tyranny of Distance: How Distance Shaped Australia's History* (London: Macmillan, 1966).

Bloomfield, Paul, *Edward Gibbon Wakefield: Builder of the British Commonwealth* (London: Longmans, 1961).

Bodkin, Thomas, 'James Collinson', *Apollo* 31 (1940), pp. 128–33.

Boehmer, Elleke, *Colonial and Postcolonial Literature: Migrant Metaphors* (Oxford: Oxford University Press, 2005).

Borchardt, D. H., 'Printing Comes to Australia', in D. H. Borchardt and W. Kirsop (eds), *The Book in Australia: Essays Towards a Cultural and Social History* (Melbourne: Australian Reference Publications, in association with the Centre for Bibliographical and Textual Studies, Monash University, 1988), pp. 1–15.

Borzello, Frances, 'Pictures for the People', in Ira Bruce Nadel and F. S. Scharzbach (eds), *Victorian Artists and the City: A Collection of Critical Essays* (New York: Pergamon, 1980), pp. 30–40.

Bossche, Chris R. Vanden, *Carlyle and the Search for Authority* (Columbus: Ohio State University Press, 1991).

Bowen, H. V, John G. Reid and Elizabeth Mancke (eds), *Britain's Oceanic Empire: Atlantic and Indian Ocean Worlds, c. 1550–1850* (Cambridge: Cambridge University Press, 2012).

Boyd, Shelley, '"Transplanted into our Gardens": Susanna Moodie and Catharine Parr Traill', *Essays on Canadian Writing* 84 (2009), pp. 35–57.

Brake, Laurel, Bill Bell and David Finkelstein, 'Introduction', in Laurel Brake, Bill Bell and David Finkelstein (eds), *Nineteenth-Century Media and the Construction of Identities* (Basingstoke: Palgrave, 2000), pp. 1–7.

Brant, Clare, *Eighteenth-Century Letters and British Culture* (Basingstoke: Palgrave Macmillan, 2006).

Brantlinger, Patrick, *Rule of Darkness: British Literature and Imperialism, 1830–1914* (London: Cornell University Press, 1988).

— *Dark Vanishings: Discourse on the Extinction of Primitive Races, 1800–1930* (London: Cornell University Press, 2003).

Brennan, Timothy, 'The National Longing for Form', in Homi K. Bhabha (ed.), *Nation and Narration* (London: Routledge, 1990), pp. 44–70.

Brooks, Ann and Brian Haworth, *It Paid to Advertise: A Look at Newspaper Advertisements from Early Pre-Victorian Newspapers* (Bury: Printwise, 1993).
Brooks, Chris and Peter Faulkner (eds), *The White Man's Burdens: An Anthology of British Poetry of the Empire* (Exeter: University of Exeter Press, 1996).
Brown, Bill, *The Material Unconscious: American Amusement, Stephen Crane and the Economies of Play* (London: Harvard University Press, 1996).
— *A Sense of Things: The Object Matter of American Literature* (Chicago: University of Chicago Press, 2003).
— 'Thing Theory', in Bill Brown (ed.), *Things* (Chicago: University of Chicago Press, 2004), pp. 1–17.
Brown, Lucy, *Victorian News and Newspapers* (Oxford: Clarendon, 1985).
Brown, Mary Markham, *An Index to the* Literary Garland, *Montreal 1838–1851* (Toronto: Bibliographical Society of Canada, 1962).
Burns, Patricia, *Fatal Success: A History of the New Zealand Company*, ed. Henry Richardson (London: Heinemann Reed, 1989).
Buss, Helen M., 'Women and the Garrison Mentality: Pioneer Women Autobiographers and their Relation to the Land', in Lorraine McMullen (ed.), *Re(dis)covering Our Foremothers: Nineteenth-Century Canadian Women Writers* (Ottawa: University of Ottawa Press, 1990), pp. 123–36.
Butler, Judith, *Gender Trouble: Feminism and the Subversion of Identity* (London: Routledge, 1990).
Byerly, Alison, 'Effortless Art: The Sketch in Nineteenth-Century Painting and Literature', *Criticism* 41 (1999), pp. 349–64.
Cameron, Wendy and Mary McDougall Maude, *Assisting Emigration to Upper Canada: The Petworth Project, 1832–1837* (Montreal: McGill-Queen's University Press, 2000).
Cameron, Wendy, Sheila Haines and Mary McDougall Maude (eds), *English Immigrant Voices: Labourers' Letters from Upper Canada in the 1830s* (Montreal: McGill-Queen's University Press, 2000).
Camus, Marianne, *Women's Voices in the Fiction of Elizabeth Gaskell: 1810–1865* (Lampeter: Edwin Mellen, 2002).
Candlin, Fiona, *Art, Museums and Touch* (Manchester: Manchester University Press, 2010).
Cannadine, David, *Ornamentalism: How the British Saw Their Empire* (London: Penguin, 2001).
Carter, *The Road to Botany Bay: An Exploration of Landscape and History* (Minneapolis: University of Minnesota Press, 2010).
Casarino, Cesare, *Modernity at Sea: Melville, Marx, Conrad in Crisis* (Minneapolis: University of Minnesota Press, 2002).
Casteras, Susan P., '"Oh! Emigration! Thou'rt the Curse . . .": Victorian Images of Emigration Themes', *Journal of Pre-Raphaelite Studies* 6 (1985), pp. 1–24.

— '"Green Lanes and Chequered Shade": The Landscapes of Richard Redgrave', in Susan Casteras and Ronald Parkinson (eds), *Richard Redgrave, 1804–1888* (London: Yale University Press, 1988), pp. 71–85.
— '"Social Wrongs": The Painted Sermons of Richard Redgrave', in Susan P. Casteras and Ronald Parkinson (eds), *Richard Redgrave, 1804–1888* (New Haven, CT: Yale University Press, 1988), pp. 2–28.
— 'Seeing the Unseen: Pictorial Problematics and Victorian Images of Class, Poverty, and Urban Life', in Carol T. Christ and Jordan O. Jordan (eds), *Victorian Literature and the Victorian Visual Imagination* (London: University of California Press, 1995), pp. 264–88.
— 'Painted Fictions: Commemorating the Everyday in Victorian Art', in *Pre-Raphaelite and Other Masters: The Andrew Lloyd Webber Collection* (London: The Royal Academy of Arts, 2003), pp. 204–27.
Cauldie, Enid, *Cruel Habitations: A History of Working-Class Housing 1780–1918* (London: George Allen & Unwin, 1974).
Chan, Winnie, *The Economy of the Short Story in British Periodicals of the 1890s* (London: Routledge, 2007).
Charlwood, Don, *Settlers under Sail*, 3rd edn (Melbourne: Burgewood Books, 1999).
Chartier, Roger, Alain Boureau and Cécile Dauphin, *Correspondence: Models of Letter-Writing from the Middle Ages to the Nineteenth Century*, trans. Christopher Woodall (Princeton: Princeton University Press, 1997).
Chilton, Lisa, *Agents of Empire: British Female Migration to Canada and Australia, 1860s–1930* (Toronto: University of Toronto Press, 2007).
Christ, Carol T. and John O. Jordan, 'Introduction', in Carol T. Christ and Jordan O. Jordan (eds), *Victorian Literature and the Victorian Visual Imagination* (London: University of California Press, 1995), pp. xix–xxix.
Christopher, Emma, Cassandra Pybus and Marcus Rediker, 'Introduction', in Emma Christopher, Cassandra Pybus and Marcus Rediker (eds), *Many Middle Passages: Forced Migration and the Making of the Modern World* (Berkeley: University of California Press, 2007), pp. 1–19.
Clark, Charles R., *Women and Children Last: The Burning of the Emigrant Ship* Cospatrick (Dunedin: Otago University Press, 2006).
Clarke, G. N. G., 'Taking Possession: The Cartouche as Cultural Text in Eighteenth-Century American Maps', *Word & Image* 4 (1988), pp. 455–74.
Classen, Constance (ed.), *The Book of Touch* (Oxford: Berg, 2005).
Claybaugh, Amanda, *The Novel of Purpose: Literature and Social Reform in the Anglo-American World* (Ithaca: Cornell University Press, 2007).
Clemm, Sabine, *Dickens, Journalism, and Nationhood: Mapping the World in* Household Words (London: Routledge, 2009).
Clunas, Craig, 'China in Britain: The Imperial Collections', in Tim Barringer and Tom Flynn (eds), *Colonialism and the Object: Empire, Material Culture and the Museum* (London: Routledge, 1998), pp. 41–51.

Codell, Julie F., 'Artists' Professional Societies: Production, Consumption and Aesthetics', in Brian Allen (ed.), *Towards a Modern Art World* (London: Yale University Press, 1995), pp. 169–87.

— 'Introduction: Imperial Co-Histories and the British and Colonial Press', in Julie F. Codell (ed.), *Imperial Co-Histories: National Identities and the British and Colonial Press* (Madison: Fairleigh Dickinson University Press, 2003), pp. 15–26.

Cohen, Margaret, *The Novel and the Sea* (Princeton: Princeton University Press, 2010).

Colby, Vineta, *Yesterday's Women: Domestic Realism in the English Novel* (Princeton: Princeton University Press, 1974).

Collins, Philip, *Dickens and Crime*, 3rd edn (London: Macmillan, 1994).

Constantine, Stephen and Marjory Harper, *Migration and Empire* (Oxford: Oxford University Press, 2010).

Conway, Jill Kathryn, 'Introduction', in *Her Own Words: Women's Memoirs from Australia, New Zealand, Canada, and the United States* (New York: Vintage Books, 1999), pp. vii–xi.

Crary, Jonathan, *Techniques of the Observer: On Vision and Modernity in the Nineteenth Century* (London: MIT Press, 1990).

Cresswell, Tim, *On the Move: Mobility in the Modern Western World* (London: Routledge, 2006).

Crone, Rosalind, 'Attempts to (Re)shape Common Reading Habits: Bible Reading on the Nineteenth-Century Convict Ship', in Beth Palmer and Adelene Buckland (eds), *A Return to the Common Reader: Print Culture and the Novel, 1850–1900* (Aldershot: Ashgate, 2011), pp. 103–20.

Culler, Jonathan, *Structuralist Poetics: Structuralism, Linguistics and the Study of Literature* (London: Routledge, 2002).

Cunningham, Valentine, *Everywhere Spoken Against: Dissent in the Victorian Novel* (Oxford: Clarendon Press, 1975).

Curtis, Gerard, *Visual Words: Art and the Material Book in Victorian England* (Aldershot: Ashgate, 1999).

d'Albertis, Deirdre, *Dissembling Fictions: Elizabeth Gaskell and the Victorian Social Text* (London: Macmillan, 1997).

Daly, Suzanne, 'Kashmir Shawls in Mid-Victorian Novels', *Victorian Literature and Culture* 30 (2002), pp. 237–56.

— *The Empire Inside: Indian Commodities in Victorian Domestic Novels* (Ann Arbor: University of Michigan Press, 2011).

David, Deirdre, *Fictions of Resolution in Three Victorian Novels: North and South, Our Mutual Friend, Daniel Deronda* (London: Macmillan, 1981).

Davis, Fred, *Yearning for Yesterday: A Sociology of Nostalgia* (New York: Collier Macmillan, 1979).

Davis, Lennard J., *Factual Fictions: The Origins of the English Novel* (New York: Columbia University Press, 1983).

de Bolla, Peter, Nigel Leask and David Simpson (eds), *Land, Nation and Culture, 1740–1840: Thinking the Republic of Taste* (Basingstoke: Palgrave Macmillan, 2005).

de Certeau, Michel, *The Practice of Everyday Life*, trans. Steven Rendall (London: University of California Press, 1984).

de Sapio, Joseph, 'Transient Communities: Travel, Knowledge, and the Victorian Railway Carriage, 1840–90', *Mobilities* 8 (2013), pp. 201–19.

Dean, Misao, 'Concealing Her Blue Stockings: Femininity and Self-Representation in Susanna Moodie's Autobiographical Works' in Gillian Whitlock and Helen Tiffin (eds), *Re-Siting Queen's English: Text and Tradition in Post-Colonial Literature* (Amsterdam: Rodopi, 1992), pp. 25–36.

Dening, Greg, 'Deep Times, Deep Spaces: Civilizing the Sea', in Bernhard Klein and Gesa Mackenthun (eds), *Sea Changes: Historicizing the Ocean* (London: Routledge, 2004), pp. 1–12.

Diamond, Marion, *Emigration and Empire: The Life of Maria S. Rye* (London: Garland, 1999).

Dickens, Charles, *The Letters of Charles Dickens: 1842–1843*, ed. Madeline House, Graham Storey and Kathleen Tillotson, 12 vols (Clarendon: Oxford, 1965–2002), iii (1974).

— *The Letters of Charles Dickens: 1844–1846*, ed. Kathleen Tillotson, 12 vols (Oxford: Clarendon Press, 1965–2002), iv (1977).

— *The Letters of Charles Dickens: 1850–1852*, ed. Graham Storey, Kathleen Tillotson and Nina Burgis, 12 vols (Oxford: Clarendon Press, 1965–2002), vi (1988).

Dickerson, Vanessa, *Keeping the Victorian House: A Collection of Essays* (London: Garland, 1995).

Djwa, Sandra, 'Canadian Poets and the Great Tradition', *Canadian Literature* 65 (1975), pp. 42–52.

Donald, James and David Morley, 'No Place Like *Heimat*: Images of Home(land) in European Culture', in Erica Carter, James Donald and Judith Squires (eds), *Space and Place: Theories of Identity and Location* (London: Lawrence & Wishart, 1993), pp. 3–31.

Donald, Stephanie, Devleena Ghosh and Heather Goodall, 'Introduction', in *Water, Sovereignty and Borders in Asia and Oceania* (London: Routledge, 2009), pp. 1–13.

Donovan, Josephine, 'Sarah Orne Jewett and the World of Mothers', in *New England Local Color Literature: A Women's Tradition* (New York: Frederick Ungar, 1983), pp. 99–118.

Douglas, Daymond and Leslie Monkman, *Canadian Novelists and the Novel* (Ottawa: Borealis, 1981).

Douglas, Mary, 'Foreword', in Marcel Mauss, *The Gift: The Form and Reason for Exchange in Archaic Societies* (London: Routledge, 1990), pp. ix–xxiii.

Dunn, Maggie and Ann Morris, *The Composite Novel: The Short Story Cycle in Transition* (New York: Twayne, 1995).

Dzelzainis, Ella, 'The Victorians and America', in Sally Ledger and Holly Furneaux (eds), *Charles Dickens in Context* (Cambridge: Cambridge University Press, 2011), pp. 211–18.
— 'Dickens, Democracy, and Spit', in Ella Dzelzainis and Ruth Livesey (eds), *The American Experiment and the Idea of Democracy in British Culture, 1776–1914* (Aldershot: Ashgate, 2013), pp. 45–60.
Earle, Rebecca (ed.), *Epistolary Selves: Letters and Letter-Writers, 1600–1945* (Aldershot: Ashgate, 1999).
Earnshaw, Steven, *Beginning Realism* (Manchester: Manchester University Press, 2010).
Easson, Angus, 'Elizabeth Gaskell and the Novel of Local Pride', *Bulletin of the John Rylands University Library of Manchester* 67 (1985), pp. 688–709.
Edwards, Peter D., *Idyllic Realism from Mary Russell Mitford to Hardy* (Basingstoke: Macmillan, 1988).
Edwards, Philip, *The Story of the Voyage: Sea Narratives in Eighteenth-Century England* (Cambridge: Cambridge University Press, 2009).
Elce, Erika Behrisch, '"One of the Bright Objects that Solace Us in these Regions": Labour, Leisure, and the Arctic Shipboard Periodical, 1820–1852', *Victorian Periodicals Review* 46 (2013), pp. 343–67.
Erickson, Charlotte, *Invisible Immigrants: The Adaptation of English and Scottish Immigrants in Nineteenth-Century America* (London: Weidenfeld and Nicolson, 1972).
— (ed.), *Emigration from Europe, 1815–1914: Select Documents* (London: A. and C. Black, 1976).
— *English Women Immigrants in America in the Nineteenth Century: Expectations and Reality* (London: LLRS, 1983).
— *Leaving England: Essays on British Emigration in the Nineteenth Century* (Ithaca: Cornell University Press, 1994).
Ermarth, Elizabeth Deeds, *Realism and Consensus in the English Novel: Time, Space and Narrative* (Edinburgh: Edinburgh University Press, 1998).
Errington, Lindsay, *Social and Religious Themes in English Art, 1840–1860* (London: Garland, 1984).
Evans, Julie, Patricia Grimshaw, David Philips and Shurlee Swan, *Equal Subjects, Unequal Rights: Indigenous Peoples in British Settler Colonies, 1830–1910* (Manchester: Manchester University Press, 2003).
Fabian, Johannes, *Time and the Other: How Anthropology Makes Its Object* (New York: Columbia University Press, 1983).
Felber, Lynette, 'Gaskell's Industrial Idylls: Ideology and Formal Incongruence in *Mary Barton* and *North and South*', *Clio* 18 (1988), pp. 55–72.
Fender, Stephen, *Sea Changes: British Emigration and American Literature* (Cambridge: Cambridge University Press, 1992).
Ferris, Ina, 'Review of Mrs Gaskell's *Tales of Mystery and Horror*', *Nineteenth-Century Fiction* 34 (1979) pp. 95–6.

Finn, Margot, 'Victorianism at the Frontier: The White Settler Colonies', in Martin Hewitt (ed.), *The Victorian World* (London, Routledge, 2012), pp. 656–70.

Fitzpatrick, David, *Oceans of Consolation: Personal Accounts of Irish Migration to Australia* (Cork: Cork University Press, 1994).

— 'Irish Emigration and the Art of Letter-Writing', in Bruce S. Elliott, David A. Gerber and Suzanne M. Sinke (eds), *Letters across Borders: The Epistolary Practices of International Migrants* (Basingstoke: Palgrave Macmillan, 2006), pp. 97–106.

Flaxman, Rhoda L., Victorian *Word-Painting and Narrative: Toward the Blending of Genres* (Saginaw: UMI Research, 1987).

Fletcher, Pamela, '"To wipe a manly tear": The Aesthetics of Emotion in Victorian Narrative Painting', *Victorian Studies* 51 (2009), pp. 457–69.

Flint, Kate, *The Victorians and the Visual Imagination* (Cambridge: Cambridge University Press, 2000).

Floyd, Janet, *Writing the Pioneer Woman* (Columbia: University of Missouri Press, 2002).

Forbes, Duncan, '"The Advantages of Combination": The Art Union of London and State Regulation in the 1840s', in Paul Barlow and Colin Trodd (eds), *Governing Cultures: Art Institutions in Victorian London* (Aldershot: Ashgate, 2000), pp. 128–42.

Foster, Shirley, *Across New Worlds: Nineteenth-Century Women Travellers and their Writings* (London: Harvester Wheatsheaf, 1990).

Foucault, Michel, *Discipline and Punish: The Birth of the Prison*, trans. Alan Sheridan (London: Allen Lane, 1977).

— 'Of Other Spaces', trans. Jay Miskowiec, *Diacritics* 16 (1986), pp. 22–7.

Fowler, Marian, '*Roughing It in the Bush*: A Sentimental Novel', in John Moss (ed.), *Beginnings*. Series: *The Canadian Novel*, rev. edn, 4 vols (Toronto: Ontario Arts Council and Canada Council), ii, pp. 80–96.

Fox, Celina, 'Wood Engravers and the City', in Ira Bruce Nadel and F. S. Scharzbach (eds), *Victorian Artists and the City: A Collection of Critical Essays* (New York: Pergamon, 1980), pp. 1–13.

Foxhall, Katherine, *Health, Medicine, and the Sea: Australian Voyages, c.1815–60* (Manchester: Manchester University Press, 2012).

Franits, Wayne, *Dutch Seventeenth-Century Genre Painting: Its Stylistic and Thematic Evolution* (London: Yale University Press, 2004).

Fraser, Hilary, Stephanie Green and Judith Johnston (eds), *Gender and the Victorian Periodical* (Cambridge: Cambridge University Press, 2003).

Fredeman, William E. (ed.), *The P. R. B. Journal: William Michael Rossetti's Diary of the Pre-Raphaelite Brotherhood 1849–1853, Together with Other Pre-Raphaelite Documents* (Oxford: Clarendon, 1975).

Freedgood, Elaine, *The Ideas in Things: Fugitive Meaning in the Victorian Novel* (Chicago: University of Chicago Press, 2006).

— 'What Objects Know: Circulation, Omniscience and the Comedy of Dispossession in Victorian It-Narratives', *Journal of Victorian Culture* 15 (2010), pp. 83–100.

Freiwald, Bina, '"The Tongue of Woman": The Language of the Self in Moodie's *Roughing It in the Bush*', in *Re(dis)covering Our Foremothers: Nineteenth-Century Canadian Women Writers* (Ottawa: University of Ottawa Press, 1990), pp. 155–72.

Frow, John, 'Spectacle Binding: On Character', *Poetics Today* 7 (1986), pp. 227–50.

Frye, Northrop, 'Conclusion to a Literary History of Canada', in *The Bush Garden: Essays on the Canadian Imagination* (Toronto: Anansi, 1971), pp. 213–51.

Fyfe, Gordon, 'On the Impersonalisation of Cultural Power: Aspects of Victorian Art Institutions', in Martin Hewitt (ed.), *Culture Institutions* (Leeds: Leeds Centre for Victorian Studies, 2002), pp. 9–23.

Gallagher, Catherine, *The Industrial Reformation of English Fiction: Social Discourse and Narrative Form 1832–1867* (Chicago: University of Chicago Press, 1985).

Garcha, Amanpal, *From Sketch to Novel: The Development of Victorian Fiction* (Cambridge: Cambridge University Press, 2009).

Gardellini, Giuliana, 'A Gender-Mapped Geography of Canada: *Roughing It in the Bush*, by Susanna Moodie', in Isabella Maria Zoppi (ed.), *Routes of the Roots: Geography and Literature in the English-Speaking Countries* (Roma: Bulzoni, 1998), pp. 129–38.

Gaskell, Elizabeth, *The Letters of Mrs Gaskell*, ed. J. A. V. Chapple and Arthur Pollard (Manchester: Mandolin, 1997).

Gay, Penny, Judith Johnston and Catherine Waters (eds), *Victorian Turns, Neovictorian Returns: Essays on Fiction and Culture* (Newcastle upon Tyne: Cambridge Scholars, 2008).

Gerber, David A., 'Epistolary Masquerades: Acts of Deceiving and Withholding in Immigrant Letters', in Bruce S. Elliott, David A. Gerber and Suzanne M. Sinke (eds), *Letters across Borders: The Epistolary Practices of International Migrants* (Basingstoke: Palgrave Macmillan, 2006), pp. 141–57.

— *Authors of their Lives: The Personal Correspondence of British Immigrants to North America in the Nineteenth Century* (New York: New York University Press, 2006).

Gerson, Carole, *A Purer Taste: The Writing and Reading of Fiction in English in Nineteenth-Century Canada* (Toronto: University of Toronto Press, 1989).

— 'Nobler Savages: Representations of Native Women in the Writings of Susanna Moodie and Catharine Parr Traill', *Journal of Canadian Studies* 32 (1997), pp. 5–21.

Ghosh, Devleena and Stephen Muecke (eds), *Cultures of Trade: Indian Ocean Exchanges* (Newcastle-upon-Tyne: Cambridge Scholars, 2007).

Giddens, Anthony, *Modernity and Self-Identity: Self and Society in the Late Modern Age* (Cambridge: Polity Press, 1991).

Giffard, Ann and Basil Greenhill, *Travelling by Sea in the Nineteenth Century: Interior Design in Victorian Passenger Ships* (London: A. and C. Black, 1972).

Gilbert, Helen and Anna Johnston (eds), *In Transit: Travel, Text, Empire* (New York: Peter Lang, 2002).

Gill, Stephen, *Wordsworth and the Victorians* (Oxford: Oxford University Press, 1998).

Gilmour, Robin, 'Regional and Provincial in Victorian Literature', in Ronald Philip Draper (ed.), *The Literature of Region and Nation* (Basingstoke: Macmillan, 1989), pp. 51–60.

Gilroy, Amanda and W. M. Verhoeven, 'Introduction', in Amanda Gilroy and W. M. Verhoeven (eds), *Epistolary Histories: Letters, Fiction, Culture* (London: University Press of Virginia, 2000), pp. 1–29.

Giltrow, Janet, '"Painful Experience in a Distant Land": Mrs Moodie in Canada and Mrs Trollope in America', *Mosaic: A Journal for the Interdisciplinary Study of Literature* 14 (1981), pp. 131–44.

Glennie, Paul and N. J. Thrift, *Shaping the Day: A History of Timekeeping in England and Wales, 1300–1800* (Oxford: Oxford University Press, 2009).

Glickman, Susan, *The Picturesque and the Sublime: A Poetics of the Canadian Landscape* (Montreal: McGill-Queen's University Press, 1998).

Golland, Jim (ed.), *Pinner to Paradise: The Langthorn Letters* (Pinner: Pinner Local History Society, 1995).

Goodlad, Lauren, *The Victorian Geopolitical Aesthetic: Realism, Sovereignty and Transnational Experience* (Oxford: Oxford University Press, 2015).

Goodman, Gemma and Charlotte Mathieson (eds), *Gender and Space in Rural Britain* (London: Pickering and Chatto, 2014).

Gopal, Priyamvada, *The Indian English Novel: Nation, History, and Narration* (Oxford: Oxford University Press, 2009).

Gothard, Jan, *Blue China: Single Female Migration to Colonial Australia* (Carlton: Melbourne University Press, 2001).

Grande, James, *William Cobbett, the Press and Rural England: Radicalism and the Fourth Estate, 1792–1835* (Basingstoke: Palgrave Macmillan, 2014).

Grant, Robert D., *Representations of British Emigration, Colonisation and Settlement: Imagining Empire, 1800–1860* (Basingstoke: Palgrave Macmillan, 2005).

Gray, Charlotte, *Sisters in the Wilderness: The Lives of Susanna Moodie and Catharine Parr Traill* (London: Duckworth, 2001).

Gray, Peter, '"Shovelling out your paupers": The British State and Irish Famine Migration 1846–50', *Patterns of Prejudice* 33 (1999), pp. 47–65.

Greenblatt, Stephen, 'Cultural Mobility: An Introduction', in Stephen Greenblatt (ed.), *Cultural Mobility: A Manifesto* (Cambridge: Cambridge University Press, 2010), pp. 1–23.

Greg, Andrew, *The Cranbrook Colony: F. D. Hardy, G. Hardy, J. C. Horsley, A. E. Mulready, G. B. O'Neil, T. Webster* (Wolverhampton: Central Art Gallery, 1977).

Griffith, George V., 'What Kind of Book is *Cranford*?', *ARIEL* 14 (1983), pp. 53–65.

Habermann, Ina and Bernhard Klein, 'Death by Water: The Theory and Practice of Shipwrecking', in *Fictions of the Sea: Critical Perspectives on the Ocean in British Literature and Culture* (Aldershot: Ashgate, 2002), pp. 104–20.

Haig-Brown, Celia and David A. Nock (eds), *With Good Intentions: Euro-Canadian and Aboriginal Relations in Colonial Canada* (Vancouver: University of British Columbia Press, 2006).

Haines, Robin F., *Doctors at Sea: Emigrant Voyages to Colonial Australia* (Basingstoke: Palgrave Macmillan, 2005).

— *Life and Death in the Age of Sail: The Passage to Australia* (Sydney: University of New South Wales Press, 2006).

Haines, Sheila, *Poor Cottages and Proud Palaces: The Life and Work of the Reverend Thomas Sockett of Petworth, 1777–1859*, ed. Leigh Lawson (Hastings: Hastings Press, 2007).

Hall, Roger and Nick Whistler, 'Galt, John', *Dictionary of Canadian Biography* <http://www.biographi.ca/en/bio/galt_john_7E.html> [accessed 30 May 2017].

Hammill, Faye, *Literary Culture and Female Authorship in Canada, 1760–2000* (Amsterdam: Rodopi, 2003).

Hanson, Carter F., *Emigration, Nation, Vocation: The Literature of English Emigration to Canada, 1825–1900* (East Lansing: Michigan State University Press, 2009).

Hardy, Barbara, 'Cousin Phillis: The Art of the Novella', *Gaskell Society Journal* 19 (2005), pp. 25–33.

Hardy, John (ed.), *Stories of Australian Migration* (Sydney: New South Wales University Press, 1988).

Hardy, Patricia, 'Victorian Images of Emigration' (unpublished doctoral thesis, Courtauld Institute of Art, 2008).

Harper, Marjory, 'British Migration and the Peopling of the Empire', in Andrew Porter (ed.), *The Nineteenth Century* (Oxford: Oxford University Press, 1999), pp. 75–87.

— 'Introduction', in Marjory Harper (ed.), *Emigrant Homecomings: The Return Movement of Emigrants, 1600–2000* (Manchester: Manchester University Press, 2005), pp. 1–14.

Harris, Michael and Robin Myers, *Serials and their Readers, 1620–1914* (Winchester: St Paul's Bibliographies, 1993).

Harris, Wendell V., 'Vision and Form: The English Novel and the Emergence of the Short Story', in Charles E. May (ed.), *The New Short Story Theories* (Athens: Ohio University Press, 1994), pp. 182–91.

Harrison, Dick, *Unnamed Country: The Struggle for a Canadian Prairie Fiction* (Edmonton: University of Alberta Press, 1977).

Harrison, Jane E., *Until Next Year: Letter Writing and the Mails in the Canadas, 1640–1830* (Waterloo: Wilfrid Laurier University Press, 1997).

Hartley, Jenny, *Charles Dickens and the House of Fallen Women* (London: Methuen, 2008).

Hartley, Lucy, 'Putting the Drama into Everyday Life: The Pre-Raphaelite Brotherhood and a Very Ordinary Aesthetic', *Journal of Victorian Culture* 7 (2002), pp. 173–95.

Harvey, David, *The Condition of Postmodernity: An Enquiry into the Origins of Cultural Change* (Oxford: Blackwell, 1989).

Hassam, Andrew, '"Our Floating Home": Social Space and Group Identity on Board the Emigrant Ship' (London: Sir Robert Menzies Centre for Australian Studies, 1992).

— *Sailing to Australia: Shipboard Diaries by Nineteenth-Century British Emigrants* (Manchester: Manchester University Press, 1994).

— *No Privacy for Writing: Shipboard Diaries 1852–1879* (Melbourne: Melbourne University Press, 1995).

Helsinger, Elizabeth K., *Rural Scenes and National Representation, Britain: 1815–1850* (Princeton: Princeton University Press, 1997).

Henderson, Jennifer, *Settler Feminism and Race Making in Canada* (Toronto: University of Toronto Press, 2003).

Henkin, David M., *The Postal Age: The Emergence of Modern Communications in Nineteenth-Century America* (Chicago: University of Chicago Press, 2006).

Hensley, Nathan, *Forms of Empire: The Poetics of Victorian Sovereignty* (Oxford: Oxford University Press, 2016).

Hernadi, Paul, *Beyond Genre: New Directions in Literary Classification* (Ithaca: Cornell University Press, 1972).

Hindley, Diana and Geoffrey Hindley, *Advertising in Victorian England, 1837–1901* (London: Wayland, 1972).

Hitchins, Fred H., *The Colonial Land and Emigration Commission* (Philadelphia: University of Pennsylvania Press, 1931).

Hoffenberg, Peter H., 'Nothing Very New or Very Showy to Exhibit?: Australia at the Great Exhibition and After', in Jeffrey A. Auerbach and Peter H. Hoffenberg (eds), *Britain, the Empire, and the World at the Great Exhibition of 1851* (Hampshire: Ashgate, 2008), pp. 93–120.

Hofmeyr, Isabel, *The Portable Bunyan: A Transnational History of* The Pilgrim's Progress (Princeton: Princeton University Press, 2004).

Homans, Margaret, *Bearing the Word: Language and Female Experience in Nineteenth-Century Women's Writing* (Chicago: University of Chicago Press, 1986).

Houghton, Walter E., 'Periodical Literature and the Articulate Classes', in Joanne Shattock and Michael Wolff (eds), *The Victorian Periodical Press: Samplings and Soundings* (Leicester: Leicester University Press, 1982), pp. 3–27.

Houston, Gail Turley, '"Pip" and "Property": The (Re)Production of the Self in *Great Expectations*', *Studies in the Novel* 24 (1992), pp. 13–25.

Howells, Gary, '"For I was tired of England Sir": English Pauper Emigrant Strategies, 1834–60', *Social History* 23 (1998), pp. 181–94.

Hueffer, Ford M., *Ford Madox Brown: A Record of his Life and Work* (London: Longmans, Green, 1896).

Huett, Lorna, 'Commodity and Collectivity: *Cranford* in the Context of *Household Words*', *The Gaskell Society Journal* 17 (2003), pp. 34–49.

Hughes, Linda K. and Michael Lund, *The Victorian Serial* (London: University Press of Virginia, 1991).

— *Victorian Publishing and Mrs Gaskell's Work* (Charlottesville: University of Virginia Press, 1999).

Hughes, Robert, *The Fatal Shore: A History of the Transportation of Convicts to Australia, 1887–1868* (London: Vintage, 2003).

Hugill, Peter J., 'The Shrinking Victorian World', in Martin Hewitt (ed.), *The Victorian World* (London, Routledge, 2012), pp. 73–89.

Hunt, William Holman, *Pre-Raphaelitism and the Pre-Raphaelite Brotherhood*, 2 vols (London: Macmillan & Co, 1905), i.

Hunter, Adrian, *The Cambridge Introduction to the Short Story in English* (Cambridge: Cambridge University Press, 2007).

Hutchings, Kevin and Julia M. Wright, *Transatlantic Literary Exchanges, 1790–1870: Gender, Race, and Nation* (Farnham: Ashgate, 2011).

Ingrams, Richard, *The Life and Adventures of William Cobbett* (London: Harper, 2005).

Inness, Sherrie A., '"An Act of Severe Duty": Emigration and Class Ideology in Susanna Moodie's *Roughing It in the Bush*', in *Imperial Objects: Essays on Victorian Women's Emigration and the Unauthorized Imperial Experience* (London: Twayne, 1998), pp. 190–210.

Jackson, Thomas Alfred, *Charles Dickens: The Progress of a Radical* (London: Lawrence & Wishart, 1937).

Jackson-Houston, Caroline, 'Cranford: Elizabeth Gaskell's Most Radical Novel?', *The Gaskell Journal* 23 (2009), pp. 16–31.

James, Simon, 'Pip's Counterfeit Money: Forgery and Great Expectations', in Peter Knight and Jonathan Long (eds), *Fakes and Forgeries* (Amersham: Cambridge Scholars Press, 2004), pp. 41–9.

Johnson, H. J. M., *British Emigration Policy, 1815–30: Shovelling Out Paupers* (Oxford: Clarendon Press, 1972).

Johnston, Anna, '"Greater Britain": Late Imperial Travel Writing and the Settler Colonies', in Richard D. Fulton (ed.), *Oceania and the Victorian Imagination: Where All Things are Possible* (Surrey: Ashgate, 2013), pp. 32–43.

Johnston, Susan, *Women and Domestic Experience in Victorian Political Fiction* (London: Greenwood Press, 2001).

Jones, William D., 'Going into Print: Published Immigrant Letters, Webs of Personal Relations, and the Emergence of the Welsh Public Sphere', in Bruce S. Elliott, David A. Gerber and Suzanne M. Sinke (eds), *Letters across Borders: The Epistolary Practices of International Migrants* (Basingstoke: Palgrave Macmillan, 2006), pp. 175–99.

Kaplan, Caren, *Questions of Travel: Postmodern Discourses of Displacement* (Durham, NC: Duke University Press, 1998).

Kaplan, Fred, *Sacred Tears: Sentimentality in Victorian Literature* (Princeton: Princeton University Press, 1987).

Kapor, Vladimir, *Local Colour: A Travelling Concept* (Oxford: Peter Lang, 2009).

Keahey, Deborah, *Making it Home: Place in Canadian Prairie Literature* (Winnipeg: University of Manitoba Press, 1998).

Keating, J., *The Working Classes in Victorian Fiction* (London: Routledge and Kegan Paul, 1979).

Kelly, Kristine, 'Speaking Up: Caroline Chisholm's Rhetoric of Emigration Reform', in *Nineteenth-Century Studies* 23 (2009), pp. 17–35.

Kelly, Mary Ann, 'The Functions of Wemmick of Little Britain and Wemmick of Walworth', *Dickens Studies Newsletter* 14 (1983), pp. 145–8.

Killick, Tim, *British Short Fiction in the Early Nineteenth Century: The Rise of the Tale* (Basingstoke: Ashgate, 2008).

King, Amy M., 'Dilatory Description and the Pleasures of Accumulation: Towards a History of Novelistic Length', in Caroline Levine and Mario Ortiz-Robles (eds), *Narrative Middles: Navigating the Nineteenth-Century British Novel* (Columbus: Ohio State University Press, 2011).

Klancher, Jon P., *The Making of English Reading Audiences, 1790–1832* (Wisconsin: The University of Winconsin Press, 1987).

Klein, Bernhard and Gesa Mackenthun, 'Introduction: Britain and the Sea', in Bernhard Klein and Gesa Mackenthun (eds), *Fictions of the Sea: Critical Perspectives on the Ocean in British Literature and Culture* (Aldershot: Ashgate, 2002), pp. 1–12.

— 'Introduction: The Sea is History', in *Sea Changes: Historicizing the Ocean* (London: Routledge, 2004), pp. 1–12.

Kopytoff, Igor, 'The Cultural Biography of Things: Commoditization as Process', in Arjun Appadurai (ed.), *The Social Life of Things: Commodities in Cultural Perspective* (Cambridge: Cambridge University Press, 1986), pp. 64–91.

Korte, Barbara, 'The Temporalities of Travel, Travel Writing and Reading', in John Zilcosky (ed.), *Writing Travel: The Poetics and Politics of the Modern Journey* (Toronto: University of Toronto Press, 2008), pp. 26–53.

Kranidis, Rita S. (ed.), *Imperial Objects: Essays on Victorian Women's Emigration and the Unauthorized Imperial Experience* (New York: Twayne, 1998).
— *The Victorian Spinster and Colonial Emigration: Contested Subjects* (Basingstoke: Macmillan, 1999).
Kreuger, Christine L., '"Speaking Like a Woman": How to Have the Last Word on Sylvia's Lovers', in Alison Booth (ed.), *Famous Last Words: Changes in Gender and Narrative Closure* (London: University Press of Virginia), pp. 135–53.
Lamb, R. C. and R. S. Gormack, *Biscuit and Butter: A Colonist's Shipboard Fare, the Journal Kept by William & Laurence Kennaway on the Emigrant Ship* Canterbury, *London to Lyttelton, 1851* (Christchurch: Nag's Head Press, 1973).
Lambart, David and Alan Lester, 'Imperial Spaces, Imperial Subjects', in David Lambart and Alan Lester (eds), *Colonial Lives across the British Empire: Imperial Careering in the Long Nineteenth Century* (Cambridge, Cambridge University Press, 2006), pp. 1–31.
Lambourne, Lionel, *An Introduction to 'Victorian' Genre Painting: From Wilkie to Frith* (London: HMSO, 1982).
— *Victorian Painting* (London: Phaidon, 1999).
Landau, Aaron, 'Great Expectations, Romance and Capital', *Dickens Studies Annual* 35 (2005), pp. 157–77.
Langton, Anne, *A Gentlewoman in Upper Canada: The Journals, Letters, and Art of Anne Langton*, ed. Barbara Williams (Toronto: University of Toronto Press, 2008).
Lansbury, Coral, *Arcady in Australia: The Evocation of Australia in Nineteenth-Century English Literature* (Melbourne: Melbourne University Press, 1970).
— *Elizabeth Gaskell: The Novel of Social Crisis* (London: Elek, 1975).
Lanser, Susan Sniader, *Fictions of Authority: Women Writers and Narrative Voice* (Ithaca: Cornell University Press, 1992).
Lape, Noreen Groover, 'The Frontier Origins of North American Realism: Metarealism and the Travel Writings of Susanna Moodie and Caroline Kirkland', *Western American Literature* 44 (2008), pp. 363–94.
Latour, Bruno, *Reassembling the Social: An Introduction to Actor-Network-Theory* (Oxford: Oxford University Press, 2007).
Law, Graham, 'Periodicalism', in Martin Hewitt (ed.), *The Victorian World* (London, Routledge, 2012), pp. 537–54.
Leane, Elizabeth, 'The *Adelie Blizzard*: The Australasian Antarctic Expedition's Neglected Newspaper', *Polar Record* 41 (2005), pp. 11–20.
Lefebvre, Henri, *The Production of Space*, trans. Donald Nicholson-Smith (Oxford: Basil Blackwell, 1991).
Lehmann, R. C. (ed.), *Charles Dickens as Editor: Being Letters Written by Him to William Henry Wills His Sub-Editor* (London: Smith & Elder, 1912).

Levine, George, *The Realistic Imagination: English Fiction from Frankenstein to Lady Chatterley* (Chicago: University of Chicago Press, 1981).
Lewis, Hyde, *The Gift: Imagination and the Erotic Life of Property* (New York: Vintage, 1983).
Lindner, Christoph, *Fictions of Commodity Culture: From the Victorian to the Postmodern* (Aldershot: Ashgate, 2003).
Lister, Raymond, *Victorian Narrative Paintings* (London: Museum Press, 1966).
Liu, Alan, 'Local Transcendence: Cultural Criticism, Postmodernism, and the Romanticism of Detail', *Representations* 32 (1990), pp. 75–113.
Livesey, Ruth, *Writing the Stage Coach Nation: Locality on the Move in Nineteenth-Century British Literature* (Oxford: Oxford University Press, 2016).
Livingstone, David N., 'Science, Text and Space: Thoughts on the Geography of Reading', *Transactions of the Institute of British Geographers* 30 (2005), pp. 391–401.
Loeb, Lori Anne, *Consuming Angels: Advertising and Victorian Women* (Oxford: Oxford University Press, 1994).
Logan, Thad, *The Victorian Parlour* (Cambridge: Cambridge University Press, 2001).
Lohrli, Anne, Household Words, *Conducted by Charles Dickens: Table of Contents, List of Contributors and their Contributions* (Toronto: University of Toronto Press, 1973).
Loney, Jack and Peter Stone, *The Australia Run*, Series: Australian Shipwrecks, VI (Benalla: Marine History Publications, 2000).
Long, Jeremy, *Strugglers and Settlers: Darvall Family Letters 1849–1849* (Springwood: Butterfly Books, 1994).
Lubbock, Basil, *The Colonial Clippers* (Glasgow: Brown, Son & Ferguson, 1968).
Lucas, Alec, 'The Function of the Sketches in Susanna Moodie's *Roughing It in the Bush*', in Lorraine McMullen (ed.), *Re(dis)covering Our Foremothers: Nineteenth-Century Canadian Women Writers* (Ottawa: University of Ottawa Press, 1990), pp. 146–54.
Lucas, John, *The Literature of Change: Studies in the Nineteenth-Century Provincial Novel* (Sussex: Harvester Press, 1980).
Lucassen, Jan and Leo Lucassen, *Globalising Migration History: The Eurasian Experience: 16th–21st Centuries* (Leiden: Brill, 2014).
Lynch, Deidre Shauna, *The Economy of Character: Novels, Market Culture, and the Business of Inner Meaning* (Chicago: University of Chicago Press, 1998).
Lyon-Jenness, Cheryl, 'Planting a Seed: The Nineteenth-Century Horticultural Boom in America', *The Business History Review* 78 (2004), pp. 381–421.
MacDonagh, Oliver, *A Pattern of Government Growth, 1800–1860: The Passenger Acts and their Enforcement* (London: MacGibbon & Kee, 1961).

MacDonald, Norman, *Canada, 1763–1841, Immigration and Settlement: The Administration of Imperial Land Regulations* (London: Longmans, 1939).
Macherey, Pierre, *A Theory of Literary Production*, trans. Geoffrey Wall (London: Routledge and Kegan Paul, 1986).
Magee, Gary B. and Andrew S. Thompson, *Empire and Globalisation: Networks of People, Goods and Capital in the British World, c.1850–1914* (Cambridge: Cambridge University Press, 2010).
Maidment, Brian, 'Readers Fair and Foul: John Ruskin and the Periodical Press', in Joanne Shattock and Michael Wolff (eds), *The Victorian Periodical Press: Samplings and Soundings* (Leicester: Leicester University Press, 1982), pp. 29–58.
— *Reading Popular Prints, 1790–1870* (Manchester: Manchester University Press, 1996).
Maitzen, Rohan Amanda (ed.), *The Victorian Art of Fiction: Nineteenth-Century Essays on the Novel* (Peterborough: Broadview Press, 2009).
Makdisi, Saree, *Romantic Imperialism: Universal Empire and the Culture of Modernity* (Cambridge: Cambridge University Press, 1998).
Manogue, Ralph A., 'James Ridgway and America', *Early American Literature* 31 (1996), pp. 264–88.
Marriott, John A. R., *Empire Settlement* (Oxford: Oxford University Press, 1927).
Marsh, Jan, *The Pre-Raphaelites: Their Lives in Letters and Diaries* (London: Collins & Brown, 1996).
Martin, Jay, 'Scopic Regimes of Modernity', in Hal Foster (ed.), *Vision and Visuality* (Seattle: Bay Press, 1988), pp. 2–23.
Marx, Karl, *Capital: A Critique of Political Economy*, intro. Ernest Mandel, trans. Ben Fowkes, 3 vols (London: Penguin, 1990), i.
Massey, Doreen, 'Politics and Space/Time', in Steve Pile and Michael Keith (eds), *Place and the Politics of Identity* (London: Routledge, 1993), pp. 141–61.
— *For Space* (London: Sage, 2005).
Mathieson, Charlotte, *Mobility in the Victorian Novel: Placing the Nation* (Basingstoke: Palgrave Macmillan, 2015).
Matthew, H. C. G., 'Herbert, Sidney, First Baron Herbert of Lea (1810–1861)', in *Oxford Dictionary of National Biography* <http://www.oxforddnb.com/view/article/13047> [accessed 14 May 2017].
Matus, Jill L. (ed.), *The Cambridge Companion to Elizabeth Gaskell* (Cambridge: Cambridge University Press, 2007).
Mauss, Marcel, *The Gift: The Form and Reason for Exchange in Archaic Societies* (London: Routledge, 1990).
May, Charles E., *The Short Story: The Reality Artifice* (New York: Twayne, 1995).
McClintock, Anne, *Imperial Leather: Race, Gender, and Sexuality in the Colonial Conquest* (London: Routledge, 1995).

McDonagh, Josephine, 'Space, Mobility and the Novel: "The Spirit of Place is a Great Reality"', in Matthew Beaumont (ed.), *Adventures in Realism* (Oxford: Blackwell, 2007), pp. 50–67.
— 'Adam Bede and Emigration', *The George Eliot Review: Journal of the George Eliot Fellowship* 41 (2010), pp. 35–40.
— 'On Settling and Being Unsettled: Legitimacy and Settlement around 1850', in Margot Finn, Michael Lobban and Jenny Bourne Taylor (eds), *Legitimacy and Illegitimacy in Nineteenth-Century Law, Literature and History* (Basingstoke: Palgrave Macmillan, 2010), pp. 48–66.
— 'Urban Migration and Mobility', in Sally Ledger and Holly Furneaux (eds), *Charles Dickens in Context* (Cambridge: Cambridge University Press, 2011), pp. 268–75.
— 'Place, Region and Migration', in John Kucich and Jenny Bourne Taylor (eds), *The Nineteenth-Century Novel, 1820–1880* (Oxford: Oxford University Press, 2012), pp. 361–76.
— 'Rethinking Provincialism in Mid-Nineteenth-Century Fiction: *Our Village* to *Villette*', *Victorian Studies* 55 (2013), pp. 399–424.
McDowell, Linda, *Gender, Identity and Place: Understanding Feminist Geographies* (Cambridge: Polity Press, 1999).
McParland, Robert, *Charles Dickens's American Audience* (Plymouth: Lexington, 2010).
Meisel, Martin, *Realizations: Narrative, Pictorial, and Theatrical Arts in Nineteenth-Century England* (Princeton: Princeton University Press, 1983).
Merish, Lori, '"The Hand of Refined Taste" in the Frontier Landscape: Caroline Kirkland's "A New Home: Who'll Follow?" and the Feminization of American Consumerism', *American Quarterly* 45 (1993), pp. 485–523.
Metz, Nancy Aycock, '"Fevered with Anxiety for Home": Nostalgia and the "New" Emigrant in *Martin Chuzzlewit*', *Dickens Quarterly* 18 (2001), pp. 49–61.
Miller, Daniel, *Stuff* (Cambridge: Polity Press, 2000).
Miller, Joseph H., 'The Fiction of Realism', in *Victorian Subjects* (London: Harvester Wheatsheaf, 1990), pp. 119–77.
Millett, Timothy, 'Leaden Hearts', in Michele Field and Timothy Millett, *Convict Love Tokens: The Leaden Hearts Convicts Left Behind* (Kent Town: Wakefield, 1998), pp. 5–30.
Mitchell, Sally, *The Fallen Angel: Chastity, Class and Women's Reading 1835–1880* (Bowling Green: Bowling Green University Press, 1981).
Mitchell, W. J. T., *Iconology: Image, Text, Ideology* (London: University of Chicago Press, 1986).
Monod, Sylvère, *Martin Chuzzlewit* (London: Allen & Unwin, 1985).
Moore, Grace, *Dickens and Empire: Discourses of Class, Race and Colonialism in the Works of Charles Dickens* (Aldershot: Ashgate, 2004).
Moretti, Franco, *Atlas of the European Novel, 1800–1900* (London: Verso, 1998).

Morgan, Marjorie, *National Identities and Travel in Victorian Britain* (Basingstoke: Palgrave, 2000).
Morgan, Rosemary, 'The Debatable Land: Frontier Women Writers', in Norman Page and Peter Preston (eds), *The Literature of Place* (Basingstoke: Macmillan, 1993), pp. 180–92.
Morris, Emily Jane, '"Ready to Hear and Help": Female Agency and the Reclamation of the Fallen Woman in Elizabeth Gaskell's *Lizzie Leigh*', *The Gaskell Journal* 23 (2009), pp. 40–53.
Morris, Paul, 'A European Journey to the Bush: Susanna Moodie's *Roughing It in the Bush* as Travel Literature', in Klaus Martens (ed.), *Pioneering North America: Mediators of European Culture and Literature* (Würzburg: Königshausen & Neumann, 2000), pp. 171–83.
Moss, Sarah, 'Class War and the Albatross: The Politics of Ships as Social Space and the *Rime of the Ancient Mariner*', in Bernhard Klein (ed.), *Fictions of the Sea: Critical Perspectives on the Ocean in British Literature and Culture* (Aldershot: Ashgate, 2002), pp. 77–88.
Moyles, R. G. and Doug Owram, *Imperial Dreams and Colonial Realities: British Views of Canada, 1880–1914* (Toronto: University of Toronto Press, 1988).
Mudford, Peter, *Memory and Desire: Representations of Passion in the Novella* (London: Duckworth, 1996).
Murdoch, Alexander, *British Emigration: 1603–1914* (Basingstoke: Palgrave Macmillan, 2004).
Mussell, James, *Science, Time and Space in the Late Nineteenth-Century Periodical Press: Movable Types* (Aldershot: Ashgate, 2007).
Myers, Janet C., *Antipodal England: Emigration and Portable Domesticity in the Victorian Imagination* (Albany: State University of New York Press, 2009).
Nead, Lynda, *Myths of Sexuality: Representations of Women in Victorian Britain* (Oxford: Basil Blackwell, 1988).
— *Victorian Babylon: People, Streets, and Images in Nineteenth-Century London* (New Haven, CT: Yale University Press, 2000).
— 'The History in Pictures', *Cultural and Social History* 7 (2010), pp. 485–92.
— 'The Layering of Pleasure: Women, Fashionable Dress and Visual Culture in the Mid-Nineteenth Century', *Nineteenth-Century Contexts: An Interdisciplinary Journal* 35 (2013), pp. 489–509.
— 'The Secret of England's Greatness', *Journal of Victorian Culture* 19 (2014), pp. 161–82. Nestor, Pauline, *Female Friendships and Communities: Charlotte Brontë, George Eliot, Elizabeth Gaskell* (Oxford: Clarendon Press, 1985).
New, William Herbert, *Land Sliding: Imagining Space, Presence, and Power in Canadian Writing* (Toronto: University of Toronto Press, 1997).
Newman, Teresa and Raymond Watkinson, *Ford Madox Brown and the Pre-Raphaelite Circle* (London: Chatto & Windus, 1991).

Nicholson, Ian, *Log of Logs: A Catalogue of Logs, Journals, Shipboard Diaries, Letters, and all Forms of Voyage Narratives, 1788–1998, for Australia and New Zealand, and Surrounding Oceans*, 3 vols (Nambour: Roebuck, 1999).

Nock, David A., 'Horatio Hale: Forgotten Victorian Author of Positive Aboriginal Representation', in Celia Haig-Brown and David A. Nock (eds), *With Good Intentions: Euro-Canadian and Aboriginal Relations in Colonial Canada* (Vancouver: University of British Columbia Press, 2006), pp. 32–50.

Nord, Deborah Epstein (ed.), 'Editor's Introduction', in John Ruskin, *Sesame and Lilies*, with essays by Elizabeth Helsinger et al. (London: Yale University Press, 2002), pp. xiii–xxiv.

Nunn, Pamela Gerrish, *Problem Pictures: Women and Men in Victorian Painting* (Aldershot: Scolar, 1995).

Nuttall, Sarah, 'Subjectivities of Whiteness', in Annie E. Coombes (ed.), *Rethinking Settler Colonialism: History and Memory in Australia, Canada, Aotearoa New Zealand and South Africa* (Manchester: Manchester University Press, 2006), pp. 245–62.

O'Brien, Jean M., *Firsting and Lasting: Writing Indians out of Existence in New England* (London: University of Minnesota Press, 2010).

O'Conner, Frank, *The Lonely Voice: A Study of the Short Story* (London: Macmillan, 1965).

O'Farrell, Patrick James and Brian Trainor (eds), *Letters from Irish Australia, 1825–1929* (Sydney: New South Wales University Press; Belfast: Ulster Historical Foundation, 1984).

Ogborn, Miles, *Indian Ink: Script and Print in the Making of the English East India Company* (Chicago: University of Chicago Press, 2007).

Ogborn, Miles and Charles W. J. Withers, 'Introduction: Book Geography, Book History', in Miles Ogborn and Charles W. J. Withers (eds), *Geographies of the Book* (Farnham: Ashgate, 2010), pp. 1–25.

Orel, Harold, *The Victorian Short Story: Development and Triumph of a Literary Genre* (Cambridge: Cambridge University Press, 1986).

Outka, Elizabeth, *Consuming Traditions: Modernity, Modernism, and the Commodified Authentic* (Oxford: Oxford University Press, 2009).

Øverland, Orm, 'Learning to Read Immigrant Letters: Reflections towards a Textual Theory', in Øyvind T. Gulliksen, David. C. Mauk and Dina Tolfsby (eds), *Norwegian-American Essays* (Oslo: Norwegian American Historical Association, 1996), pp. 207–25.

Page, Norman, 'Introduction', in Norman Page and Peter Preston (eds), *The Literature of Place* (Basingstoke: Macmillan, 1993), pp. xi–xii.

Palmegiano, E. M., *The British Empire in the Victorian Press, 1832–1867: A Bibliography* (London: Garland Publishing Press, 1987).

Parkinson, Ronald, 'James Collinson', in Leslie Parris (ed.), *Pre-Raphaelite Papers* (London: Tate Gallery/Allen Lane, 1984), pp. 61–75.

Parry, John, *The Discovery of the Sea* (London: Weidenfeld and Nicolson, 1975).
Payne, Christiana, *Toil and Plenty: Images of the Agricultural Landscape in England, 1780–1890* (New Haven, CT: Yale University Press, 1994).
— *Rustic Simplicity: Scenes of Cottage Life in Nineteenth-Century British Art* (London: Lund Humphries, 1998).
Penn, W. S, 'The Tale as Genre in Short Fiction', in Charles E. May, *The New Short Story Theories* (Athens: Ohio University Press, 1994), pp. 44–53.
Perera, Suvendrini, *Reaches of Empire: The English Novel from Edgeworth to Dickens* (New York: Columbia University Press, 1991).
Peterman, Michael A., '"Splendid Anachronism": The Record of Catharine Parr Traill's Struggles as an Amateur Botanist in Nineteenth-Century Canada', in Lorraine McNullen (ed.), *Re(dis)covering Our Foremothers: Nineteenth-Century Canadian Women Writers* (Ottawa: University of Ottawa Press, 1990), pp. 173–85.
— 'Editor's Introduction', in Catharine Parr Traill, *The Backwoods of Canada* (Ottawa: Carleton University Press, 1997 [1836]), pp. xix–lxix.
— *Susanna Moodie: A Life* (Toronto: ECW, 1999).
— 'Introduction', in Susanna Moodie, *Roughing It in the Bush*, ed. Michael A. Peterman (London: Norton, 2007 [1852]), pp. vii–xvii.
Pettitt, Clare, 'Monstrous Displacements: Anxieties of Exchange in *Great Expectations*', *Dickens Studies Annual* 30 (2001), pp. 243–62.
— 'On Stuff', *19: Interdisciplinary Studies in the Long Nineteenth Century* 6 (2008), pp. 1–12 <http://19.bbk.ac.uk/index.php/19/article/viewFile/474/334> [accessed 30 March 2017].
— 'Travel in Print: Wonders, Miscellanies and News Culture', unpublished paper presented at 'Modes of Transport: Travel Writing and Form', King's College London, 26 May 2011.
Piesse, Jude, '2012 Van Arsdel Prize Essay. Dreaming across Oceans: Emigration and Nation in the Mid-Victorian Christmas Issue', *Victorian Periodicals Review* 46 (2013), pp. 37–60.
— *British Settler Emigration in Print, 1832-1877* (Oxford: Oxford University Press, 2016).
Plotz, John, *Portable Property: Victorian Culture on the Move* (Princeton: Princeton University Press, 2008).
Ponsonby, Margaret, 'Ideals, Reality and Meaning: Homemaking in England in the First Half of the Nineteenth Century', *Journal of Design History* 16 (2003), pp. 201–14.
Pooley, Colin G. and Ian D. Whyte (eds), *Migrants, Emigrants and Immigrants: A Social History of Migration* (London: Routledge, in association with the Social History Society of the United Kingdom, 1991).
Pratt, Mary Louise, 'The Short Story: The Long and Short of It', in Charles E. May (ed.), *The New Short Story Theories* (Athens: Ohio University Press, 1994), pp. 91–113.

— *Imperial Eyes: Travel Writing and Transculturation*, 2nd edn (London: Routledge, 2006).

Prentis, Malcolm, 'Haggis on the High Seas: Shipboard Experiences of Scottish Emigrants to Australia, 1821–1897', *Australian Historical Studies* 36 (2008), pp. 294–311.

Pre-Raphaelite and Other Masters: The Andrew Lloyd Webber Collection (London: The Royal Academy of Arts, 2003).

Price, Leah, *The Anthology and the Rise of the Novel: From Richardson to George Eliot* (Cambridge: Cambridge University Press, 2000).

— *How to Do Things with Books in Victorian Britain* (Princeton: Princeton University Press, 2012).

Pybus, Cassandra, 'Bound For Botany Bay: John Martin's Voyage to Australia', in Emma Christopher, Cassandra Pybus and Marcus Rediker (eds), *Many Middle Passages: Forced Migration and the Making of the Modern World* (Berkeley: University of California Press, 2007), pp. 92–108.

Randall, Craig, 'Fictional License: The Case of (and in) *Great Expectations*', *Dickens Studies Annual* 35 (2005), pp. 109–32.

Rappaport, Erika, 'Imperial Possessions, Cultural Histories, and the Material Turn: Response', *Victorian Studies* 50 (2008), pp. 289–96.

Redford, Bruce, *The Converse of the Pen: Acts of Intimacy in the Eighteenth-Century Familiar Letter* (Chicago: University of Chicago Press, 1986).

Reynolds, Henry, *The Other Side of the Frontier: Aboriginal Resistance to the European Invasion of Australia* (Sydney: University of New South Wales Press, 2006 [1982]).

Richards, Eric, 'Voices of British and Irish Migrants in Nineteenth-Century Australia', in *Migrants, Emigrants and Immigrants: A Social History of Migration*, ed. Colin G. Pooley and Ian D. Whyte (London: Routledge, 1991), pp. 19–41.

— *Britannia's Children: Emigration from England, Scotland, Wales and Ireland since 1600* (London: Hambledon and London, 2004).

— 'Running Home from Australia: Intercontinental Mobility and Migrant Expectations in the Nineteenth Century', in Marjory Harper (ed.), *Emigrant Homecomings: The Return Movement of Emigrants, 1600–2000* (Manchester: Manchester University Press, 2005), pp. 77–104.

— 'The Limits of the Australian Emigrant Letter', in Bruce S. Elliott, David A. Gerber and Suzanne M. Sinke (eds), *Letters across Borders: The Epistolary Practices of International Migrants* (Basingstoke: Palgrave Macillan, 2006), pp. 56–74.

Ricoeur, Paul, *Freud and Philosophy: An Essay on Interpretation*, trans. Denis Savage (London: Yale University Press, 1970).

— *Time and Narrative*, trans. Kathleen McLaughlin and David Pellauer, 4 vols (Chicago: University of Chicago Press, 1985), ii.

Robbins, Bruce, 'How to Be a Benefactor without any Money: The Chill of Welfare in *Great Expectations*', in Suzy Anger (ed.), *Knowing the Past: Victorian Literature and Culture* (London: Cornell University Press, 2001), pp. 172–91.

'Robert Best Ede', *British Book Trade Index* <http://www.bbti.bham.ac.uk/Details.htm?TraderID=21833> [accessed 21 September 2017].

Roberts, Helene E., 'Art Reviewing in the Early Nineteenth-Century Art Periodicals', *Victorian Periodicals Newsletter* 19 (March 1973), pp. 9–20.

— 'Exhibition and Review: The Periodical Press and the Victorian Art Exhibition System', in Joanne Shattock and Michael Wolff (eds), *The Victorian Periodical Press: Samplings and Soundings* (Leicester: Leicester University Press, 1982), pp. 79–107.

Roberts, Janine, *Massacres to Mining: The Colonisation of Aboriginal Australia* (Bristol: Investigative Media Productions, 2008).

Rose, Michael E., 'Settlement, Removal and the New Poor Law', in Derek Fraser (ed.), *The New Poor Law in the Nineteenth Century* (Basingstoke: Macmillan, 1976), pp. 25–44.

Roston, Murray, *Victorian Contexts: Literature and the Visual Arts* (Basingstoke: Macmillan, 1996).

Rotunno, Laura, *Postal Plots in British Fiction, 1840–1898: Readdressing Correspondence in Victorian Culture* (New York: Palgrave Macmillan, 2013).

Rubery, Matthew, *The Novelty of Newspapers: Victorian Fiction after the Invention of the News* (Oxford: Oxford University Press, 2009).

Rudy, Jason R., 'Floating Worlds: Emigre Poetry and British Culture', *ELH* 81 (2014), pp. 325–50.

Russell, Shannon, 'Recycling the Poor and Fallen', in Rita S. Kranidis (ed.), *Imperial Objects: Essays on Victorian Women's Emigration and the Unauthorized Imperial Experience* (New York: Twayne Publishers, 1998), pp. 43–53.

Said, Edward W., *The World, the Text, and the Critic* (Cambridge: Harvard University Press, 1983).

— *Culture and Imperialism* (London: Chatto & Windus, 1993).

Schor, Hilary M., *Scheherazade in the Marketplace: Elizabeth Gaskell and the Forms of the Heroine's Plot* (Oxford: Oxford University Press, 1992).

Schrift, Alan, *The Logic of the Gift: Toward an Ethic of Generosity* (London: Routledge, 1997).

Scott, Jennifer, 'Reciprocal Investments: John Galt, the Periodical Press, and the Business of North American Emigration', *Victorian Periodicals Review* 46 (2013), pp. 368–82.

Scott, Paul Henderson, 'Galt, John (1779–1839)', *Oxford Dictionary of National Biography* <http://www.oxforddnb.com/view/article/10316> [accessed 15 June 2017].

Scott-Baumann, Alison, *Ricoeur and the Hermeneutics of Suspicion* (London: Continuum, 2009).

Secord, James A., 'Knowledge in Transit', *Isis* 95 (2004), pp. 654–72.

Sells, A. Lytton, *Oliver Goldsmith: His Life and Works* (London: George Allen & Unwin, 1974).

Sha, Richard, *The Visual and Verbal Sketch in British Romanticism* (Philadelphia: University of Pennsylvania Press, 1998).
— 'The Power of the English Nineteenth-Century Visual and Verbal Sketch: Appropriation, Discipline, Mastery', *Nineteenth-Century Contexts* 24 (2002), pp. 73–100.
Sharps, John Geoffrey, *Mrs Gaskell's Observation and Invention: A Study of her Non-Biographic Works* (London: Linden, 1970).
Shaw, A. G., *Convicts and the Colonies: Studies of Penal Transportation from Great Britain and Ireland to Australia and Other Parts of the British Empire* (Carlton: Melbourne University Press, 1978).
Shaw, Bernard, 'Foreword', in *Great Expectations* (London: Hamish Hamilton, 1947), pp. v–xxiii.
Shaw, Christopher and Malcolm Chase (eds), *The Imagined Past: History and Nostalgia* (Manchester: Manchester University Press, 1989).
Sheehan, Paul, 'Marx, Money, and Monstrosity in *Great Expectations*', *Q/W/E/R/T/Y* 9 (1999), pp. 97–104.
Shepperson, Wilbur Stanley, *Emigration and Disenchantment: Portraits of Englishmen Repatriated from the United States* (Norman: University of Oklahoma Press, 1965).
Shoemaker, Adam, 'Landscapes and Mindscapes: Regionalism and Nationalism in Canadian and Australian Culture', in Gillian Whitlock and Helen Tiffin (eds), *Re-Siting Queen's English: Text and Tradition in Post-Colonial Literature* (Amsterdam: Rodopi, 1992), pp. 117–29.
Silver, Arthur W., *Manchester Men and Indian Cotton, 1847–1872* (Manchester: Manchester University Press, 1966).
Smith, Barbara Herrnstein, *On the Margins of Discourse: The Relation of Literature to Language* (Chicago: University of Chicago Press, 1978).
Smith, Grahame, *Dickens, Money, and Society* (Berkeley: University of California Press, 1968).
Smith, Sheila M., '"Savages and Martyrs": Images of the Urban Poor in Victorian Literature and Art', in Ira Bruce Nadel and F. S. Scharzbach (eds), *Victorian Artists and the City: A Collection of Critical Essays* (New York: Pergamon, 1980), pp. 14–29.
Snell, K. D. M., *Parish and Belonging: Community, Identity, and Welfare in England and Wales, 1700–1950* (Cambridge: Cambridge University Press, 2006).
Soja, Edward W., *Thirdspace: Journeys to Los Angeles and Other Real-and-Imagined Places* (Oxford: Blackwell, 1996).
Sokoll, Thomas, *Essex Pauper Letters, 1731–1837* (Oxford: Published for the British Academy by Oxford University Press, 2001).
Spence, Catherine Helen, *Ever Yours, C. H. Spence: Catherine Helen Spence's An Autobiography (1825–1910), Diary (1894) and Some Correspondence (1894–1910)*
, ed. Susan Magarey and Barbara Wall (Kent Town: Wakefield Press, 2005).
Spencer, Jane, *Elizabeth Gaskell* (Basingstoke: Macmillan, 1993).

Spivak, Gayatri, 'Translator's Preface', in Jacques Derrida, *of Grammatology* (Baltimore: Johns Hopkins University Press, 1976), pp. ix–xc.
Stafford, Fiona, *Local Attachments: The Province of Poetry* (Oxford: Oxford University Press, 2010).
Stam, David H. and Deirdre C. Stam, 'Bending Time: The Function of Periodicals in Nineteenth-Century Polar Naval Expeditions', *Victorian Periodicals Review* 41 (2008), pp. 301–22.
Stammers, M. K., *The Passage Makers: The History of the Black Ball Line of Australian Packets, 1852–1871* (Brighton: Teredo, 1978).
Stegner, Wallace, *Where the Bluebird Sings to the Lemonade Springs: Living and Writing in the West* (New York: Random House, 1992).
Stein, Richard L., *The Ritual of Interpretation: The Fine Arts as Literature in Ruskin, Rossetti, and Pater* (London: Harvard University Press, 1975).
Steinberg, Philip E., *The Social Construction of the Ocean* (Cambridge: Cambridge University Press, 2001).
Steinitz, Rebecca, *Time, Space, and Gender in the Nineteenth-Century British Diary* (Basingstoke: Palgrave Macmillan, 2011).
Stevenson, Robert Louis, *The Amateur Emigrant and the Silverado Squatters*, ed. James Michie (London: Folio Society, 1991).
Stewart, Susan, *On Longing: Narratives of the Miniature, the Gigantic, the Souvenir, the Collection* (London: Duke University Press, 1993).
Stoneman, Patsy, *Elizabeth Gaskell* (Sussex: Harvester Press, 1987).
Strathern, Marilyn, *The Gender of the Gift: Problems with Women – Problems with Society in Melanesia* (London: University of California Press, 1988).
Surtees, Virginia, *The Diary of Ford Madox Brown* (London: Yale University Press, 1981).
Teukolsky, Rachel, *The Literate Eye: Victorian Art Writing and Modernist Aesthetics* (Oxford: Oxford University Press, 2009).
Thacker, Andrew, *Moving through Modernity: Space and Geography in Modernism* (Manchester: Manchester University Press, 2003).
Thom, Molly, *The Bush-Ladies in their Own Words: Susanna Moodie, Catharine Parr Traill, Anne Langton, Anna Jameson* (Victoria: Scirocco Drama, 2000).
Thomas, Christa Zeller, '"I had never seen such a shed called a house before": The Discourse of Home in Susanna Moodie's *Roughing It in the Bush*', *Canadian Literature* 203 (2009), pp. 105–21.
Thomas, Clara McCandless, 'Strickland, Samuel', *Dictionary of Canadian Biography* <http://www.biographi.ca/en/bio/strickland_samuel_9E.html> [accessed 30 May 2014].
Thomas, Julia, *Victorian Narrative Painting* (London: Tate Publishing, 2000).
— *Pictorial Victorians: The Inscription of Values in Word and Image* (Athens: Ohio University Press, 2004).
Thomas, Nicholas, *Entangled Objects: Exchange, Material Culture, and Colonialism in the Pacific* (London: Harvard University Press, 1991).

Thompson, Elizabeth, *The Pioneer Woman: A Canadian Character Type* (Montreal: McGill-Queen's University Press, 1991).

Thornton, Sara, *Advertising, Subjectivity and the Nineteenth-Century Novel: Dickens, Balzac and the Language of the Walls* (Basingstoke: Palgrave Macmillan, 2009).

Tick, Stanley, 'Sidney, Samuel (1813–1883)', *Australian Dictionary of Biography* < http://adb.anu.edu.au/biography/sidney-samuel-2662/text3599> [accessed 16 June 2017].

Tomalin, Claire, *Charles Dickens: A Life* (London: Penguin, 2012).

Tosh, John, *A Man's Place: Masculinity and the Middle-Class Home in Victorian England* (New Haven, CT: Yale University Press, 2007).

Treuherz, Julian, with contributions by Susan P. Casteras, Lee M. Edwards, Peter Keating and Louise van Tilborgh, *Hard Times: Social Realism in Victorian Art* (London: Lund Humphries in association with Manchester City Art Galleries, 1988).

Trodd, Colin, 'Representing the Victorian Royal Academy: The Properties of Culture and the Promotion of Art', in Paul Barlow and Colin Trodd (eds), *Governing Cultures: Art Institutions in Victorian London* (Aldershot: Ashgate, 2000), pp. 56–68.

Tromans, Nicholas, 'Museum or Market?: The British Institution', in Paul Barlow and Colin Trodd (eds), *Governing Cultures: Art Institutions in Victorian London* (Aldershot: Ashgate, 2000), pp. 44–55.

Trotter, David, *Circulation: Defoe, Dickens and the Economies of the Novel* (London: Macmillan, 1988).

— 'Introduction', in *Great Expectations*, ed. Charlotte Mitchell (London: Penguin, 2003), pp. vii–xx.

— 'Household Clearances in Victorian Fiction', *19: Interdisciplinary Studies in the Long Nineteenth Century* 6 (2008), pp. 1–19 <http://www.19.bbk.ac.uk/index.php/19/article/viewFile/472/332> [accessed 30 March 2017].

Trumpener, Katie, *Bardic Nationalism: The Romantic Novel and the British Empire* (Princeton: Princeton University Press, 1997).

Tuck, Robert Critchlow (ed.), *The Island Family Harris: Letters of an Immigrant Family in British North America, 1856–1866* (Charlottetown: Ragweed Press, 1983).

Turner, Mark W., 'Periodical Time in the Nineteenth Century', *Media History* 8 (2002), pp. 183–96.

— 'Time, Periodicals, and Literary Studies', *Victorian Periodicals Review* 39 (2006), pp. 309–16.

Uglow, Jenny, *Elizabeth Gaskell: A Habit of Stories* (London: Faber and Faber, 1993).

van Binsbergen, Wim M. J. and Peter Geschiere (eds), *Commodification: Things, Agency, and Identities* (Münster: Lit, 2005).

Vanarsdel, Rosemary T., 'The "Wellesley Index" Forty Years Later (1966–2006)', *Victorian Periodicals Review* 39 (2006), pp. 257–65.

Veracini, Lorenzo, *Settler Colonialism: A Theoretical* Overview (Basingstoke: Palgrave Macmillan, 2010).
Wagner, Tamara S., 'Introduction: Narrating Domestic Portability: Emigration, Domesticity and Genre Formation', in *Victorian Settler Narratives: Emigrants, Cosmopolitans and Returnees in Nineteenth-Century Literature* (London: Pickering & Chatto, 2011), pp. 1–22.
— *Domestic Fiction in Colonial Australia and New Zealand* (London: Routledge, 2015).
— *Victorian Narratives of Failed Emigration: Settlers, Returnees, and Nineteenth-Century Literature in English* (London: Routledge, 2016).
Walker, Carole, *A Saviour of Living Cargoes: The Life and Work of Caroline Chisholm* (North Melbourne: Australian Scholarly Pub, 2009).
Walkowitz, Judith R., *Prostitution and Victorian Society: Women, Class and the State* (Cambridge: Cambridge University Press, 1980).
Warren, Lynne, '"Women in Conference": Reading the Correspondence Columns in *Woman* 1890–1910', in Laurel Brake, Bill Bell, and David Finkelstein (eds), *Nineteenth-Century Media and the Construction of Identities* (Basingstoke: Palgrave, 2000), pp. 122–34.
Waters, Catherine, *Commodity Culture in Dickens's* Household Words: *The Social Life of Goods* (Aldershot: Ashgate, 2008).
Waterston, Elizabeth, *John Galt: Reappraisals* (Guelph: University of Guelph, 1985).
Webby, Elizabeth, 'Writers, Printers, Readers: The Production of Australian Literature before 1855', in *The Penguin New Literary History of Australia* (London: Penguin, 1988), pp. 113–25.
Weiner, Annette B., *Inalienable Possessions: The Paradox of Keeping-While-Giving* (Oxford: University of California Press, 1992).
Whitley, William T., *Art in England: 1827–1837* (Cambridge: Cambridge University Press, 1930).
Whitlock, Gillian, 'Exiles from Tradition: Women's Life Writing', in Gillian Whitlock and Helen Tiffin (eds), *Re-Siting Queen's English: Text and Tradition in Post-Colonial Literature* (Amsterdam: Rodopi, 1992), pp. 11–24.
Williams, Merryn, *Women in the English Novel, 1800–1900* (London: Macmillan, 1984).
Williams, Raymond, *The Country and the City* (London: Vintage, 2016).
Woloch, Alex, *The One vs the Many: Minor Characters and the Space of the Protagonist in the Novel* (Princeton: Princeton University Press, 2003).
Wood, Christopher, *Victorian Panorama: Paintings of Victorian Life* (London: Faber, 1976).
Wood, Gillen d'Arcy, *The Shock of the Real: Romanticism and Visual Culture, 1760–1860* (Basingstoke: Palgrave Macmillan, 2001).
Woolcock, Helen R., *Rights of Passage: Emigration to Australia in the Nineteenth Century* (London: Tavistock, 1986).

Woollacott, Angela, *Settler Society in the Australian Colonies: Self-Government and Imperial Culture* (Oxford: Oxford University, 2015).
Wright, Edgar, *Mrs Gaskell: The Basis for Reassessment* (Oxford: Oxford University Press, 1965).
Wright, Terence, *Elizabeth Gaskell, 'We Are Not Angels': Realism, Gender, Values* (Basingstoke: Macmillan, 1995).
Yeazell, Ruth Bernard, *Art of the Everyday: Dutch Painting and the Realist Novel* (Princeton: Princeton University Press, 2008).
Young, Paul, *Globalization and the Great Exhibition: The Victorian New World Order* (Hampshire: Palgrave, 2009).
Zagarell, Sandra A., 'Narrative of Community: The Identification of a Genre', *Signs* 13 (1988), pp. 498–527.
Zemka, Sue, 'Chronometrics of Love and Money in *Great Expectations*', *Dickens Studies Annual* 35 (2005), pp. 133–56.
Zilcosky, John, 'Introduction: Writing Travel', in John Zilcosky (ed.), *Writing Travel: The Poetics and Politics of the Modern Journey* (Toronto: University of Toronto Press, 2008), pp. 3–21.

Index

Page numbers in *italics* refer to illustrations.

Absolon, John, 160n, 192
advertisements for emigration, 6, 33, 36, 132, 133, 151–5; *see also* promotion of emigration
aesthetics of distance, 8, 14–15, 185, 192; *see also* spatial relations in emigration literature
aesthetics of textual mobility and materiality, 17–18, 155, 193; *see also* mobility of emigration texts
affective engagement with place, 7–8, 106, 108–10, 115, 117, 120; *see also* home
Alfred (newspaper), 63–72, *66*, *67*, 74–7, 79–80, 82–3, 85–7, 186; *see also* shipboard newspapers
Alfred (ship), 63, 71, 76–7, 79–80, 89n, 186
America
  emigration to, from and via, 16, 21, 30, 55, 167–75
  print culture, 18, 97, 107, 121, 193
Anderson, Benedict, 81, 88

anthologies of letters
  Barthes, Roland, 38
  Letters from Settlers & Labouring Emigrants in the New Zealand Company's Settlements of Wellington, Nelson & New Plymouth, 39–41, 44
  Price, Leah, 38
  Sussex Emigrants, 36–7, 41, 51, 53
  Twenty-Four Letters from Labourers in America to their Friends in England, 43, 50
  see also letters: publication; Sockett, Thomas
art *see* paintings of emigration
Australia
  colonial violence, 21, 192
  distance, 2, 187
  First Fleet, 19, 91n
  gold rush, 130, 136
  image as penal colony, 9, 65–6
  literary representations, 66, 185
  literature from, 162, 178–83
  trading routes, 19
  voyage to, 63–4, 89n, 177

authenticity of emigration
    literature
  anxiety about, 193
  authenticity effect, 49–56
  preoccupation of emigration
    literature, 6, 17, 100–6,
    123, 161
  printed letters, 33–5, 49–56
  see also unreliability of
    emigration literature

back-migration, 19, 26n, 28n,
  87, 167–8
Baines, Dudley, 19, 37
Barrell, John, 108, 110, 150
Barthes, Roland, 38, 54–5
Belich, James, 5, 12, 20–1
Bell, Bill, 65, 75–6, 79, 93n
Benjamin, Walter, 55
Bentley, Richard, 105, 121
*Blackwood's Edinburgh
  Magazine*, 66, 121–2
booster literature
  authenticity, 123
  bias, 100–6
  influence on novels, 178
  as propaganda, 5, 96, 122–3,
    175
  success narratives, 33, 123,
    133
  writing back to, 97–102,
    105, 118, 133
  see also promotion of
    emigration; unreliability of
    emigration literature
Brontë, Charlotte, 95, 179
Brontë, Emily, 95, 165
Brown, Ford Madox, 130,
  132, *134*, 136–7,
  138–40
Buller, Charles, 10–11
Byerly, Alison, 97–8, 105

Cameron, Wendy, et al., 34,
  48, 51
Canada
  cultivation of attachment,
    118–19
  difficulties of settling, 103–6,
    122–3
  emigration schemes, 31–2,
    35–7, 41–2
  First Nation people, 29n,
    113–14
  landscape, 106–11, 120
  letters from, 36–7, 41, 51,
    53, 96
  literary representations of,
    163
  literature of, 95–123
  promotion of emigration to,
    99–101
  publishing, 97, 104–7, 120–1
  reconstruction of English life
    in, 48–9
  society, 111–15
Carlyle, Thomas, 8–9, 163–4,
  166, 180
Casteras, Susan, 148–9
Cattermole, William, 99–100,
  122, 175
*Chambers's Edinburgh
  Journal*, 66, 121, 124n
Chisholm, Caroline, 11, 37–8,
  52–5, 65–6, 119
Clare, John, 108, 110
class
  aspirations of emigrants, 68
  audience for different genres,
    112, 131–2
  implications in language
    of emigration and
    colonisation, 21, 64
  politics on board ship, 74,
    76–80, 92n, 167–8

in settler communities, 112–13, 115, 122–3, 139
Cobbett, William, 50, 61n
Collins, S. H., 44, 49
Collinson, James, 130, 132, 133, 144–9, *145*, 151, 154, 155n, 158n
Colonial Land and Emigration Commission, 9, 73
colonisation, 10–13, 21, 64, 88, 123, 192; *see also* settlement
Curtis, Gerard, 132, 153

diarists
　Charlwood, Edward, 87–88
　Clapham, John, 64, 78
　Curr, Henry, 88
　Darvall, Eliza and Emily, 63, 77, 82, 89nn, 92n
　Gosling, Francis, 78
　Hopkins, James, 64
　Kennaway, William and Laurence, 64
　Lines, Charles Henry, 1–4
　Wakefield, Edward Jerningham, 64, 78
Dickens, Charles
　American Notes, 167–8, 170
　David Copperfield, 162, 175–8, 183–6
　emigration schemes, 11, 175
　Great Expectations, 165
　Martin Chuzzlewit, 161–2, 167–75, 177, 181
　sketches, 105
　Urania Cottage, 175
Dilke, Charles, 18; *see also* Greater Britain

distance
　affective, 7–8, 56, 161, 194
　geographical, 2, 6, 65, 164–6, 186–8, 194
　reducing sense of, between colonies, 7, 13–14, 48–9, 55–6, 65, 71, 81, 155, 161–2, 180–1, 187
　temporal, 2, 22, 87, 180–1
　unity between Britain and colonies, 12–14
　see also aesthetics of distance; spatial relations in emigration literature
Doyle, Martin, 3, 11

Egremont, Earl of, 35–7, 51
Eliot, George, 179
emigrant guidebooks
　advances in print technology, 33
　Counsel for Emigrants, 5, 44, 46
　Emigrant Voyager's Manual, 78, 85
　Emigrant's Guide (Cobbett), 50
　Emigrant's Guide (Collins), 44
　emphasis on idea of home, 7, 87, 185
　The Female Emigrant's Guide and Hints on Canadian Housekeeping, 102
　Hints on Emigration to Upper Canada, 3, 11
　maps in, 3, 146–7
　women's exclusion from, 97, 118, 123, 124n
emigrant periodicals, 66
emigrants' tokens, 51–6

emigration
  assisted, 9–10, 11–12, 37, 51
  change in national sentiment, 9–10, 21
  from countries other than Britain, 18–20, 191
  economic reasons for, 4, 8–12, 31, 96, 137–40, 148–9, 164
  free emigration, 12, 65
  history of, 4, 8–12
  pervasiveness in nineteenth-century life, 7–8
  scale of, 4, 12
  see also emigration societies; transportation
emigration literature
  authenticity as preoccupation of, 6, 17, 100–6, 123, 161
  definition of, 5–7
  home in, 7, 14, 20–1, 87, 106, 177
  influence on the novel, 162, 174–5, 178, 194
  materiality of settler life in, 7, 49, 55–6, 121
  as motif in the novel, 162, 172–4, 177–8, 181, 183–5, 194
  nation-building rhetoric in, 6, 88
  production of familiarity, 6–7, 14, 35, 161
  publication of, 3–6, 32–7, 44, 96–7, 120–1, 193
  settlement in, 20, 115, 187
  unreliability of, 19, 33, 58n, 99–101, 161, 167–75
  see also anthologies of letters; booster literature; emigrant guidebooks; emigrant periodicals; genre; mobility of emigration texts; shipboard newspapers; spatial relations in emigration literature
emigration societies
  Family Colonisation Loan Society, 37
  opposition to, 9–10
  Petworth Emigration Scheme, 35–7, 41, 51–2
  as source of information, 4, 22, 34
  see also Chisholm, Caroline; Dickens, Charles: emigration schemes; New Zealand Company
Erickson, Charlotte, 34, 60n, 61n

familiarity, production of in emigration literature, 6–7, 14, 35, 161
family, importance in emigration rhetoric, 13, 136–7, 150–1; see also mothers
Family Loan Colonization Society, 37
Fender, Stephen, 48, 49
Foucault, Michel, 65, 73
Frye, Northrop, 106, 112, 127

Garcha, Amanpal, 98, 102–3
Gaskell, Elizabeth
  Cranford, 16
  emigration as philanthropy, 187
  Mary Barton, 162–7, 175, 178, 186
  North and South, 166
  Ruth, 176

gender
  attention to detail in female writing, 115–17
  criticism of female writing, 115–17
  female experience of emigration, 37, 97–8, 101–2, 112–17, 122–3, 147–8
  female solidarity, 114, 121
  gender structures on board ship, 80
  lack of female writing about colonial life, 97, 102, 123
  male domination of science, 108
  married women's role in emigration, 118–20
  single women emigrants, 4, 37–8, 86, 118
  sketch as form for female writers, 102–6, 115–17
  women's contributions to shipboard newspapers, 79–80
  see also mothers
genre, 5–7, 102–3, 112, 131, 192–3
Gerber, David, 34, 58n
gold rush, 4, 65, 130, 136, 138, 140, 148, 153–4, 180
Goldsmith, Oliver, 137–8
Great Exhibition, 154, 182–3
Greater Britain, 12–14; see also systematic colonisation

Harvey, David, 21
Heaphy, Charles, 33
home
  in emigration literature, 7, 14, 20–1, 87, 106, 177
  in emigration paintings, 133, 140, 148, 151
  gender, 95, 98, 117, 119–20
  leaving, 129n, 133, 134–40
  making new, 18, 20–1, 46, 98, 133, 151, 192
  meaning of, 174, 182
  recreation of British home abroad, 46, 48–9, 133, 140, 194
  relationship between old and new, 8, 14–15, 56, 148, 155, 185
  representation in novels and art, 18, 133–7, 140, 148, 150
  ship as, 72, 192
Home Circle, 120, 121
Household Words, 18–19, 33–4, 37, 66

India, 12, 18, 19
indigenous peoples, 21–2, 29n, 109, 113–14, 192
internal migration, 72

Kingsley, Charles: *Alton Locke*, 165–6
Kingston, William Henry Giles, 78, 85, 91n
knowable communities, 111–15, 163–7, 188

landscape, writing about, 106–11
leave-taking in art and literature, 120, 134–40
letter writers
  Boxall, Edward, 35–6, 39, 42, 52
  Boxall, George, 39, 47
  Cooper, William, 39, 52
  Hasted, Frederick, 31–3, 39, 49, 143

letter writers (*cont.*)
  Holden, Mary, 51–2, *53*
  Langthorn, Catherine, 16–17
  Neal, Richard, 41–2
  Phillips, William, 36, 39
  Stinson, Alexander, 3
  Watson family, 43–4, 51
  Wyly, Isabella, 2–3
letters
  authenticity of printed, 34–5, 49–56
  bias, 34
  connection to home, 12, 16–17, 31, 42–3, 55–6
  distance, 2–3, 6–7, 48–9, 56, 155
  integral to emigrant experience, 177–8
  letter scenes in art, 140–8
  materiality, 16–17
  overlap of public and private, 41–4
  promoting emigration, 34–5, 38–41
  publication, 32–4, 36–7
  as source of information about life in colonies, 32, 35, 44–9
  success narratives, 34–41
  touch, 16, 56, 142
  transition to print, 22–3, 35, 42, 50, 193
  see also anthologies of letters; letter writers
Literary Garland, 104, 105, 107, 121
Lovell, James, 104, 121; *see also Literary Garland*

McDonagh, Josephine, 15, 72, 110
magazines *see* periodicals

Magee, Gary and Andrew Thompson, 19–20
Malthus, Thomas, 8
manuscript texts
  authenticity, 34–5, 50–1, 55
  mimicking printed texts, 68, 70, 88–9
  relationship to printed texts, 22–3, 47, 56
  transition to print, 22–3, 35, 42, 50, 193
maps, 3, 132, 144, 146–7, 171–2
Meisel, Martin, 131–2
Metz, Nancy, 169–70
Mitford, Mary Russell, 98, 110
mobility of emigration texts
  aesthetics of distance, 14–15
  authenticity, 17, 23, 51, 161, 193
  delocalising effect, 6
  influence on form and genre, 7, 16–17, 56–7, 193
  initiation of movement, 133, 148, 155
  materiality of emigration literature, 17–18, 68–70, 142, 193
  see also aesthetics of textual mobility and materiality
Moodie, John, 96, 113
Moodie, Susanna, 95–6, 106–7, 147, 175
  Roughing It in the Bush, 97–106, 109–15, 118–23, 177, 191, 193
Moretti, Franco, 65, 192
mothers
  affective attachment to children's birthplace, 120

in emigration paintings,
136–7, 144
integral to successful
emigration, 118–20
metaphor for Britain, 13,
118–19, 121
see also family, importance in
emigration rhetoric

nation-building
emigration as contributing
to, 11, 86, 143, 166
emigration as threat to, 11,
138
rhetoric in emigration
literature, 6, 88
Nead, Lynda, 133, 150
New Zealand, 18, 33, 39–40,
44
New Zealand Company, 33,
39–40
newspapers
American, 169, 170
articles on emigration, 4, 5,
32
colonial, 18, 179, 181, 184
global circulation, 183,
184
publication of emigrants'
letters, 33–4, 176
see also periodicals;
shipboard newspapers
novels
distance in, 161–2, 180–7,
194
emigration as escape in,
164–6, 175
emigration literature as motif
in, 162, 172–4, 177–8,
181, 183–5, 194
genre of mobility, 15, 162
as guide to emigration, 169

representations of settler
life in, 163–7, 170–8,
180–3, 187
shaped by emigration
literature, 162, 174–5,
178, 194

Open Sea, 63–72, *69*, 74–7,
79–81, 83–6, *84*; see also
shipboard newspapers;
True Briton
opposition to emigration,
9–11, 138, 140, 167–8
oral emigration narratives, 83,
163, 173–4, 181
overpopulation, 8–9

paintings of emigration, *134,
135, 141, 145, 152*
families in, 136–7, 140, 144,
150–1
growth of genre, 130–1
homes in, 133, 140, 148,
151
lack of social realism in genre
painting, 149–50
leave-taking in, 134–40
letters in, 140–8
reception, 131–2, 137, 138,
140–1, 144–6
relationship between word
and image, 132–3,
136, 137–9, 151–5,
194
rural settings in, 148–51
Parks, James and Harriot, 45,
175
Parr Traill, Catharine, 95–7,
106–13, 115–23, 147
The Backwoods of Canada,
97–103, 107, 111, 116–17,
120–1, 193

Parr Traill, Catharine (*cont.*)
  *The Female Emigrant's
    Guide and Hints on
    Canadian Housekeeping*,
    102
  *Studies of Plant Life in
    Canada*, 108
  The Young Emigrants, 96
penal colonies, 9, 66, 91n;
  see also transportation
Perera, Suvendrini, 65–6
periodicals
  British periodicals, 16, 33–4,
    66, 120–2, 124n
  Canadian and North
    American, 104, 105,
    107, 121
  emigrant periodicals, 66
  importance to settlement,
    16, 72
  *see also Household Words;
    Sharpe's London Journal*
philanthropy, 11, 175, 179,
  187; *see also* emigration
  societies
Piesse, Jude, 15
place names, 108–10, 115
Plotz, John, 15, 17, 46
Poole, Paul Falconer, 136–7,
  159n
population growth, 8–9
Pre-Raphaelite Brotherhood,
  130, 144, 158n
Prince, Mary, 124n, 139n
Pringle, Thomas, 96, 124n
print culture
  creation of community, 88,
    123
  linking Britain to colonies,
    3–4, 81, 162, 180–1,
    183–5, 193
  mobility, 193

  performance of print in
    shipboard newspapers, 56,
    66–70, 75, 177
  promoting emigration, 32–3,
    65–6, 140
  role in settlement, 91n, 180
  see also manuscript texts
promotion of emigration,
  4, 32–5, 38–41, 65–6,
  99–101, 140; *see also*
  advertisements for
  emigration; booster
  literature; success
  narratives
propaganda *see* booster
  literature; promotion of
  emigration
publication of emigration
  literature, 3–6, 32–7, 44,
  96–7, 120–1, 193

'reality effect', 54–5
Redgrave, Richard, 130, 132,
  134–40, *135*, 148–9, 151
Rossetti, William, 144–5
Royal Academy of Arts, 130,
  131–2, 159n
Rudy, Jason, 81
rural settings in emigration
  paintings, 148–51

Seeley, John Robert, 12–14
settlement
  central concern of emigration
    literature, 20, 115, 187
  effect on indigenous peoples,
    21–2
  performance of, 64–5, 71–2,
    85–6, 177, 186
  terminology, 21
  violence, 21, 192
  see also colonisation; home

Sha, Richard, 97, 115–16
*Sharpe's London Journal
(Sharpe's London Magazine)*,
10–11, 66, 119, 121, 127n
shipboard newspapers, 66, 67, 69, 84
  class, 76–80
  creation of community, 57, 65, 70–80, 86–7
  creation of settlement, 64–5, 86
  ephemerality, 64
  expression of cultural proximity to Britain, 65, 71, 86–8
  mobility of emigration texts, 6, 16, 56–7
  spatial imaginaries, 70–2, 80, 85, 88
  unconventional mode of reporting news, 81–4
  use of print conventions, 56, 66–70, 75, 88–9
  see also Alfred (newspaper); *Open Sea*
ships *see Alfred* (ship); shipboard newspapers; *True Briton*; voyage out
sketch as literary form, 97–8, 102–6, 115–17
Smith, Benjamin, 43, 50
Sockett, Thomas, 31–2, 35–9, 41–2, 50–5, 53
Solomon, Abraham, 130, 132, 151–5, *152*
South Africa, 96
spatial relations in emigration literature
  exclusionary spatial politics, 76–7, 92n
  hybrid spatial imaginary, 85–8, 194
  overlapping spatial imaginaries, 65, 70–2, 80, 85, 88
  representation of distance between colonies, 7, 161, 194
  skewed, 187
  spatial synchronicity, 88
  see also aesthetics of distance; familiarity, production of in emigration literature
Spence, Catherine Helen, 178–9, 192
  Clara Morison, 162, 179–83, 186–7
  Mr Hogarth's Will, 179
  Tender and True, 102, 180, 186–7
stigma of emigration, 9–10, 21
Strickland, Agnes, 121, 129n
Strickland, Jane, 121, 129n
success narratives
  exclusion of women's experiences, 97, 118, 123, 124n
  key feature of emigration literature, 6
  in letters, 34–41
  in novels, 176–8, 185
  paintings that respond to, 133, 136, 140, 155
  unreliability, 19, 33, 58n, 99–101, 118, 161, 167–75
  see also authenticity of emigration literature; booster literature; unreliability of emigration literature
systematic colonisation, 10–11, 40; *see also* Greater Britain

technological advances
  publishing, 15, 33, 154
  sense of distance changed by, 13–14, 21–2, 81
  socioeconomic change caused by, 31
Teukolsky, Rachel, 132
Thackeray, William Makepeace, 105, 180
Thornton, Sara, 153–5
transportation, convict, 52, 64, 91n; *see also* penal colonies
travel literature, 6–7, 20, 115
True Briton, 63, 89n, 186; *see also Open Sea*; ships

unreliability of emigration literature, 19, 33, 58n, 99–101, 161, 167–75; *see also* authenticity of emigration literature; booster literature: bias

Victoria Magazine, 104, 105
voyage out
  creation of communities, 57, 65, 70–80, 86–7
  liminality, 1–2, 65, 85–9
  living conditions on board, 76–80, 92n, 167–8
  performance of settlement on board, 64–5, 71–2, 85–6, 177, 186
  reading on board, 78–9, 93n
  regulations, 73–4, 81–2
  time of preparation, 64–5, 85–6, 186
  see also Alfred (ship); shipboard newspapers; *True Briton*

Wakefield, Edward Gibbon, 10–11, 40, 64
Webster, Thomas, 130, 132, 133, 140–3, *141*, 146, 148–9, 151, 166
Wilkie, David, 144, 149
Williams, Raymond, 112, 151, 165; *see also* knowable communities
women *see* gender
Woollacott, Angela, 11, 18
Woolner, Thomas, 130, 148, 157n

EU Authorised Representative:
Easy Access System Europe Mustamäe tee 50, 10621 Tallinn, Estonia
gpsr.requests@easproject.com

Printed and bound by CPI Group (UK) Ltd, Croydon, CR0 4YY
16/01/2026
02036336-0001